Voting in America

Recent Titles in Contemporary Debates

The Affordable Care Act: Examining the Facts
Purva H. Rawal

Climate Change: Examining the Facts
Daniel Bedford and John Cook

Immigration: Examining the Facts
Cari Lee Skogberg Eastman

Marijuana: Examining the Facts
Karen T. Van Gundy and Michael S. Staunton

Muslims in America: Examining the Facts
Craig Considine

Prisons and Punishment in America: Examining the Facts
Michael O'Hear

American Journalism and "Fake News": Examining the Facts
Seth Ashley, Jessica Roberts, and Adam Maksl

Free Speech and Censorship: Examining the Facts
H. L. Pohlman

Poverty and Welfare in America: Examining the Facts
David Wagner

Voting in America

Examining the Facts

H. L. Pohlman

Contemporary Debates

BLOOMSBURY ACADEMIC
NEW YORK · LONDON · OXFORD · NEW DELHI · SYDNEY

BLOOMSBURY ACADEMIC
Bloomsbury Publishing Inc
1385 Broadway, New York, NY 10018, USA
50 Bedford Square, London, WC1B 3DP, UK
29 Earlsfort Terrace, Dublin 2, Ireland

BLOOMSBURY, BLOOMSBURY ACADEMIC and the Diana logo
are trademarks of Bloomsbury Publishing Plc

First published in the United States of America by ABC-CLIO 2020
Paperback edition published by Bloomsbury Academic 2024

Copyright © Bloomsbury Publishing Inc, 2024

Cover photo: Union members in New York City demonstrate against the Koch Brothers' paid influence on the manipulation of voting rights in the United States. (David Grossman/Alamy Stock Photo)

All rights reserved. No part of this publication may be reproduced or transmitted in any form or by any means, electronic or mechanical, including photocopying, recording, or any information storage or retrieval system, without prior permission in writing from the publishers.

Bloomsbury Publishing Inc does not have any control over, or responsibility for, any third-party websites referred to or in this book. All internet addresses given in this book were correct at the time of going to press. The author and publisher regret any inconvenience caused if addresses have changed or sites have ceased to exist, but can accept no responsibility for any such changes.

Library of Congress Cataloging-in-Publication Data
Names: Pohlman, H. L., 1952–author.
Title: Voting in America : examining the facts / H.L. Pohlman.
Description: Santa Barbara, California : ABC-CLIO, 2020. |
Series: Contemporary debates | Includes bibliographical references and index.
Identifiers: LCCN 2020035485 (print) | LCCN 2020035486 (ebook) |
ISBN 9781440873287 (hardcover) | ISBN 9781440873294 (ebook)
Subjects: LCSH: Voting—United States. | Representative government
and representation—United States.
Classification: LCC JK1967 .P648 2020 (print) |
LCC JK1967 (ebook) | DDC 324.60973—dc23
LC record available at https://lccn.loc.gov/2020035485
LC ebook record available at https://lccn.loc.gov/2020035486

ISBN: HB: 978-1-4408-7328-7
PB: 979-8-7651-2697-4
ePDF: 978-1-4408-7329-4
eBook: 979-8-2161-6281-0

Series: Contemporary Debates

To find out more about our authors and books visit www.bloomsbury.com
and sign up for our newsletters.

To Jonathan and Kaveri

Contents

How to Use This Book   xi
Introduction   xiii

1   Voting and Political Representation in the Constitution   1
    Q1. Did the original Constitution give all citizens a right to vote in presidential elections?   2
    Q2. Did the original Constitution of the United States grant citizens the right to vote for members of Congress?   6
    Q3. Did any African Americans have a right to vote in federal elections prior to the Civil War?   9
    Q4. Did the ratification of the Fifteenth Amendment in 1870 end the practice of states denying or abridging the right of African American men to vote in federal or state elections?   14
    Q5. After Reconstruction ended in 1877, did northern and western states in general comply with the letter of the Fifteenth Amendment?   20
    Q6. As it doubled the size of the American electorate, did the Nineteenth Amendment (1920) granting women the right to vote immediately transform American politics?   25

Q7. Was the Twenty-Sixth Amendment (1971), which dropped the voting age from twenty-one to eighteen, ratified primarily because the federal government was drafting eighteen-, nineteen-, and twenty-year-old men to fight in the Vietnam War? 30

Q8. Are there any other amendments to the U.S. Constitution that affected the right of American citizens to vote in federal and state elections? 35

2 **Electoral Districting and the Warren Court** 43

Q9. During the nineteenth century and the first half of the twentieth, did Congress allow state legislatures to determine the geographical lines of electoral districts for elections to the House of Representatives? 44

Q10. Did the Republican Guarantee Clause of the Constitution (Article IV, Section 4) provide the Supreme Court with a legal basis to invalidate House electoral districts if they contained unequal populations? 49

Q11. If federal courts were unable to rely on the Republican Guarantee Clause to require states to equalize the populations of House electoral districts, could they invalidate a change in a state's electoral district lines based on race or ethnicity? 53

Q12. As the Supreme Court rejected the argument that the Republican Guarantee Clause was an appropriate basis to invalidate malapportioned House electoral districts, was there some other constitutional provision that the Court could utilize to invalidate malapportioned state electoral districts? 57

Q13. When the Supreme Court ruled in *Reynolds v. Sims* and *Wesberry v. Sanders* that unequal electoral districts violated either the Equal Protection Clause or Article I, Section 2, did the Supreme Court invalidate the nature of representation underlying the U.S. Senate, the Electoral College, and the U.S. House of Representatives? 63

Q14. Did the Warren Court permit a state to maintain unequal electoral districts if the state's voters overwhelmingly approved this type of inequality via referendum or initiative? 67

Q15. Did the Warren Court apply the principle of "one person, one vote" flexibly, allowing relatively small variations in population between electoral districts without requiring the state to explain or justify them?	71
Q16. Did the Warren Court hand down any major decisions on the right to vote besides those related to apportionment and electoral districting?	76

3 The Voting Rights Act in the Twenty-First Century   81

Q17. Was the Voting Rights Act of 1965 politically uncontroversial as it passed by large margins in both the Senate (77–19) and the House of Representatives (333–85)?	82
Q18. As the Voting Rights Act of 1965 authorized an unprecedented degree of federal control and supervision over state electoral practices, was its constitutionality in doubt when it was enacted?	89
Q19. Do federal "examiners" and "observers" of elections continue to play an important role in states subject to the "special provisions" of Section 5 of the Voting Rights Act?	94
Q20. Was Section 2 of the Voting Rights Act redundant because it only banned what the Fifteenth Amendment already prohibited?	99
Q21. Could a state use race as a factor in drawing electoral district lines to comply with Section 5 of the Voting Rights Act to such an extent that it violated the Equal Protection Clause of the Fourteenth Amendment?	105
Q22. Did Congress ever broaden the Voting Rights Act to prohibit discrimination against nonracial minorities, and to require states and political subdivisions to provide assistance to these minorities in exercising their voting rights?	111
Q23. Has the constitutionality of all the provisions of the Voting Rights Act regarding its scope and coverage been consistently upheld by the Supreme Court?	116

4 Partisan Gerrymandering   125

Q24. Has partisan gerrymandering evolved significantly throughout American political electoral history?	127
Q25. Has the Supreme Court ever invalidated an extreme partisan gerrymander on constitutional grounds?	133

Q26. Even if the Supreme Court will not consider the constitutionality of partisan gerrymandering, can state courts strike down gerrymanders for violating state constitutions? 139

Q27. If no state judicial remedy is available, are there any political remedies that disaffected citizens can pursue to rectify extreme partisan gerrymandering? 147

Q28. As state courts have recently ruled that extreme partisan gerrymandering violates their state constitutions (Q26) and a number of states have established independent redistricting commissions (Q27), is it likely that partisan gerrymandering will soon disappear from American political life? 153

5 Ongoing Challenges 161

Q29. Is voter fraud a serious problem in the modern United States? 163

Q30. Do state voter identification (ID) laws have any legitimate purpose? 170

Q31. Does the federal Constitution require states to disfranchise convicted felons? 176

Q32. Even if there are legitimate reasons why states purge their voter registration lists, can such purges be used to suppress voting rights? 183

Q33. Is it constitutional for a state to require that an elector of the Electoral College pledge to vote for the presidential candidate who won the state's popular vote and punish the elector if the pledge is not honored? 189

Q34. Is there any way to circumvent or abolish the role of the Electoral College in presidential elections in favor of a national popular vote? 195

Q35. Did Russia interfere in the 2016 presidential election to undermine American confidence in U.S. elections and the value of the right to vote? 201

Q36. Apart from foreign interference in the 2016 presidential election, are there additional reasons why voters have lost confidence in the value of the right to vote and the integrity of American democracy itself? 209

Index 215

How to Use This Book

Voting in America: Examining the Facts is part of ABC-CLIO's Contemporary Debates reference series. Each title in this series, which is intended for use by high school and undergraduate students as well as members of the general public, examines the veracity of controversial claims or beliefs surrounding a major political/cultural issue in the United States. The purpose of this series is to give readers a clear and unbiased understanding of current issues by informing them about falsehoods, half-truths, and misconceptions—and confirming the factual validity of other assertions—that have gained traction in America's political and cultural discourse. Ultimately, this series has been crafted to give readers the tools for a fuller understanding of controversial issues, policies, and laws that occupy center stage in American life and politics.

Each volume in this series identifies 30 to 40 questions swirling about the larger topic under discussion. These questions are examined in individualized entries, which are in turn arranged in broad subject chapters that cover certain aspects of the issue being examined, for example, history of concern about the issue, potential economic or social impact, or findings of latest scholarly research.

Each chapter features 4 to 10 individual entries. Each entry begins by stating an important and/or well-known Question about the issue being studied—for example, "Was the Twenty-Sixth Amendment (1971), which dropped the voting age from twenty-one to eighteen, ratified primarily because the federal government was drafting eighteen-, nineteen-, and twenty-year-old men to fight in the Vietnam War?" and "Is voter fraud a serious problem in the modern United States?"

The entry then provides a concise and objective one- or two-paragraph **Answer** to the featured question, followed by a more comprehensive, detailed explanation of **The Facts**. This latter portion of each entry uses quantifiable, evidence-based information from respected sources to fully address each question and provide readers with the information they need to be informed citizens. Importantly, entries will also acknowledge instances in which conflicting data exists or data is incomplete. Finally, each entry concludes with a **Further Reading** section, providing users with information on other important and/or influential resources.

The ultimate purpose of every book in the Contemporary Debates series is to reject "false equivalence," in which demonstrably false beliefs or statements are given the same exposure and credence as the facts; to puncture myths that diminish our understanding of important policies and positions; to provide needed context for misleading statements and claims; and to confirm the factual accuracy of other assertions. In other words, volumes in this series are being crafted to clear the air surrounding some of the most contentious and misunderstood issues of our time—not just add another layer of obfuscation and uncertainty to the debate.

Introduction

The right to vote is arguably the most important right that Americans have because it is the means by which they are able to protect their other rights and liberties. Of course, one of the main responsibilities of judges is to protect the rights of citizens and, with some well-known exceptions, they generally do so. However, Americans are deluding themselves if they depend totally on courts to preserve their freedoms. As Judge Learned Hand argued in 1944, during the dark days of World War II, it is a "false hope" to rely only on constitutions, laws, and courts to protect one's rights. In a speech titled the "Spirit of Liberty," he said, "Liberty lies in the hearts of men and women; when it dies there, no constitution, no law, and no court can save it; no constitution, no law, no court can even do much to help it." The "spirit of liberty" in the "hearts of men and women," according to Hand, consisted of "the spirit which is not too sure that it is right," the "spirit which seeks to understand the minds of other men and women," the spirit which "weighs their interest alongside" the interest of others "without bias," and, lastly, the spirit to strive to make America "a signal, a beacon, a standard to which the best hopes of mankind will ever turn." Hand gave this speech in New York City's Central Park at an "I am an American Day" event when newly naturalized American citizens swore their allegiance to the flag "and the republic for which it stands," thereby gaining their right to vote in the U.S. elections. It is arguably in the exercise of the right to vote that Americans most fully express what Hand called the "spirit of liberty." By its exercise, Americans not only can protect their rights and liberties but also have the opportunity to realize their vision of the "best hopes of mankind."

Judge Hand's speech implied that the right to vote had a twofold function: one is protective of the past; the other, constructive of the future. Regarding the first function, it is easy in a large representative democracy, such as the United States, for the individual to underappreciate the importance of the right to vote as a protective shield. After all, each of us only has one vote, and one vote rarely makes a difference in an election, especially at the national level. However, as an individual, each of us is also a member of groups that are central to our identity, to who we are, whether the identifying groups are based on race, ethnicity, gender, sexual orientation, class, or some combination thereof. If any of the groups to which one belongs is denied the right to vote, history shows conclusively that public policy will disfavor its members. This reality is what President Lyndon B. Johnson was referring to when he said, "A man without a vote is a man without protection." Johnson knew that in American history, individuals were not denied the right to vote as individuals, but rather as members of groups that were excluded from the franchise. Of course, the individual voter who does not belong to a disfranchised group has the luxury, if he or she so wills, to be a "free rider," that is, someone who relies on others to protect his or her liberties. But if the individual is a member of a disfranchised group, he or she has no "free rider" protection, but instead is vulnerable to the effects of popular passions and prejudices. The protective role of the right to vote should be understood from the perspective of a vulnerable member of a disfranchised group.

The constructive function of the right to vote consists of participation in shaping the country's future. Hand asserted that this participation was vital in making the United States "a signal, a beacon, a standard to which the best hopes of mankind will ever turn." This function is unlike voting's protective role in that the individual can only gain the benefits of it by engaging in voting with what Judge Hand called "the spirit of liberty"—a spirit acknowledging that one does not know everything, a spirit that tries to see the world as other voters do, and a spirit that considers everyone's interest with fairness and impartiality.

This view of the constructive role of voting is, of course, very idealistic. It is doubtful whether most American voters go to the polls with anything like this elevated perspective. However, even if a voter's perspective is one of narrow self-interest, without any thought regarding how the candidate's policies will affect others or the common welfare, this voter is yet trying to do his or her part to shape the future of America. His or her vote may only have a minimal impact, but it is nonetheless an expression of personal values and principles. It is, in short, a form of standing up for what one believes in.

However, Judge Hand clearly thought that the voter whose first priority was the best interests of society, rather than narrow personal self-interest, was more aligned with the spirit of liberty and its importance as a social good. An individual cannot be free unless he or she lives in a free society where the great majority of citizens respect each other—even those they sharply disagree with. They acknowledge others equally as citizens and at least consider what they think and believe. No matter how convinced they are of the correctness of their own values and beliefs, they cannot be certain that they are right about what is or is not in the public interest. Voters sincerely trying to push the United States in the direction of "the best hopes of mankind" understand voting not just as a means to an end but as an end in itself and its own reward. By trying to improve American society through the realization of American ideals, they gain personal enrichment, become better American citizens, and even better human beings.

It is arguable, however, that modern voting in America does not fulfill either of Judge Hand's two functions. It neither protects the liberties that the American people have gained in the past or helps secure the liberties that the American people aspire to bestow upon their sons, daughters, and grandchildren. One troubling indication of the poor health of American democracy is the abysmal turnout rate of American voters, which is typically around 60 percent of the eligible voting population during presidential elections and 40 percent during midterm elections. The turnout rate reflects a general lack of confidence in the federal government and U.S. elections and a lack of conviction that their engagement in the political process makes a difference in their lives. Big policy problems, from climate change to issues of race and gender, the ever-mounting federal debt, and a decaying infrastructure, go unaddressed while partisan polarization has intensified, dividing the American people into hostile warring tribes.

This antagonistic partisan environment has raised new and troubling challenges to the American right to vote, from extreme political gerrymandering to partisan attempts to suppress the right to vote. The Russian interference in the 2016 election and the impeachment of President Donald Trump, even though it did not result in a conviction by the Senate, have further complicated American electoral life. Political controversies pile up and no remedy or solution is visible on the horizon.

This book is an attempt to make some sense of today's right to vote from a dispassionate perspective. It is part of a series dedicated to examining the facts about contemporary controversies of American political and social life. Voting in America is a topic that has an empirical dimension, but it is a subject that also includes the right to vote. This right is not discovered or analyzed by empirical analysis, but rather by an understanding of the evolution of rules, principles, and norms. The most fundamental set of norms regarding the American right to vote is contained in the Constitution of the United States. This study will begin with a discussion of how the Constitution has shaped and extended the right to vote from the founding until today. The second chapter will examine crucial Supreme Court decisions interpreting the Constitution during the 1960s, decisions that established the basic framework of contemporary U.S. elections. The book then turns to Congress's major contribution to the right to vote: The Voting Rights Act of 1965. This law, along with Congress's later amendments of it, has had an enormous impact on the right to vote, especially in terms of providing federal protection of the voting rights of racial and language minorities. Such federal protection of the voting rights of minorities continues to be of fundamental importance. The fourth chapter explores political gerrymandering, a practice that is arguably eroding the contemporary value of the American right to vote. The last chapter examines ongoing challenges to the right to vote that have yet to be resolved in any meaningful way. The book, in general, focuses on the realities of voting and the nature of the right to vote, making every effort to stick to the facts. The goal is to give students an unvarnished understanding of what is arguably the most fundamental right of Americans.

1

Voting and Political Representation in the Constitution

The Constitution of the United States consists of the original seven articles ratified in 1788 and the twenty-seven amendments that the two houses of Congress have since approved by a two-thirds vote and that three-fourths of the state legislatures have ratified. Fundamental to our system of government, the U.S. Constitution grants the legal authority to the three branches of the federal government, sets the federal limits on the powers of state governments, and establishes the constitutional rights of individual residents and citizens, including the right to vote. Under the initial Constitution, the right to vote was fairly narrow, requiring direct election of only members of the House of Representatives and granting states considerable leeway to establish voting qualifications, such as property ownership, tax, and residency requirements. Consistent with this practice, voting at the time of the founding, and through much of the nineteenth century, was generally considered a "privilege" one had to earn, not a "right" to which one was entitled. This point of view slowly changed as Americans fought to extend the franchise after the Civil War through the constitutional amendment process, but progress was slow. It was not until the mid-twentieth century that voting became a firmly rooted right, but even then universal suffrage was not yet a reality. Universal suffrage had to wait for Congress's enactment of the Voting Rights Act of 1965 (see chapter 3), but the broadening of the electorate through the process of constitutional amendment was nonetheless an important step in this direction.

To better understand the historical evolution of the right to vote, it is helpful to know how the federal government and state governments differ from a constitutional point of view. Both forms of government cannot enact laws that violate their constitutions, including the individual rights protected by their constitutions, but the federal government is a government of "enumerated" powers. This means that before the federal government can initiate any legislation, it must be able to point to the clause of the federal Constitution that "affirmatively" gives it the authority to do so. In contrast, state governments are governments of "reserved" powers, which means that they can exert authority not "explicitly" granted to them on the assumption that the authority in question is "reserved" to them. Of course, even with this assumption, state assertions of authority cannot violate either the state or the federal constitution. The above understanding of the authority of the federal government is one of the reasons why it was reluctant to intrude itself into how states limited the franchise prior to the Civil War—and why it was necessary to utilize the constitutional amendment process to extend and enlarge the right to vote. These basic underlying principles have neither been changed nor abandoned; they still form the foundation of today's right to vote.

Q1. DID THE ORIGINAL CONSTITUTION GIVE ALL CITIZENS A RIGHT TO VOTE IN PRESIDENTIAL ELECTIONS?

Answer: No. The Constitution of 1788 did not grant any citizen or resident the right to vote in presidential elections, including the one that made George Washington the nation's first president.

The Facts: The Constitutional Convention of 1787 considered a number of options for selecting the president of the United States: selection by Congress, by the state legislatures, or by a popular vote of qualified voters, but it could come to no consensus. It, therefore, established a special committee to recommend a compromise. Balancing the relevant interests, the committee recommended the following system of presidential electors: "Each State shall appoint, in such Manner as the Legislature thereof may direct, a Number of Electors, equal to the whole Number of Senators and Representatives to which the State may be entitled in the Congress." The electors were to meet "in their respective States, and vote by Ballot for two Persons, of whom one at least shall not be an Inhabitant of the same State with themselves." As to the timing of presidential selection, "Congress may determine the Time of chusing the Electors, and the Day on which they shall give their Votes" (Article II, Section 1). Whoever received the highest number of electoral votes became president and the second highest became vice president. If the vote resulted in a tie, then the House of Representatives chose the president, but the vote was taken by state, the representatives of each state having one vote. If no person received a majority of electoral votes, then the House would use the same process to select the president from the five candidates who received the highest number of votes.

The Committee that made this recommendation argued that it was consistent with the principle of separation of powers, buttressed the independence of the president from Congress, granted states two "senatorial" votes despite their small population, reduced the impact of popular factions, and, finally, allowed a degree of popular influence through state legislatures. In *Federalist No. 39*, James Madison justified this system on the ground that it had both a "national" and a "federal" dimension. "The executive power," he argued, "will be derived from a very compound source. The immediate election of the President is to be made by the States in their political characters. The votes allotted to them are in a compound ratio, which considers them partly as distinct and coequal societies [each state having two senatorial votes], partly as unequal members of the same society [each state having additional votes equal to the number of representatives it had based on its population]." The advantage of this "compound" source of executive power, according to Madison, was that it was both "republican," in the sense that political authority "derived all its powers directly or indirectly from the great body of the people," and "federal," in the sense that the Constitution recognized the new "Union as a *Confederacy* of sovereign states."

In *Federalist No. 68*, Alexander Hamilton called the system of presidential electors "excellent," if "not perfect." He assumed that state legislatures would adopt some form of popular selection of electors because "the sense of the people should operate in the choice of the person to whom so important a trust was to be confided." However, despite the value of popular input, Hamilton argued that "the *immediate* election [of the president] should be made by men most capable of analyzing the qualities adapted to the station, and acting under circumstances favorable to deliberation, and to a judicious combination of all the reasons and inducements which were proper to govern their choice" (emphasis added). Such an indirect election of the president would afford "as little opportunity as possible to tumult and disorder." This was so, in Hamilton's view, because the "choice of *several*, to form an intermediate body of electors, will be much less apt to convulse the community with any extraordinary or violent movements, than the choice of *one* who was himself to be the final object of the public wishes." In addition, having the appointed electors vote in their separate states "will expose them much less to heats and ferments, which might be communicated from them to the people, than if they were all to be convened at one time, in one place." Accordingly, for Hamilton, the highest priority was "that every practicable obstacle should be opposed to cabal, intrigue, and corruption" in the choice of the president. There was no better method than assigning this responsibility to a "dispersed" and "transient" body of electors who have the trust and confidence of the qualified voters in each state.

Following the ratification of the Constitution in 1788, the first presidential election was held in 1789. Six state legislatures used some form of popular election to select the presidential electors, but about the same number selected their electors themselves. The six states that used some form of popular election, however, did not grant the right to vote for the presidential electors to all their citizens. High property ownership qualifications and strict residency requirements radically reduced the number of male eligible voters. For example, in the six states that used popular elections to choose their electors, only 38,818 voted (35,866 for Washington's Federalist Party Electors and 2,952 for Anti-Federalist Electors), a figure less than 2 percent of the total population of the country (*Our Campaigns*). In the end, all presidential electors selected in 1789, whether by state legislatures or by popular election, voted for Washington, who repeated this feat in the election of 1792. No other president save Washington has received the unanimous endorsement of the Electoral College—and he received it twice!

However, the harmony of the country's first two presidential elections did not last long. The rise of political parties during the 1790s eroded consensus, and the resulting competition exposed a flaw in the system of presidential electors. In 1796, the Federalist Party backed John Adams, who won a majority of the elector votes, but Thomas Jefferson, the candidate for the Democratic-Republican Party, gained the second highest number of votes. The result was a president who perceived the vice president as a political adversary. To guard against this result in the presidential election of 1800, each party worked hard to ensure that its electors voted only for the party's candidates. The effort was successful, but the result was not: all Democratic-Republican electors cast their ballots for Jefferson and his running mate, Aaron Burr, resulting in a tie vote between candidates of the same party. The unexpected result threw the presidential election into the House of Representatives, which was then controlled by the Federalist Party. Many Federalists supported Burr over Jefferson, making it difficult for Jefferson to gain the support of a majority of the representatives from more than eight of the sixteen states. Finally, after thirty-six ballots, the Federalists from Maryland and Vermont abstained, giving these two states to Jefferson, who won the presidential election by a 10–4 vote, with Delaware and South Carolina casting blank ballots.

The 1796 and 1800 presidential elections were the impetus behind the Twelfth Amendment to the Constitution, which was ratified in 1804. This amendment modified the procedure by which electors cast their votes for president and vice president. Rather than each elector voting for two persons (either of whom could become president), the Twelfth Amendment required each elector to vote one person for president and another for vice president. The president of the Senate would then count these votes separately; the candidate having the highest number of votes for the presidency would become president and the individual receiving the highest number for the vice presidency would become vice president. If no person had the highest number of votes for the presidency, whether because of a tie or a lack of majority, then the House, voting by state, would choose the president from the three persons receiving the highest number of votes.

In the early nineteenth century, the term "Electoral College" became the customary way to designate the dispersed set of electors as a collective entity. More state legislatures adopted popular election as their method for selecting presidential electors, but South Carolina refused to take this step until 1860. A second change that arose in the twentieth century was that state legislatures began to allow voters to vote for a slate of electors pledged to a particular candidate, with the winning slate casting all the state's electoral votes in favor of the slate's candidate. This approach increased the electoral influence of small states because no candidate was likely to ignore a state, even if it had a modest number of electoral votes, if there was a reasonable chance of winning them all.

As of 2019, only Maine and Nebraska have not adopted this "winner-take-all" system. Both states reserve two electoral votes for the winner of the popular vote but allow each congressional district to elect its own elector. However, the general trend in favor of the "winner-take-all" model has fundamentally changed the nature of the Electoral College. In a presidential election, the electors no longer mirror the preferences of the nation's popular vote, but rather the preferences of the majority or plurality of all the states. The end result is that the "winner-take-all" system increases the likelihood that a presidential candidate can win the electoral vote but lose the nation's popular vote. This is precisely what happened in the presidential elections of George W. Bush in 2000 and Donald Trump in 2016. For this reason, the Electoral College has become quite controversial, with some commentators calling for its abolition (see Q34).

FURTHER READING

Alexander, Robert M. *Representation and the Electoral College.* Oxford: Oxford University Press, 2019.

Amar, Akhil. "Electoral College Reform, Lincoln-Style." *Northwestern University Law Review* 112 (2017): 63–81.

Bennett, Robert W. *Taming the Electoral College.* Stanford, CA: Stanford University Press, 2006.

Burin, Eric. *Picking the President: Understanding the Electoral College.* Grand Forks, ND: University of North Dakota Press, 2017.

Our Campaigns. "U.S. President—National Vote," available at https://www.ourcampaigns.com/RaceDetail.html?RaceID=59542.

Pierce, Neal R., and Longley, Lawrence D. *The People's President: The Electoral College in America and the Direct Vote Alternative.* New Haven, CT: Yale University Press, 1981.

Rossiter, Clinton, ed. *The Federalist Papers.* New York: Mentor, 1961.

Wilmerding, Lucius. *The Electoral College.* New Brunswick, NJ: Rutgers University Press, 1958.

Q2. DID THE ORIGINAL CONSTITUTION OF THE UNITED STATES GRANT CITIZENS THE RIGHT TO VOTE FOR MEMBERS OF CONGRESS?

Answer: No. The Constitution did not give citizens or residents the right to vote for members of either the Senate or the House of Representatives.

The Facts: The U.S. Congress is a bicameral legislature with two separate houses: the Senate and the House of Representatives. As indicated in Article I, Section 3, the Senate is composed of two senators from each state, each of whom has "attained the Age of thirty Years" and has been a citizen of the United States for nine years or more. The elections of senators (who serve six-year terms) are staggered, with roughly one-third coming up for election every two years. As each state sent two Senators regardless of population, it balanced the power of small states against large ones. According to the 1788 Constitution, state legislatures, not voters, selected their senators. The six-year term of office for each senator, coupled with the method of election, strongly suggests that the framers intended the Senate to function as an upper house of Congress—a deliberative and stable body of experienced statesmen that could check illegitimate exercises of executive power, as well as the passions and whims of public opinion, as they were reflected in the House of Representatives, often referred to as the "people's house." Some specific functions the Constitution assigned to the Senate reflect this vision of the Senate as the "upper house." For example, the Senate had the "sole Power to try all Impeachments," and only the Senate gave its "Advice and Consent" to the president on treaties and the appointment of "ambassadors, other public Ministers and Consuls, Judges of the Supreme Court, and all other Officers of the United States" (Article 1, Section 3, and Article II, Section 2). In the view of the framers, it was better for these functions to be performed by a house of Congress somewhat insulated from direct popular control.

Unlike the Senate, the states did not have equal representation within the House of Representatives. Although each state had to have at least one representative, the number allotted to each state depended upon the population of that state by "adding to the whole Number of free Persons, including those bound to Service for a Term of Years, and excluding Indians not taxed, three fifths of all other Persons" (Article 1, Sections 2 and 7). The southern states insisted on the last clause to ensure that slaves (who constituted a significant percentage of the population of the southern states) were counted, if only fractionally, for the purpose of increasing their allotment of seats in the House.

The right to be counted for the purpose of appropriating House seats to individual states, of course, in no way implied a right to vote for the Representative who filled the seat. Instead, the Constitution mandated that for House elections, "Electors in each State shall have the Qualifications requisite for Electors of the most numerous Branch of the State Legislature" (Article I, Section 2). Accordingly, although the framers envisioned the House of Representatives as the popular branch of Congress, it did not require anything approaching universal manhood suffrage for House elections. By delegating the authority to decide who could vote in House elections indirectly to states, the Constitution permitted considerable variation in the size of the franchise in House elections from state to state.

It is commonly estimated that only 6 percent of the population of the country could vote for members of the House in the first election held under the Constitution in 1789. The primary reason for this low level of participation was that the original thirteen states typically limited the right to vote to white men who owned a substantial amount of personal property or paid a significant amount of taxes, but a few states also barred certain religions from the franchise. However, state suffrage laws were complex and subject to change. For example, New Jersey and Pennsylvania initially permitted free African Americans to vote, but both states later revoked this right: the former in 1807, and the latter in 1838. New Jersey also granted women the right to vote during this early period, as did Massachusetts and New York, but these states quickly withdrew this right. Property qualifications gradually disappeared, with the new state of Kentucky initiating the trend in 1792.

In part to encourage immigration, new states that entered the Union in the early nineteenth century tended not to erect property barriers to the franchise. The original states eventually followed suit and, by 1840, only three (Rhode Island, Virginia, and North Carolina) of the original thirteen states retained property qualifications. North Carolina was the last state to abandon them, doing so in 1856. Taxpaying requirements also withered away during the mid-nineteenth century but survived in Pennsylvania and Rhode Island until the twentieth century. A number of states barred Catholics and Jews from voting, including Maryland, which in 1828 became the last state to lift this type of restriction. Virtually, the only voting convention that prevailed across the country in America's formative years was that, all other things being equal, a white male who owned substantial property could vote.

Although the Constitution grants states the power to regulate the "Times, Places and Manner" of federal elections, it gives Congress the authority to "make or alter such Regulations, except as to the Places of chusing Senators" (Article I, Section 4). Congress has exercised this power in multiple ways. For example, in the mid-nineteenth century, Congress passed a law in 1842 requiring all states entitled to more than one seat in the House of Representatives to conduct House elections by "districts" within the state, not by at-large elections of the entire state. Congress also passed a law in 1872 designating the first Tuesday following the first Monday in November as a national election day. In 1907, Congress prohibited national banks and corporations from contributing money to candidates in federal elections. However, there were limits to Congress's power to regulate the "manner" of the elections. It could not, for example, add qualifications for voting in House elections beyond the age, citizenship, and residency requirements of the Constitution. In general, courts decide if federal and state regulations of House elections are reasonable and lawful or an unreasonable infringement of the right to vote. Accordingly, a complex set of both federal and state laws, subject to judicial review, regulates the details of House elections.

FURTHER READING

Engerman, L. Stanley, and Sokoloff, Kenneth L. "The Evolution of Suffrage Institutions in the New World." In *Economic Development in the Americas Since 1500: Endowments and Institutions.* Cambridge: Cambridge University Press, 2011.

Keyssar, Alexander. *The Right to Vote: The Contested History of Democracy in the United States.* Revised ed. New York: Basic Books, 2009.

Lichtman, Allan J. *The Embattled Vote in America.* Cambridge, MA: Harvard University Press, 2018.

Rossiter, Clinton, ed. *The Federalist Papers.* New York: Mentor, 1961.

Tolson, Franita. "The Spectrum of Congressional Authority over Elections." *Boston University Law Review* 99 (2019): 320–393.

Q3. DID ANY AFRICAN AMERICANS HAVE A RIGHT TO VOTE IN FEDERAL ELECTIONS PRIOR TO THE CIVIL WAR?

Answer: Yes. During the eighteenth century, several of the newly formed states, mostly in the north, did not formally exclude free African American men from the franchise, but such exclusion became the norm during the nineteenth century until the Civil War and the subsequent ratification of the Fifteenth Amendment in 1870.

The Facts: Following the Constitutional Convention of 1787, the thirteen states that ratified the new Constitution had different rules on whether Catholics, Jews, Native American Indians, and free African Americans had the right to vote. Prior to the American Revolution, some colonies excluded one or more of these groups from the franchise, while others did not. However, many states at the time of the founding rewrote their state constitutions and abandoned some or all of these types of exclusions. For example, most states granted Jews and Catholics the right to vote, although North Carolina required each voter to "acknowledge the being of God." Connecticut, Delaware, Maryland, Massachusetts, New Hampshire, New Jersey, New York, North Carolina, Pennsylvania, Rhode Island, and the new state of Vermont (admitted to the Union in 1791) did not explicitly bar free African Americans from voting, but southern states, such as Georgia, South Carolina, and Virginia, did so, even those who had fought in the Revolutionary War. Of course, all states denied African American slaves the right to vote because the law designated them "chattel," moveable property subject to the will of their masters.

However, even if a few states did not formally deny free African Americans the right to vote, they were still subject to the state's property ownership, taxpaying, and residency qualifications. Many free African Americans were disfranchised on these grounds, rather than on race. For example, Massachusetts limited the right to vote to men who owned "freehold estate" (complete legal title without any lease or mortgage) that earned three pounds of income per year or was worth sixty pounds (Keyssar, 2009). At the time, this was a high property qualification and it kept most of the relatively small number of African Americans living in Massachusetts from voting. Of course, this property qualification applied to all races and ethnic groups, thereby sharply limiting the size of the electorate, but the effect on African Americans was especially severe because they were often subject to social and economic discrimination by local white elites and were typically trapped in relatively low-paying jobs, with little opportunity to acquire the property needed to meet the property qualification. The residency requirement, which typically ranged from six months to two years depending on the state, compounded the problem for free African Americans because many of their jobs were transient in nature, working as agricultural or manual laborers. This combination of hurdles effectively barred most free African Americans from legally voting in the late eighteenth century.

However, many states at the beginning of the nineteenth century began to lower or eliminate their property (or taxpaying) qualifications for voting. For example, in the eighteenth century, Maryland had enforced a property qualification of a "freehold" of fifty acres of property above the value of thirty pounds, but it eliminated this voting eligibility requirement in 1801; Connecticut dropped its "freehold" requirement in 1817, Massachusetts in 1821, and New Jersey in 1844 (Keyssar, 2009). Also, new states that joined the Union in the early nineteenth century, such as Ohio (1803), Illinois (1818), and Michigan (1837), never imposed a property qualification for voting. But as states reduced, eliminated, or rejected property qualifications, they increasingly adopted racial exclusions that confined the franchise to whites only. For example, Maryland excluded free African Americans from the franchise in 1801, Ohio in 1802, New Jersey in 1807, Indiana in 1816, Connecticut and Illinois in 1818, Alabama in 1819, Michigan and North Carolina in 1835, Pennsylvania in

1838, and California in 1849 (Keyssar, 2009). By 1850, only Maine, Massachusetts, New Hampshire, New York, and Rhode Island among America's thirty-one states permitted free African Americans to vote if—and it was a big "if"—they satisfied the relevant residency, property, and taxpaying requirements.

Another barrier to the ballot box for African Americans was that states often required citizenship as a qualification for voting. It was possible that children of free African Americans born in the United States might qualify as U.S. citizens, but Congress limited naturalized citizenship to "free white persons" by the Naturalization Act of 1790, a rule that remained in effect until after the Civil War. Accordingly, states that limited their electorate to U.S. citizens indirectly excluded aliens who were neither "free" nor "white." Accordingly, states that limited voting to citizens routinely excluded from their franchises alien indentured servants, emancipated slaves born in Africa, or even free African Americans born outside the United States. Not all states imposed this type of citizenship requirement, but those that did not could simply restrict the franchise to whites. For example, Illinois's Constitution of 1818 did not have a citizenship requirement, presumably as an enticement for recent white immigrants to move to Indiana, but only granted whites the right to vote (Keyssar, 2009).

In contrast, Maine did not explicitly bar African Americans from the franchise, but it did require U.S. citizenship, which could not be obtained by African Americans born outside the United States. Because so few African Americans resided in Maine, it is not clear how it applied its rule to native-born free African Americans or to those who gained their freedom through manumission. Of course, a slave who gained his *de facto* freedom by escaping from a slave state could not become a citizen because he was, under the Federal Fugitive Slave Act, a "fugitive" who legally should be returned to his owner. However, the citizenship status of free African Americans or of slaves freed by their owners, assuming they were born in the United States, was not clear during the first half of the nineteenth century.

The Supreme Court took up the issue of the eligibility of African Americans born in the United States for national citizenship in *Dred Scott v. Sandford* (1857). In this infamous decision, the Court held that a slave who temporarily resided in a free state/territory did not thereby become free on his return to Missouri. In reaching this result, Chief Justice Roger B. Taney's majority opinion raised the question whether emancipated descendants of slaves "imported into this country" could "become a member of the political community formed and brought into existence by the Constitution of the United States." The Court answered this question with a decisive "no," holding that even if a particular state recognized a free African American descended from slaves as a citizen, such state citizenship did not mean he was a citizen of either the state or the United States in terms of federal law. In Taney's words, the "Constitution has conferred on Congress the right to establish an uniform rule of naturalization, and this right is evidently exclusive, and has always been held by this court to be so." Accordingly, in Taney's view, a state might give the right to vote in federal elections to "negroes and mulattoes, but that does not make them citizens of the State, and still less of the United States." In effect, Taney's opinion in *Dred Scott* authorized any state to bar free African Americans from voting in both state and federal elections by simply requiring U.S. citizenship as a qualification.

Arguably, the first significant step in the process of federal African American enfranchisement was the Emancipation Proclamation of January 1, 1863. This document, issued by President Abraham Lincoln as a war measure to weaken the military strength of the South, declared that on this date "all persons held as slaves within any State or designated part of a State, the people whereof shall then be in rebellion against the United States, shall be then, thenceforward, and forever free." The Proclamation also permitted African American men to join the ranks of the Union Army and Navy "to garrison forts, positions, stations, and other places, and to man vessels of all sorts in said service." This Proclamation did not affect the status of slavery in loyal border states, such as Delaware, Kentucky, Maryland, or Missouri, or in the seceded states already under Northern military occupation, but nonetheless it was a substantial step toward emancipation. If the North was victorious and if the Proclamation was honored, it meant that no slave in a seceded state yet in rebellion in 1863 could be barred from voting after the war based on their slave status. It also opened a possible avenue to citizenship and the franchise through military service. By the end of the Civil War, nearly two hundred thousand black African American soldiers and sailors, both free blacks and ex-slaves, had fought in the conflict.

Lincoln himself, at the beginning of the war, opposed slavery but was not in favor of the enfranchisement of African Americans. However, by January 1864, he had partially changed his mind, at least in regard to African Americans who had fought for the North. He wrote that he considered it his

> religious duty, as the nation's guardian of these people, who have so heroically vindicated their manhood on the battle-field, where, in assisting to save the life of the Republic, they have demonstrated in blood their right to the ballot, which is but the humane protection of the flag they have so fearlessly defended. (Basler, 1953/2001)

Following the ratification of the Thirteenth Amendment, the Radical Republicans addressed black suffrage through the Fourteenth Amendment, which was ratified in 1868. The first section reads as follows: "All persons born or naturalized in the United States and subject to the jurisdiction thereof, are citizens of the United States and of the State wherein they reside." The amendment, therefore, reversed Taney's conclusion in *Dred Scott* that free African Americans descended from slaves could not be citizens neither of the United States nor of the state in which they resided. As citizens of the United States and of the state in which they lived, no state could exclude African Americans born in the United States from the franchise based on their lack of citizenship.

The second section of the amendment indirectly penalized any reconstituted southern state for denying male African Americans the right to vote. It did so by reducing a state's representation in the Electoral College and the House of Representatives to the degree that it "denied to any of the male inhabitants of such State, being twenty-one years of age, and citizens of the United States" the "right to vote at any election for the choice of electors for President and Vice President of the United States, Representative in Congress, the Executive and Judicial officers of a State, or the members of the Legislature thereof," except for "participation in rebellion, or other crime." Because the number of African Americans in the North was much less than in the South, this section of the Fourteenth Amendment had a far greater impact on southern than northern states. For example, in the 1868 election, Republican candidate Ulysses S. Grant won a narrow victory based on southern black votes even though he lost the state of New York, one of the northern states that continued to deny African Americans the right to vote despite the ratification of the Fourteenth Amendment.

Recognizing that Grant had only won the presidential election because of southern black votes, the Republican Party proposed the Fifteenth Amendment, which prohibited either the United States or any state from denying or abridging the right to vote "on account of race, color, or previous condition of servitude." Republicans favored this amendment for two reasons: first, it would provide additional constitutional protection to African Americans in reconstituted southern states; second, it would ensure the support of African Americans for the Republican Party. Ratified in February 1870, the Fifteenth Amendment formally granted male African American citizens the right to vote in federal and state elections, but this right was in practice nullified to a great extent following the disputed election of 1876. In this electoral contest, Republican candidate Rutherford B. Hayes won the electoral vote by promising to end Reconstruction and withdraw federal troops from the South (see Q4).

FURTHER READING

Avins, Alfred. *The Reconstruction Amendments' Debate The Legislative History and Contemporary Debates in Congress on the 13th, 14th, and 15th Amendments.* Richmond, VA: Virginia Commission on Constitutional Government, 1967.

Basler, Roy P., ed. *The Collected Works of Abraham Lincoln.* Ann Arbor, MI: University of Michigan Digital Library, 2001, initially published by The Abraham Lincoln Association, 1953, Vol. VII, pp. 101–102 (Letter to James S. Wadsworth, January 1864), available at http://abrahamlincolnassociation.org/lincoln-repository/collected-works/.

Bell, Derrick. *Race, Racism and American Law.* 6th ed. New York: Aspen Publishers, 2008.

Cantu, Edward. "Normative History and Congress's Enforcement Power under the Reconstruction Amendments." *Texas Review of Law and Politics* 21 (2016): 119–199.

Foner, Eric. *The Second Founding: How the Civil War and Reconstruction Remade the Constitution.* New York: Norton, 2019.

Keyssar, Alexander. *The Right to Vote: The Contested History of Democracy in the United States.* Revised ed. New York: Basic Books, 2009.

Lincoln, Abraham. "The Emancipation Proclamation." January 1, 1863, available at https://www.ourdocuments.gov/doc.php?flash=false&doc=34&page=transcript.

Q4. DID THE RATIFICATION OF THE FIFTEENTH AMENDMENT IN 1870 END THE PRACTICE OF STATES DENYING OR ABRIDGING THE RIGHT OF AFRICAN AMERICAN MEN TO VOTE IN FEDERAL OR STATE ELECTIONS?

Answer: No. Although the right of male African Americans to vote was initially respected to a limited degree, southern states utilized a number of techniques, such as literacy tests and white primaries, to disfranchise African American male voters after the federal government ended southern Reconstruction and withdrew its troops from the South in 1877.

The Facts: The Radical Republicans who controlled Congress at the end of the Civil War refused to grant the seceded states representation in either the Senate or the House of Representatives until each of them ratified the Thirteenth Amendment (ratified in 1865), the Fourteenth

Amendment (in 1868), and the Fifteenth Amendment (in 1870). Congress also enacted a number of statutes to implement these Reconstruction Amendments, such as the Civil Rights Act of 1866 and the Reconstruction Acts of 1867 and 1868. Regarding the right to vote, Congress included in the Enforcement Act of 1870 a provision that prohibited any "wrongful act or omission" that interfered with the right of African Americans to vote in state and federal elections. However, in *United States v. Reese* (1875), the Supreme Court invalidated this provision on the ground that it was beyond Congress's power under the Fifteenth Amendment. In the Court's view, the enforcement clause of the Fifteenth Amendment only gave Congress the power to prevent racial discrimination in voting, not to prevent all "wrongful" acts, such as threats or physical assaults, that might prevent an African American from voting.

In 1871, Congress enacted the Ku Klux Klan Act, which authorized the use of the army to suppress white supremacists from threatening, assaulting, and lynching black voters, but this legislation did not end the violence. For example, Louisiana's contested 1872 gubernatorial election pitted southern white Democrats against the Republican Party. After the Republican president Ulysses S. Grant sent federal troops to support the Republican candidate, white and black militias were formed, with each side heavily armed. The situation erupted into violence in April 1873, ending in the massacre of dozens of black militiamen. Federal authorities criminally prosecuted several whites, but the Supreme Court invalidated these convictions in *United States v. Cruikshank* (1876), concluding that the federal government did not have the power to impose criminal sanctions on *private* conduct that violated the rights of citizens to peaceably assemble together "for lawful purposes." Any such right to assemble "was not created by the [First] amendment," the Court argued, and "neither was its continuance guaranteed, except as against congressional interference." To protect this broad right of assembly from *private* interference, "the people must look to the States. The power for that purpose was originally placed there, and it has never been surrendered to the United States."

Cruikshank was ominous for the southern black community for at least two reasons: first, members of the Klan and other racist vigilante groups no longer had to worry about federal criminal law enforcement; second, it gave white supremacists greater latitude to suppress the political rights of African Americans to the degree they regained control of southern state governments. Moreover, despite the fact that Congress enacted a new Civil Rights Act in 1875, one that prohibited racial discrimination in privately owned public accommodations, such as restaurants or hotels, the white supremacists' goal of returning to power in southern states was within their reach. During the 1870s, the Grant Administration and many conflict-weary northern Republicans were focusing more on economic issues than the southern reconstruction effort.

Matters came to a head in the disputed election of 1876, which pitted Democrat Samuel J. Tilden, who won the popular vote and 184 electoral votes (one shy of the majority needed to win), against Republican Rutherford B. Hayes, who won 165 electoral votes. Twenty electoral votes from four states, including Florida, Louisiana, and South Carolina, were contested. In what is called the Compromise of 1877, Republicans and Democrats agreed that the outstanding 20 electoral votes would go to Hayes if federal troops were withdrawn from the southern states, thereby bringing an end to the Reconstruction Era. Soon thereafter, southern opponents of the Reconstruction Amendments, known as "Redeemers," reasserted themselves across the South as the southern Republican Party went into decline. The transition was gradual and uneven across the South, but the trend was unmistakably in the direction of a white Redeemer Democratic Party, a trend the Supreme Court indirectly encouraged by invalidating the Civil Rights Act of 1875 in the *Civil Rights Cases* (1883). The Court's rationale for this result was that the Fourteenth Amendment did not grant Congress the power to prohibit *private* racial discrimination in public accommodations. In a comparable vein, the Court upheld the constitutionality of southern states engaging in *public* racial segregation of public schools, parks, buses on the assumption that the facilities were "separate but equal" in *Plessy v. Ferguson* (1896). Together, these two cases arguably marked the consolidation of the Jim Crow Era in the South.

By 1890, the "Redeemers" were largely in control of the former confederate states, at which point they began to disfranchise African American voters *legally*, a process that complemented the existing *illegal* methods of fear, intimidation, and violence practiced by the Ku Klux Klan and other white vigilante groups. The key to the Redeemers' strategy to *legally* disfranchise African American men was to exclude them from the franchise without openly violating the express terms of the Fifteenth Amendment. Mississippi took the lead in this effort by extending its residency requirement from six months to two years. As African American males at the time were generally low-paid workers, they tended to be more mobile, traveling from job to job, than the wealthy property-owning white class. Accordingly, this facially lawful change in the residency requirement had a negative effect on the voting rights of African American men. The Supreme Court upheld residency requirements in *Pope v. Williams* (1904), holding that "the privilege to vote in a state is within the jurisdiction of the state itself, to be exercised as the state may direct, and upon such terms as to it may seem proper" and that the "question whether the conditions prescribed by the state might be regarded by others as reasonable or unreasonable is not a federal one."

In the same vein, Mississippi required any potential voter to pay all taxes due for two preceding years by February 1 of an election year and instituted a new $2 poll tax to vote (approximately $58 in 2019 dollars). Both provisions functioned as a clear disincentive for poor African American men to exercise their voting rights. Of course, these new tax requirements also had a depressing effect on the voting power of poor whites, but the wealthy white elite either did not consider that result a problem or saw it as a worthwhile trade-off to secure black disfranchisement. Lastly, Mississippi's 1890 constitution imposed a new literacy test for potential voters. The test required that "every elector shall . . . be able to read any section of the constitution of this State; or he shall be able to understand the same when read to him, or give a reasonable interpretation thereof." The county clerks who administered the test were invariably white and had complete discretion to decide what section to assign and whether a black potential voter passed the test. The failure rate among black voters was high as well as predictable.

During the 1890s, other southern states followed Mississippi's example, but several also added to their constitutions a so-called "grandfather clause" that permitted a clerk to register anyone, despite the results of a literacy test, if the person's grandfather had been qualified to vote prior to the Civil War. Such provisions were obviously designed to benefit illiterate white voters. The end result of these techniques of disfranchisement was that only a small percentage of African American men in the South, typically less than 10 percent, could register to vote at the turn of the century. As most could not register to vote, all African Americans suffered additional negative effects. For example, many states at the time selected jurors from the list of eligible voters, which meant that black criminal defendants typically came before all-white juries. In *Mississippi v. Williams* (1898), a black defendant—one indicted for murder by an all-white grand jury, convicted by an all-white petit jury, and sentenced to be hanged by a white judge—argued that the state's voter-registration requirements violated his rights under the Fourteenth Amendment's equal protection clause.

The Supreme Court unanimously rejected this argument on the ground that Mississippi's system of voter registration did not *explicitly* discriminate on the basis of race. As the Court noted, "it is not asserted . . . that either the constitution of the state or its laws discriminate in terms against the negro race, either as to the elective franchise or the privilege or duty of sitting on juries." The claim was rather that discrimination is "effected by the powers vested in certain administrative officers," such as the power of the county clerk to decide if a black voter had passed the literacy test. However, the Court reasoned, all that the black defendant had shown was that the discretion of the county clerks "could" be used in a racially discriminatory manner, not that the "actual administration [of the voting rules] was evil, only that evil was possible under them."

The Court invalidated the use of the grandfather clause in 1915, but at the same time reaffirmed the validity of literacy tests, writing that "no time need be spent on the question of the validity of the literacy test, considered alone [without the grandfather clause], since, as we have seen, its establishment was but the exercise by the State of a lawful power vested in it not subject to our supervision, and, indeed, its validity is admitted" (*Guinn v. United States* [1915]). Of course, as these techniques of disfranchisement of African Americans solidified in southern states, the Republican Party atrophied across the region to the point that the winner of the Democratic primary was the assured winner of the general election. This situation encouraged the development of another tactic that reduced the voting power of the black community to its nadir: the white primary. Southern states claimed that a state political party, despite its role in state elections, was a private association distinguishable from the state itself and therefore not subject to the Fourteenth or Fifteenth Amendment. Relying on this assumption, South Carolina established an all-white Democratic primary election in 1896 and other southern states quickly followed suit.

Over twenty years later, the Supreme Court ruled in *Nixon v. Herndon* (1927) and *Nixon v. Condon* (1932) that Texas's white primary violated the Fourteenth Amendment because the state itself was directly or indirectly (through the party's state executive committee) participating in the exclusion of African Americans from the primary election. Texas responded to these two decisions by completely delegating its authority to establish the rules of primary elections to political parties assembled in convention. The Supreme Court upheld the constitutionality of this delegation in *Grovey v. Townsend* (1935), observing that "the primary is a party primary; the expenses of it are not borne by the state, but by members of the party seeking nomination; the ballots are furnished not by the state, but by the agencies of the party . . . ." Since the exclusion of African Americans "upon its face is not state action," the Court found there was no violation of the Constitution. Accordingly, African Americans could not legally vote in Democratic primaries and, if they satisfied the stringent residency requirements, paid their poll tax, and passed the literacy test, they might be able to vote in the general election, but their vote would not make an iota of difference in the election results.

These techniques of suppressing the voting power of African Americans in southern states continued unabated until the mid-twentieth century, at which point the Supreme Court began to slowly and unevenly restrict state authority over voter qualifications. For example, in *Smith v. Allwright* (1944), the Court reversed its decision in *Grovey*, which had upheld the constitutionality of the white primary, by holding that it "may now be taken as a postulate that the right to vote in such a primary for the nomination of candidates without discrimination by the State, like the right to vote in a general election, is a right secured by the Constitution. By the terms of the Fifteenth Amendment, that right may not be abridged by any state on account of race." However, in *Lassiter v. Northampton County Board of Elections* (1959), the Court once again upheld the constitutionality of literacy tests, writing that "The ability to read and write likewise has some relation to standards designed to promote intelligent use of the ballot . . . [and is] neutral on race, creed, color, and sex." The ruling ignored the reality of how southern states were applying literacy tests to deny African Americans the right to vote.

FURTHER READING

Foner, Eric. *Reconstruction: America's Unfinished Revolution*. New York: Harper Row, 1988.

Goldman, Robert M. *Reconstruction and Black Suffrage: Losing the Vote in Reese and Cruikshank*. Lawrence, KS: University Press of Kansas, 2001.

Harrison, John. "The Lawfulness of the Reconstruction Amendments." *University of Chicago Law Review* 68 (2001): 375–462.

Inflation Calculator, available at http://www.in2013dollars.com/us/inflation/1890.

Kousser, Morgan. *The Shaping of Southern Politics: Suffrage Restriction and the Establishment of the One-Party South, 1880–1910*. New Haven, CT: Yale University Press, 1974.

Lane, Charles. *The Day Freedom Died: The Colfax Massacre, the Supreme Court, and the Betrayal of Reconstruction*. New York: Holt Paperbacks, 2009.

Mississippi 1890 Constitution, available at http://mshistorynow.mdah.state.ms.us/articles/103/index.php?s=extra&id=270.

Perman, Michael. *Struggle for Mastery: Disfranchisement in the South, 1888–1908*. Chapel Hill, NC: University of North Carolina Press, 2001.

White, Richard. *The Republic for Which It Stands: The United States during Reconstruction and the Gilded Age, 1865–1896*. New York: Oxford University Press, 2017.

Wilson, Theodore B. *Black Codes of the South*. Tuscaloosa, AL: University of Alabama Press, 1965.

Q5. AFTER RECONSTRUCTION ENDED IN 1877, DID NORTHERN AND WESTERN STATES IN GENERAL COMPLY WITH THE LETTER OF THE FIFTEENTH AMENDMENT?

Answer: Yes. However, they arguably violated its spirit by reinstituting and tightening voter qualifications, which made it difficult for immigrants from eastern and southern Europe and Mexico to vote, and by denying Asian immigrants and many Native Americans the right to vote on the ground that they were not U.S. citizens.

The Facts: During and after the Civil War, escalating trends in the direction of corporate capitalism, industrialization, and urbanization radically transformed northern and western states from agricultural local economies into one integrated national manufacturing powerhouse. The need for labor in this expanding manufacturing economy sparked a flood of new immigrants, some from Ireland and Germany but many more from eastern and southern Europe, Mexico, and Asia. Mainly, these new immigrants were unlike the agricultural settlers who often purchased land on their arrival prior to the Civil War. These new immigrants were poor, illiterate, non-English speaking, mostly Catholic or Jewish, with cultures and manners that were foreign to native-born Americans of the nineteenth century. This influx led many northern and western states to reduce the size of their electorate by preserving, expanding, or imposing new rules for voting, including property/tax requirements (such as poll taxes), residency requirements, and literacy tests. All these types of requirements were literally consistent with the Fifteenth Amendment because they did not exclude persons from the franchise based on their race, color, or previous condition of servitude, but these exclusions were heavily correlated to nationality, ethnicity, and, to some extent, race.

For example, in 1848, the Treaty of Guadalupe Hidalgo that ended the Mexican War granted citizenship to persons of Mexican descent who chose to remain in the five hundred thousand square miles of territory annexed by the United States, territory that eventually became the states of the southwest, including Texas, Arizona, New Mexico, and California. This grant of citizenship was consistent with the federal naturalization law (which limited citizenship to "free white persons") because persons of Mexican descent were deemed "whites." But this grant of citizenship did little to stem the violence, intimidation, and discrimination Anglos inflicted on Mexican Americans during the second half of the nineteenth century, including discriminatory denials of the right to vote. For example, Texas's laws in the 1850s prohibited the Mexican American citizens "from using their native Spanish language and organizing political rallies . . . [and from] serving as election judges." During the early 1900s, "poll taxes, direct primaries, and white primaries were adopted [by Texas] with the purpose of establishing voting requirements that the vast majority of Mexican Americans could not meet, although they already constituted [based on population] a decisive voting bloc in many areas of the state" (Perales, Figueroa, and Rivas, 2006). Similar forms of discrimination against the voting rights of Mexican Americans were not uncommon in California, Arizona, and New Mexico.

Meanwhile, the influx of white immigrants from eastern and southern Europe led northeastern and midwestern states to utilize literacy tests to dampen the voting power of new citizens who had yet to master the English language. A voter in Massachusetts under its 1892 constitution had to "be able to read the Constitution in English and write his name," while Connecticut's 1902 constitution required voters to "read at least three lines of the Constitution or of the statutes of this State . . . in such manner as to show that he is not prompted nor reciting from memory" (Keyssar, 2009). In general, the literacy tests of the northern states were not as far-reaching or arbitrary as those that the southern states imposed on African American citizens or those that the southwestern states imposed on Mexican American citizens, but they nonetheless had a significant impact on newly naturalized citizens from eastern and southern Europe.

Congress enacted the Naturalization Act of 1870 the same year the Fifteenth Amendment was ratified. This law broadened naturalization by permitting "aliens of African nativity and persons of African descent" a path to citizenship, but it refused to do the same for Asian immigrants of Chinese, Japanese, or Korean nationality. California was not satisfied with the exclusion of Chinese immigrants from the electorate based on their lack of citizenship. It took the added precaution of including in its 1879 constitution a provision (Article II, Section 1) mandating that "no native of China . . . shall ever exercise the privileges of an elector in this State," language crafted so as not to violate the literal terms of the Fifteenth Amendment's prohibition of discrimination based on "race" or "color."

The purpose of this provision was to ensure that Chinese immigrants could not vote in California even if the federal government changed its mind and permitted them to become citizens. But Congress instead hardened its stance against the Chinese by enacting the Chinese Exclusion Act of 1882, which prohibited for ten years any further immigration of Chinese laborers and once again barred alien Chinese already living in the country from citizenship. This Act was renewed in 1892, made permanent in 1902, and was not repealed until 1943. Accordingly, western states routinely denied Chinese immigrants the right to vote, whether on the grounds that they were not citizens or, as in the case of California, on the grounds that they had been born in China.

The Supreme Court upheld the constitutionality of the Chinese Exclusion Act in *Chae Chan Ping v. United States* (1889). Nine years later, however, it held that children of Chinese immigrants born inside the United States were citizens even if their parents were yet subjects of the Emperor of China in *United States v. Wong Kim Ark* (1898). In the Court's view, the Fourteenth Amendment mandated birthright citizenship for everyone born in the United States unless the parents were foreign rulers, diplomats, enemies militarily occupying the United States, members of a Native American tribe "not taxed," or the birth occurred on a foreign public ship. Accordingly, California could not deny Wong the right to vote on the ground that he was not a citizen or a "native of China." So long as Wong satisfied other voting qualifications, he had the right to vote. After the 1906 San Francisco earthquake destroyed many municipal records, including immigration documents and birth certificates, many Chinese immigrants obtained citizenship by falsely claiming they had been born in the United States.

In *Ozawa v. United States* (1922), a Japanese immigrant to the United States challenged his exclusion from becoming a naturalized citizen by claiming that he was in fact a "free white person." The Supreme Court rejected this line of reasoning, holding "that the words 'white person' were meant to indicate only a person of what is popularly known as the Caucasian race." In the Court's view, color of skin was not the proper test because color "differs greatly among persons of the same race." The Court concluded that Ozawa was "clearly of a race which is not Caucasian" and therefore was "clearly ineligible for citizenship." Accordingly, even though the Fifteenth Amendment prohibited the United States and states from discriminating against the right of citizens to vote based on "race" or "color," it was constitutional for the federal government to deny citizenship on the basis of race. Of course, children born of Japanese immigrants in the United States were citizens by birth and could not be denied their right to vote based either on their "race" or "color."

The Court's reliance on "Caucasian race" as the critical term to decide if an immigrant was eligible for naturalization came under considerable strain the following year when a high-caste Hindu born in Punjab argued that he was eligible for naturalization in *United States v. Bhagat Singh Thind* (1923). As the applicant was "classified by certain scientific authorities as of the Caucasian or Aryan race," he argued he was entitled to become a U.S. citizen under *Ozawa*. In its opinion, the Court conceded that the Aryan invaders of Punjab tried "to preserve their racial purity," but nonetheless claimed that "intermarriages did occur," thereby "producing an intermingling of the two [races] and destroying to a greater or less degree the purity of the 'Aryan' blood." Accordingly, the Court held "that the words 'free white persons' are words of common speech, to be interpreted in accordance with the understanding of the common man," not in terms of scientific usage.

Congress repealed the Chinese Exclusion Act in 1943, a time when the Republic of China was an ally of the United States during World War II, and nine years later enacted the 1952 Immigration Act, which ended the tradition of denying Asian immigrants the right to become naturalized citizens. However, despite these reforms, there was one group born in the geographical United States that was historically excluded from citizenship: Native American Indians. This exclusion from U.S. citizenship did not mean that a state could not grant Native American Indians the right to vote. As early as 1869, prior to the ratification of the Fifteenth Amendment, Massachusetts granted state citizenship to all Indians within its jurisdiction and all the "rights, privileges and immunities" associated with it, including the right to vote. However, as many states restricted their electorates to U.S. citizens, Native American Indians who lived in a tribal setting on a reservation could not qualify for U.S. citizenship. For birthright citizenship, the Fourteenth Amendment required that a person (1) be born inside the country or naturalized and (2) be "subject to the jurisdiction" of the United States. Native Americans who lived in a "tribal" setting were thought not to be "subject to the jurisdiction" of the United States but rather to their "tribe."

In *Elk v. Wilkins* (1884), the Supreme Court took up the question whether a Native American Indian could become a citizen if he severed his relationship with his tribe and surrendered himself fully and completely to the jurisdiction of the United States by moving to Omaha, Nebraska and living there for more than a year. The Court began its analysis with the observation that Indian tribes "were not, strictly speaking, foreign states, but they were alien nations, distinct political communities . . . ." Accordingly, "Indians born within the territorial limits of the United States, . . . although in a geographical sense born in the United States, are no more 'born in the United States and subject to the jurisdiction thereof' . . . [than] the children born within the United States of ambassadors or other public ministers of foreign nations." The Court's conclusion was that such Indians, "not being citizens by birth, can only become citizens in the second way mentioned in the Fourteenth Amendment, by being 'naturalized in the United States,' by or under some treaty or statute."

Eventually, Congress passed the Dawes Act of 1887, which extended U.S. citizenship to Native American Indians who severed their ties with their tribe, and the Indian Citizenship Act in 1924, which granted citizenship to all Native Americans born inside the United States, whether living in tribal settings or independently of the tribe. However, despite this law, states with large Native American populations continued to deny those living on reservations the right to vote based on residency requirements, their nontaxed status, or, in the case of Arizona, identifying them as "guardians" of the United States and disqualifying them from voting on that basis. In time, however, this type of discrimination against Native American Indians slowly faded away, with Arizona ending the practice in 1948 and Utah and Maine in the 1960s ("Securing," 2016).

FURTHER READING

Ancheta, Angelo N. *Race, Rights, and the Asian American Experience*. 2nd ed. New Brunswick, NJ: Rutgers University Press, 2006.

Behnken, Brian D. *Fighting Their Own Battles: Mexican Americans, African Americans, and the Struggle for Civil Rights in Texas*. Chapel Hill, NC: University of North Carolina, 2011.

Keyssar, Alexander. *The Right to Vote: The Contested History of Democracy in the United States*. Revised ed. New York: Basic Books, 2009.

Perales, Nina, Figueroa, Luis, and Rivas, Criselda G. *Voting Rights in Texas: 1982–2006: Report of the RenewtheVRA.org*. Los Angeles, CA: Renew the VRA.org, June 2006.

Reidy, Joseph P. *Illusions of Emancipation: The Pursuit of Freedom and Equality in the Twilight of Slavery*. Chapel Hill, NC: University of North Carolina, 2019.

"Securing Indian Voting Rights: Developments in the Law." *Harvard Law Review* 129 (2016): 1731, available at http://harvardlawreview.org/wp-content/uploads/2016/04/1731-1754-Online.pdf.

Q6. AS IT DOUBLED THE SIZE OF THE AMERICAN ELECTORATE, DID THE NINETEENTH AMENDMENT (1920) GRANTING WOMEN THE RIGHT TO VOTE IMMEDIATELY TRANSFORM AMERICAN POLITICS?

Answer: No. The Nineteenth Amendment did not immediately transform American politics, but it did constitute the first wave of the women's movement, which over the course of the last century has had a profound effect on the political, economic, social, and cultural life of the United States.

The Facts: Although New Jersey allowed women to vote for a decade or so after the ratification of the Constitution, the women's suffrage movement dates its beginnings to a convention held in Seneca Falls, New York, in 1848. Organized by Elizabeth Cady Stanton and Lucretia Mott, the convention approved a "Declaration of Sentiments" that proclaimed "all men and women are created equal" but that the "history of mankind is a history of repeated injuries and usurpations on the part of man toward woman, having in direct object the establishment of an absolute tyranny over her." In proof of these statements, the Declaration noted a number of issues, but highlighted the fact that men have denied women the exercise of her "inalienable right to the elective franchise" and have forced them "to submit to laws, in the formation of which she had no voice." These arguments echoed the principles of the Declaration of Independence: that all human beings had "inalienable" rights and that the authority of government is derived from the consent of the governed, such that there can be no "taxation without representation."

At the time, the "Declaration" fell on deaf ears, at least the ears of the majority of voting men. Most men thought giving women the right to vote would make no difference because husbands would control how their wives voted. They also generally thought that many women did not need or, for that matter, want the vote because their husbands and fathers could and would represent their interests better than they could themselves. And, lastly, if granting women the right to vote would make a difference, it could do so only at the cost of introducing discord into the family, too high of a price to pay. These patriarchal attitudes were strong and commonplace in the mid-nineteenth century and were an important reason why the struggle for women's right to vote was a long and difficult one.

Their commitment to human equality inclined the early leaders of the suffrage movement to ally themselves with the abolitionists before and during the Civil War. In fact, suffrage advocates placed ending slavery before their own agenda during the war and, at its end, they expected that granting the newly freed slaves the right to vote would naturally lead to a complementary extension of the right to vote to women. However, the inclusion of the term "male" inhabitant and "male" citizen in the Fourteenth Amendment (1868), combined with the Fifteenth Amendment's (1870) focus on denials of the right to vote on account of "race, color, or previous condition of servitude," but not on account of sex, frustrated the aspirations of the early suffragists.

In response to this major disappointment, the suffrage movement split into two associations: the National Woman Suffrage Association (NWSA), organized by Stanton and Susan B. Anthony in 1869, continued to focus on a national strategy of enfranchisement; the American Woman Suffrage Association (AWSA), organized by Lucy Stone and her husband, Henry Blackwell, concentrated on encouraging states to grant women the right to vote. The latter strategy showed some early promise. The Territory of Wyoming granted women the right to vote in 1869 followed by the Territory of Utah in 1870. At the same time, the suffrage movement also turned to the courts, hoping to achieve success based on the clause of the Fourteenth Amendment that granted federal and state citizenship to "all persons born or naturalized in the United States." Their argument was the following: if women were citizens, they must have all the "privileges and immunities" of citizens, one of which must be the right to vote. Susan B. Anthony relied on this argument when she voted in defiance of state law for incumbent Ulysses S. Grant in the presidential election of 1872 in Rochester, New York. A week later she was arrested and New York Judge Ward Hunt eventually issued her a fine of $100 for illegal voting, a fine she refused to pay with the remark, "May it please your honor, I shall never pay a dollar of your unjust penalty." The Court informed Anthony that she would not be jailed if she declined to pay the fine, a tactic that prevented an incarcerated Anthony from filing a petition for a writ of habeas corpus to a federal court and thereby bringing her case to the nation's attention. Despite this judicial maneuver, Anthony's trial nonetheless quickly became a national cause célèbre and a rallying cry for the suffragist movement (Linder, 1995–2020).

Another case involved a voting official in St. Louis who refused to permit Virginia Minor to register to vote. Minor sued and her case—*Minor v. Happersett*—reached the Supreme Court in 1875. In its decision, the Court completely agreed with Minor that she was a citizen of the United States and of the state in which she resided, but rejected the implication that she necessarily had the right to vote on that basis. The Court pointed out that prior to passage of the Fourteenth Amendment, women were citizens of states in which they lived, yet in "all save perhaps New Jersey, this right [of voting] was only bestowed upon men, and not upon all of them." Moreover, in some states, "citizenship has not in all cases been made a condition precedent to the enjoyment of the right of suffrage." Thus, in a number of states, "persons of foreign birth, who have declared their intention to become citizens of the United States, may under certain circumstances vote." Accordingly, historical practice shows that citizenship and the right to vote do not imply each other. "If uniform practice long continued," the Court continued, "can settle the construction of so important an instrument as the Constitution of the United States confessedly is, most certainly it has been done here." The Court added, somewhat apologetically, "No argument as to woman's need of suffrage can be considered. We can only act upon her rights as they exist. It is not for us to look at the hardship of withholding. Our duty is at an end if we find it is within the power of a State to withhold."

Other western territories and states followed the example of Wyoming and Utah during the 1880s and 1890s, with the Territories of Washington granting women the right to vote in 1883, Montana in 1887, and the states of Colorado in 1893 and Idaho in 1896. At that point, even though the two major suffrage organizations had unified their efforts by creating the National American Woman Suffrage Association (NAWSA) in 1890, the movement stalled, perhaps because of a general opposition to extending the franchise to any new voters, especially the new immigrants from eastern and southern Europe, Mexico, and Asia (see Q5). Another factor was that the suffrage movement during the 1890s had a fairly narrow social base, generally limited to white middle-class women, many of whom opposed granting the illiterate foreign-born men of the working class the right to vote. It was, in short, difficult for women to win over the hearts and minds of male working-class voters when some members of their ranks supported literacy tests that would take away their right to vote.

However, by 1906, the NAWSA decisively broke with its earlier class- and ethnic-based strategy by dropping its support for literacy tests and allying itself with organizations representing working-class women and men, thereby transforming itself into a mass movement. More success at the territory/state level quickly followed, with California granting women the right to vote in 1911, Kansas and Oregon in 1912, the Territory of Alaska in 1913, Nevada in 1914, New York in 1917, and Michigan, Oklahoma, and South Dakota in 1918. This steady enfranchisement of women by states and territories not only created a large pool of potential voters in favor of a constitutional amendment but also undermined the argument that women's suffrage would destroy the American family and radically change the political system. It simply could not be denied that the states and territories that had extended the franchise to women had thriving families and stable republican political institutions.

The only area of the country where NAWSA had no success was the South, largely because southern states did not want any extension of the right to vote if there was the smallest chance that it might disturb the southern system of disfranchising African Americans. The lack of official southern support, however, did not deter the NAWSA. Following America's entrance into World War I in April 1917, the group pursued a national campaign publicizing the many important ways in which women were contributing to the war effort. Women around the country were joining the workforce to support their families in the absence of their husbands, selling war bonds, becoming nurses, sending gifts to soldiers, distributing food to wounded veterans, and so on. In recognition of the value of these efforts, President Woodrow Wilson threw his support behind women's suffrage by describing it as a "war measure" in January 1918, whereupon the House voted in favor of the Nineteenth Amendment, followed by the Senate in June 1919. Northeastern, midwestern, and western states quickly ratified the amendment, but southern states refused to follow suit, leaving the issue of whether women should be given a constitutional right to vote in the hands of the border states. Texas and Arkansas acted promptly in 1919, Kentucky in early 1920, and it was Tennessee that pushed the amendment over the top on August 18, 1920, by a margin of one vote. Ratified by thirty-six states, the Nineteenth Amendment became a part of the U.S. Constitution and women voted in the 1920 presidential election later that year.

However, the Nineteenth Amendment did not radically change American politics at the national level, at least not in the short term. The expectation that allowing women to vote would destroy the American family and revolutionize American political life by creating a monolithic women's bloc of voters proved to be a total myth. Although the electorate had doubled, only about 35–40 percent of women eligible to vote went to the polls in the aftermath of the ratification of the Nineteenth Amendment, and party alignment remained stable. During the 1920s, women generally voted the same way as their male family members.

Despite the fact that the Nineteenth Amendment only had a modest effect on American politics, over time it exerted a profound and enduring impact on American life. For example, the NAWSA founded the League of Women Voters in 1920 to support the voting rights of all Americans, lobby for legislation supporting women's rights and interests, and eliminate the role of secret money in U.S. elections. The League focused national attention on issues regarding labor law, women's health, child welfare, education, family law, and other family matters. The right to vote also naturally encouraged women to consider running for federal political offices. Although Montana had already elected Jeannette Pickering Rankin to the House of Representatives in 1916, prior to the Nineteenth Amendment's ratification, women became more active after its ratification. Arkansas voters elected Democrat Hattie Wyatt Caraway to the Senate in 1932, reelected her in 1938, and she had the honor of being the first woman to chair a Senate Committee and to preside over the Senate.

Reenergized by the African American civil rights movement of the 1950s and 1960s, the second wave of the women's movement supported congressional legislation that prohibited sexual discrimination in employment, housing, and education. Through litigation, women's organizations in the 1960s and 1970s won victories in federal courts that expanded the degree of control women had over reproductive health and, despite the failure to ratify the Equal Rights Amendment, established the principle that sexual equality was a constitutional imperative. Although voter turnout by women was low in the early years following suffrage, that changed by midcentury and women began voting at higher rates than men in the 1960s, a trend that has continued to this day, whether in absolute numbers or as a percentage of the vote. At the same time, a gender gap has appeared in every presidential election since 1980, with women and men diverging in their presidential preferences. This trend has coincided with steady growth in the percentage of women who identify themselves as Democrats and similar increases in the percentage of men who describe themselves as Republicans. Women also made tremendous inroads in various realms of public life in the late 1900s and early 2000s. Sandra Day O'Connor was sworn in as the first woman to serve on the Supreme Court in 1981. Janet Reno became the first female Attorney General in 1993; Madeleine Albright was confirmed as the first female Secretary of State in 1997; Nancy Pelosi became the first woman to serve as Speaker of the House in 2007; and Hillary Clinton became the first woman to receive a presidential nomination from a major political party in 2016. In the early 2020, presidential Democratic primaries, Senator Elizabeth Warren (D-MA) and Senator Amy Klobuchar (D-MN) were two of the six or seven contenders yet active. Clearly, the Nineteenth Amendment unleashed a force that has fundamentally reshaped American society, one that will continue to do so now and in the future.

FURTHER READING

Declaration of Sentiments (1848), available at https://sourcebooks.fordham.edu/mod/senecafalls.asp.

Dubois, Ellen Carol. *Feminism and Suffrage: The Emergence of an Independent Women's Movement in America, 1848–1869*. Ithaca, NY: Cornell University Press, 1999.

Isenberg, Nancy. *Sex and Citizenship in Antebellum America*. Chapel Hill, NC: University of North Carolina Press, 1998.

Lemay, Kate Clarke, ed. *Votes for Women: A Portrait of Persistence*. Princeton, NJ: Princeton University Press, 2019.

Linder, Douglas O. *Famous Trials: Susan Anthony Trial (1873)*. Kansas City, MO: University of Missouri-Kansas City School of Law, 1995–2020, available at https://www.famous-trials.com/anthony/.

Poulson, Susan L. *Suffrage: The Epic Struggle for Women's Right to Vote*. Santa Barbara, CA: Praeger, 2019.

Ware, Susan. *Why They Marched: Untold Stories of the Women Who Fought for the Right to Vote*. Cambridge, MA: Harvard University Press, 2019.

"The Woman's Vote in National Elections." *Editorial Research Reports*. Washington, DC: Congressional Quarterly Press, 1927, available at https://library.cqpress.com/cqresearcher/document.php?id=cqresrre1927053100.

Q7. WAS THE TWENTY-SIXTH AMENDMENT (1971), WHICH DROPPED THE VOTING AGE FROM TWENTY-ONE TO EIGHTEEN, RATIFIED PRIMARILY BECAUSE THE FEDERAL GOVERNMENT WAS DRAFTING EIGHTEEN-, NINETEEN-, AND TWENTY-YEAR-OLD MEN TO FIGHT IN THE VIETNAM WAR?

Answer: Yes. The Twenty-Sixth Amendment granting eighteen-year-olds the right to vote was ratified largely because men of this age were fighting and dying in Vietnam.

The Facts: In the United States, the relationship between military service and the right to vote goes back at least to the Civil War. In January 1864, President Lincoln wrote General A. Wadsworth a well-known letter in which he called himself the "nation's guardian" of black soldiers "who have so heroically vindicated their manhood on the battle-field, where, in assisting to save the life of the Republic, they have demonstrated in blood their right to the ballot, which is but the humane protection of the flag they have so fearlessly defended" (Basler, 1953/2001). Union General William Tecumseh Sherman expressed a similar perspective when he wrote, "When the fight is over, the hand that drops the musket cannot be denied the ballot" (Emberton, 2013). Consistent with Sherman's sentiments, the military service of African American men during the Civil War was a factor in the ratification of the Fifteenth Amendment in 1870. In the same vein, following World War I, Congress granted citizenship to the thousands of Native American men who served in the ranks. Although this grant did not guarantee these Native American veterans the right to vote, it removed one of the common barriers that kept them from participating in the franchise. No state could deny these Native American veterans the right to vote based on the fact that they were not citizens. They were citizens because they had fought for their country.

These extensions of the right to vote based on military service were correlated to the traditional voting age limit of twenty-one years of age or older, an age limit that colonial and British practice of the eighteenth century linked to military service. However, in World War II, President Franklin D. Roosevelt called upon Congress to lower the draft age from twenty years to eighteen. Congress did so on November 11, 1942 and Roosevelt signed the bill into law on November 13. Soon thereafter, Republican Senator Arthur Vandenberg and Democratic Representative Jennings Randolph sponsored a constitutional amendment to lower the voting age to eighteen. Supporters quickly adopted the slogan, "old enough to fight, old enough to vote." Although the House Judiciary Committee held hearings on the matter, the proposal never got out of the Committee. Following the War, President Dwight D. Eisenhower unsuccessfully urged Congress to propose a constitutional amendment. During the Korean War (1950–1953), as many as thirty-five states considered lowering the age requirement for voting, but only three such efforts at the state level met with success: Kentucky in 1955 and Alaska and Hawaii in 1959 joined Georgia, which had lowered the voting age limit in 1943 (Neale, 1983). Perhaps the issue languished because the country was at peace after 1953.

The situation quickly changed in the 1960s as the United States increasingly became entangled in the quagmire of the Vietnam War. U.S troop levels rose significantly in the second half of the decade: from 23,000 in 1964, to 385,000 in 1966, to 530,000 in 1968; U.S. casualties mirrored the increase in troop levels, with 200-plus killed in 1964, 6,000-plus in 1966, and almost 17,000 in 1968. All told, more than 58,000

Americans were killed over the course of the war (the last U.S. combat troops left in March 1973, though the war itself dragged on for another two years). The overall number of wounded American military casualties was more than one in ten of those who served: approximately 304,000 of 2.7 million. Not surprisingly, the number of men drafted into military service during the war increased sharply: about 86,000 in 1960, 112,000 in 1964, 382,000 in 1966, and 296,000 in 1968. To fulfill the military's demands for young men, local draft boards leaned heavily on those who were not in college—the poor, racial minorities, and blue-collar whites—which tended to undermine the legitimacy of the draft, especially among those who opposed American involvement in Vietnam. As conscription expanded and the war became increasingly unpopular, opposition to the draft increased and took a variety of forms: men applied for conscientious-objector status, refused to report for induction, joined demonstrations against the war, burned draft cards, claimed a disability, moved to Canada, and, if already inducted, went absent without leave (AWOL). College campuses became a focal point of protest, in part because young men lost their deferments upon graduation. Of course, men under the age of twenty-one who were drafted were keenly aware that they were being sent to fight in a war that they could not vote for or against.

In response to the growing resistance to the draft, Senator Edward Kennedy and several of his colleagues proposed amending the Voting Rights Act of 1970 to lower the voting age to eighteen, not by constitutional amendment, but by federal statute. In support of this measure, Kennedy argued that the

> well-known proposition—"old enough to fight, old enough to vote"—deserves special mention . . . [and] has great appeal. At the very least, the opportunity to vote should be granted in recognition of the risks an 18 year-old is obliged to assume when he is sent off to fight and perhaps die for his country. About 30% of our forces in Vietnam are under 21. Over 19,000, or almost half, of those who have died in action there were under 21. Can we really maintain that these young men did not deserve the right to vote? (Kennedy, 1970)

Congress accepted the amendment and passed the Voting Rights Act of 1970, and President Nixon signed it into law on June 22, 1970.

Oregon and several other states, however, immediately objected that the Act violated the reserved power of states to decide who can vote in state elections. The issue came before the Supreme Court in *Oregon v. Mitchell* (1970). In a closely divided decision, four justices affirmed that

Congress could lower the voting age for both federal and state elections under its authority to alter the election "Regulations" of states (Article I, Section 4), four justices denied the same, and one justice, Hugo Black, concluded that Congress could lower the voting age for federal but not for state elections. Justice Black's reasoning was straightforward: "The Constitution allotted to the States the power to make laws regarding national elections, but provided that, if Congress became dissatisfied with the state laws, Congress could alter them. A newly created national government could hardly have been expected to survive without the ultimate power to rule itself and to fill its offices under its own laws." However, at the same time, "The Constitution was also intended to preserve to the States the power that even the Colonies had to establish and maintain their own separate and independent governments, except insofar as the Constitution itself commands otherwise." Accordingly, while Congress could lower the voting age to eighteen in federal elections, it would take a constitutional amendment to require the states to do the same.

Following the Court's December 21, 1970, decision, Congress moved quickly to pass the Twenty-Sixth Amendment, which barred the United States and the states from denying or abridging the right of citizens eighteen years of age or older the right to vote "on account of age." The Senate voted 94–0 in favor of the measure on March 10, 1971; the House passed the measure by a lopsided 401–19 vote on March 23. The requisite thirty-eight states ratified the Amendment by July 1, 1971, less than four months after Congress submitted it for ratification, the shortest amount of time ever needed for ratification of a constitutional amendment. One reason why the states acted so expeditiously was quite simple: the Court's decision in *Mitchell* required state officials to keep two sets of voting-registration rolls and ballots—one for state and local elections, the other for federal elections—as well as polling stations that could accommodate two types of voters. The aggravation and the costs were too much for most states to bear. They quickly got behind the federal Twenty-Sixth Amendment to solve this administrative nightmare prior to the presidential election of 1972.

There is little evidence that state election officials have applied the Twenty-Sixth Amendment in a discriminatory fashion except in regard to the residency requirements of college students who attend out-of-state schools. If an out-of-state student does not intend to reside in the state where the college or university is located, he or she is not "domiciled" in that state and so has no right to vote there, but must instead vote in his or her home state. However, if a student does intend to remain in the state where the college or university is located, he or she does have the right to register and vote in that state, and election officials may not legally impose unusual evidentiary requirements on such persons by requiring them, for example, to fill out special questionnaires (see *Symm v. United States* [1979]). Forcing atypical registration requirements on college students that are not required of the general population is a violation of the Twenty-Sixth Amendment because it "abridges" a citizen's right to vote "on account of age." Moreover, as young undergraduate students tend in general to be more liberal in their outlook, values, and policy preferences, such atypical registration requirements can be politically motivated in conservative electoral districts, which today are often controlled by the Republican Party. Any denial of the right to vote of an undergraduate student eighteen years of age and a resident of the state for such political reasons is a clear violation of the Constitution.

The overall impact of the Twenty-Sixth Amendment has been tempered by the low voter turnout of young voters. For example, while the voting rates of voters over sixty years of age have over time fluctuated between 52 and 71 percent, only 42 percent of eighteen- to twenty-four-year-olds voted in 1976, 36 percent in 1988, and 32 percent in 1996 and 2000. The number rebounded somewhat in 2004 and especially in 2008, increasing to 48 percent in the presidential election of Barack Obama, before dropping to 38 percent in 2012. 2016 saw a bounce back up to 42 percent, much of it in support of Democratic candidate Bernie Sanders, but a gap of about 30 percent continued to separate the turnout rate of young voters from the 72 percent turnout rate of voters sixty-plus years of age (United States Elections Project). In 2018, 28.2 percent of young voters between ages eighteen and twenty-nine voted, nearly double the national youth vote in the 2014 midterms. According to the Pew Research Center, nearly 60 percent of eighteen- to twenty-four-year-olds identify with the Democratic Party. Currently, Democratic candidates are reaching out to the youth vote during the 2020 primaries. Whether these trends have set the stage for a strong Democratic surge by young voters in the general 2020 presidential race remains to be seen (Paz, 2019). If they do have this effect, one that could possibly determine who wins the presidential race, such a result was only made possible by the Twenty-Sixth Amendment.

FURTHER READING

Basler, Roy P., ed. *The Collected Works of Abraham Lincoln*. Ann Arbor, MI: University of Michigan Digital Library, 2001, initially published by The Abraham Lincoln Association, 1953, Vol. VII, p. 101 (Letter to James S. Wadsworth, January 1864), available at http://abrahamlincoln association.org/lincoln-repository/collected-works/.

Center for Information and Research on Civic Learning and Engagement (CIRCLE). "New National Youth Turnout Estimate: 28% of Young People Voted in 2018," available at https://civicyouth.org/new-national-youth-turnout-estimate-28-of-young-people-voted-in-2018/.

Cheng, Jenny Diamond. "Voting Rights for Millennials: Breathing New Life into the Twenty-Sixth Amendment." *Syracuse Law Review* 67 (2017): 653–678.

Cultice, Wendell W. *Youth's Battle for the Ballot: A History of Voting Age in America*. New York: Praeger, 1992.

Emberton, Carole. *Beyond Redemption: Race, Violence and the American South After the Civil War*. Chicago, IL: University of Chicago Press, 2013.

File, Thom. *Young-Adult Voting: An Analysis of Presidential Elections, 1964–2012*. Washington, DC: U.S. Census Bureau, April 2014, available at https://www.census.gov/prod/2014pubs/p20-573.pdf.

Gentry, Bobbi. *Why Youth Vote: Identity, Inspirational Leaders and Independence*. New York: Springer Publishing, 2018.

Kennedy, Edward M. "Lowering the National Voting Age to 18." March 9, 1970, available at http://www.tedkennedy.org/ownwords/event/voting_age/.

Neale, Thomas H. *The Eighteen Year Old Vote: The Twenty-Sixth Amendment and Subsequent Voting Rates of New Enfranchised Age Groups*. Report No. 83-103. Washington, DC: Congressional Research Service, 1983, available at https://www.everycrsreport.com/files/19830520_83-103GOV_f7c90f8fb698968e03f7ce5e3b45288dffcce08f.pdf.

Paz, Isabella Grullon. "Democrats Seek Young Voters, and the Memes that Move Them." *The New York Times*, April 22, 2019, available at https://www.nytimes.com/2019/04/22/us/politics/youth-voters-2020.html.

Selective Service System. "Induction Statistics," available at https://www.sss.gov/About/History-And-Records/Induction-Statistics.

United States Elections Project. "Voter Turnout Demographics," available at http://www.electproject.org/home/voter-turnout/demographics.

Q8. ARE THERE ANY OTHER AMENDMENTS TO THE U.S. CONSTITUTION THAT AFFECTED THE RIGHT OF AMERICAN CITIZENS TO VOTE IN FEDERAL AND STATE ELECTIONS?

Answer: Yes. The Seventeenth Amendment granted citizens the right to elect U.S. Senators; the Twenty-Second Amendment denied citizens the right to elect a president to a third term; the Twenty-Third Amendment gave citizens of Washington, DC, the right to select "electors" in presidential elections; and the Twenty-Fourth Amendment abolished poll taxes in federal elections.

The Facts: The Seventeenth Amendment of the Constitution, ratified in 1913, granted citizens the right to vote for the two senators of the state in which they resided. This amendment was necessary because the original Constitution granted state legislatures the power of "chusing" U.S. senators (Article 1, Section 3). In *Federalist No. 62*, James Madison summarized the constitutional convention's rationale for this method of senatorial appointment:

> Among the various modes which might have been devised for constituting this branch of the government, that which has been proposed by the convention is probably the most congenial with the public opinion. It is recommended by the double advantage of favoring a select appointment, and of giving to the State governments such an agency in the formation of the federal government as must secure the authority of the former, and may form a convenient link between the two systems.

In short, according to Madison, the public favored this method of selection; it would produce more qualified and experienced senators; states would support the federal government; and it would foster communication and cooperation between the two levels of government. Madison did not address whether this method of senatorial appointment was consistent with representative democracy. Relying on the fact that the legislatures of the states would be elected through some form of popular election, he instead assumed that the proposed "indirect" method of electing U.S. senators was compatible with a republican form of government.

However, during the nineteenth century, several problems arose with this method of selecting U.S. senators. First, it appeared that the practice was vulnerable to corruption because a candidate could possibly "purchase" a Senate seat by buying off a limited number of state legislators, whether by money or political favors. The Senate found it necessary to investigate "ten cases of bribery or corruption" between 1857 and 1900, and in three of these cases, "a Senate committee [was] able to conclude that the charges had merit." The troublesome influence that corporations and political machines had on state legislatures buttressed the problem of corruption. Another concern was that state legislatures often deadlocked and failed to elect a senator (Bybee, 1997). New Jersey, for example, ran into this predicament in 1865. John P. Stockton received only a plurality, not a majority, of the votes cast in a joint session of the two houses of the state's legislature. Stockton claimed the election was valid because the joint session had earlier voted 41–40 to permit the election by a plurality of legislators, rather than by a majority. However, Stockton's opponents argued that this change of the rules required a majority vote in each house of the state legislature and that one of the houses had not voted for the change of the rules. In the end, the U.S. Senate accepted this latter argument and refused Stockton his seat in March 1866, leaving one of New Jersey's seats in the Senate vacant for more than a year.

In response to the Stockton impasse, Congress in 1866 exercised its authority under Article I, Section 4, by enacting a law that required each house of a state legislature to meet separately when electing a U.S. senator. If both houses chose the same candidate, that candidate would be elected; if not, then the two houses would meet in joint session every day until a majority (not a plurality) of the legislators came to an agreement. However, this law did not prevent deadlocks. In fact, "Between 1891 and 1905, eight state legislatures failed to elect senators and were without full representation from periods of ten months to four years." Delaware, in particular, was in senatorial gridlock at the turn of the century, "failing to send senators in 1895, 1899, 1901, and 1905" (Bybee, 1997).

Of course, the extensions of the franchise throughout the nineteenth century contributed to the public's growing support for the direct election of senators. This idea had been proposed several times in the nineteenth century, in fact as early as 1826, but the proposals quickly died away, primarily because the U.S. Senate was composed of persons elected by state legislatures. However, a gradual movement in the direction of popular election arose in the last decade of the nineteenth century. The Populist Party incorporated direct election of senators into its platform in the mid-1890s. Oregon in 1907 required state legislators to vote for the winner of a state primary election. By 1912, twenty-nine states had followed Oregon's example, shifting the power in the Senate from those who opposed direct election to those who favored it. Congress submitted the Seventeenth Amendment to the states on May 13, 1912, and thirty-six states ratified it within a year, Connecticut passing the critical vote on April 8, 1913.

The Twenty-Second Amendment limited a president to two four-year terms. The original Constitution contained no such restriction, with Alexander Hamilton arguing in *Federalist No. 69* that a president was "re-eligible as often as the people of the United States shall think him worthy of their confidence." However, George Washington, the country's first president who served two four-year terms, refused to run for a third, explaining his reasons in a letter to Jonathan Trumbull, Jr. dated July 21, 1799. First, Washington referred to his "ardent wishes to pass through the vale of life in retirem[en]t, undisturbed in the remnant of the days I have to sojourn here, unless called upon to defend my Country." Second, although he expressed gratitude for his good health, he admits that he is "not insensible to my declination in other respects," such that he thought it would be "criminal" of him to accept the presidential office when "another would discharge [it] with more ability." And lastly, Washington feared that, if he ran for a third term, he would become "a mark for the shafts of envenomed [partisan] malice" and "charged not only with irresolution, but with concealed ambition, . . . dotage and imbicility [sic]" (Founders Online). The letter lends support to the view that Washington retired after two terms primarily because he thought it would be better for the country if he stepped down.

Washington's decision set a precedent that survived for almost a century and a half. Although Ulysses S. Grant ran for a third term in 1880, he failed to get his party's nomination. Theodore Roosevelt also lost his bid for a third term in the 1912 presidential election (albeit as the candidate of the Bull Moose Party rather than the Republican Party, which had nominated him in his two earlier presidential victories). It was not until Franklin Delano Roosevelt won the 1940 election that Washington's precedent gave way to the political imperatives of the Great Depression and the challenges of navigating America through World War II. At this time, the American economy was still plagued by persistent unemployment, numerous and costly labor strikes, and the lack of consumer purchasing power. Although the United States had not yet entered the war in 1940, Roosevelt was deeply concerned about Germany's aggressive military actions in Europe and Japan's in Asia and he did everything he could to support Britain despite the Neutrality Acts, which Congress had passed in the 1930s to limit U.S. involvement in foreign wars.

In this context, without a clear Democratic successor, Roosevelt decided that it was too dangerous to change leadership, so he ran for a third term in 1940 and a fourth in 1944, winning both. However, during the latter election, Republican candidate Thomas Dewey argued, "four terms of sixteen years is the most dangerous threat to our freedom ever proposed." He added, "That is one reason why I believe that two terms must be established as the limit by constitutional amendment." The Hoover Commission, created in 1947 by President Harry Truman (who succeeded Roosevelt after his death in 1945) to make administrative changes in the federal government, agreed with Dewey and recommended to Congress that it should submit such an amendment to the states. A

Republican-controlled Congress did so in March 1947, and the requisite number of states ratified it in 1951. The amendment limited the number of years a president could serve to ten. Accordingly, if a person became president without a presidential election and served for less than two years, then he or she could run for two additional terms, but only for one term if his or her initial term of office was more than two years.

The Twenty-Third Amendment gave the citizens of Washington, DC, the right to select the number of "electors" to the Electoral College in presidential elections to which it would be entitled if it was a state, but in no case more electors "than the least populous State." Prior to this amendment, Congress under Article I, Section 8, of the Constitution had the power to "exercise exclusive Legislation in all Cases whatsoever, over such District . . . as may . . . become the Seat of the Government of the United States." Washington, DC, became the "Seat of Government" in 1801, and from that point forward, Congress generally refused to delegate authority to elected local officials, especially after 1870, preferring instead to delegate to the President the power to appoint local DC officials and city council members. In 1881, an amendment to permit DC's participation in presidential elections was introduced in Congress, but support for it was negligible. It was not until President Dwight D. Eisenhower endorsed the idea in the 1950s that momentum for such an amendment began to build. Congress passed the Twenty-Third Amendment in 1960 and both presidential candidates of that year, Vice President Richard M. Nixon and Senator John F. Kennedy, backed the measure. Thirty-eight states ratified the proposal by March 29, 1961.

The 1964 presidential election was the first in which the citizens of DC were able to vote. Currently, the District has three electoral votes, the same number as Wyoming, the least populous state with approximately two hundred thousand fewer residents than Washington, DC. Although the Twenty-Third Amendment gave DC residents the right to participate in presidential elections, it did not give them the right to participate in congressional elections, whether of the Senate or the House of Representatives. However, in 1970, Congress granted the citizens of DC the right to vote for one *nonvoting* representative to the House of Representatives and, in 1973, enacted the Home Rule Act, which gave local residents the right to elect a mayor and a city council. Despite the importance of these concessions, Congress retained the right to overturn any of DC's municipal laws. In 1978, Congress passed the District of Columbia Voting Rights Amendment, which would have given the District full representation in Congress and full participation in the Electoral College and the federal amendment process, but only sixteen states ratified it and it expired in 1985. In 1982, DC ratified a constitution for a new state called "New Columbia," but Congress declined to move the proposal forward. To this day, the citizens of Washington, DC, remain what could be called second-class citizens, with no role in the federal constitutional amendment process or in the election of U.S. senators and only a right to speak, but not vote, in the House of Representatives.

The Twenty-Fourth Amendment, ratified in 1964, prohibited the United States or any state from denying or abridging anyone's right to vote "by reason of failure to pay any poll tax or other tax." This amendment was not a radical change of practice in most states. Property qualifications for general state elections (excluding special local elections for bond issues or school elections) had largely died by the end of the nineteenth century. However, several states retained tax requirements for voting and this practice rebounded in the South during the 1890s to discourage African Americans and poor whites from voting. But economic qualifications for voting eventually became less popular in the South, especially during the Great Depression when white unemployment was widespread. In addition, poll taxes in the South were employed with less frequency because other voter suppression measures, such as literacy tests and white primaries, had become the preferred method of disfranchising black voters.

Despite this trend against the use of poll taxes, the Supreme Court upheld their constitutionality in *Breedlove v. Suttles* (1937), which ensured their continued use in Alabama, Arkansas, Mississippi, Texas, and Virginia. These were the only states that still had poll taxes when the Twenty-Fourth Amendment was ratified in 1964. All of these states save Arkansas kept its poll tax for state elections, but two years later, the Supreme Court overruled *Breedlove* in *Harper v. Virginia Board of Elections* (1966), concluding that the use of poll taxes in state elections violated the Equal Protection Clause. In the Court's view, "Voter qualifications have no relation to wealth nor to paying or not paying this or any other tax" and the Fourteenth Amendment "restrains the States from fixing voter qualifications which invidiously discriminate" against the poor. With this decision, poll taxes disappeared from American political life.

FURTHER READING

Ackerman, Bruce, and Nou, Jennifer. "Canonizing the Civil Rights Revolution: The People and the Poll Tax." *Northwestern University Law Review* 103 (2009): 63–148.

Amar, Vikram David. "Indirect Effects of Direct Election: A Structural Examination of the Seventeenth Amendment." *Vanderbilt Law Review* 49 (1996): 1347–1405.

Berman, Ali. *Give Us the Ballot: The Modern Struggle for Voting Rights in America.* New York: Farrar, Straus and Giroux, 2015.

Bybee, Jay S. "Ulysses at the Mast: Democracy, Federalism, and the Siren's Song of the Seventeenth Amendment." *Northwestern University Law Review* 91 (1997): 500–569.

Founders Online, National Archives. "From George Washington to Jonathan Trumbull, Jr., 21 July 1799," available at https://founders.archives.gov/documents/Washington/06-04-02-0165.

Jordon, David M. *FDR, Dewey, and the Election of 1944.* Bloomington, IN: Indiana University Press, 2011.

Korzi, Michael J. *Presidential Term Limits in American History: Power, Principles, and Politics.* College Station, TX: Texas A&M University Press, 2011.

Rossiter, Clinton, ed. *The Federalist Papers.* New York: Mentor, 1961.

Rossum, Ralph A. *Federalism, the Supreme Court, and the Seventeenth Amendment: The Irony of Constitutional Democracy.* Lanham, MD: Lexington Books, 2001.

Schiller, Wendy J., and Stewart, Charles, III. *Electing the Senate: Indirect Democracy before the Seventeenth Amendment.* Princeton, NJ: Princeton University Press, 2014.

Walters, Ronald W., and Travis, Toni-Michelle. *Democratic Destiny and the District of Columbia: Federal Politics and Public Policy.* Lanham, MD: Lexington Books, 2010.

2

Electoral Districting and the Warren Court

Electoral districting is about who votes in what elections. One might think that elections are the same across the country, but that is not true. For example, following the ratification of the Seventeenth Amendment, elections for U.S. Senators are statewide contests. The state itself is the district in which the senatorial election takes place, and the candidate who wins a majority or plurality of the popular vote wins the election. In a similar way, states that are entitled to only one representative, such as Wyoming, Vermont, and Alaska, also conduct statewide popular elections to decide who will represent the people of each state in the House of Representatives. However, House elections in states that are entitled to more than one federal representative are different. Federal law currently requires these states to divide themselves into geographical districts, each of which elects its own representative. Because only Nebraska has a unicameral state legislature, state senators are also typically elected within geographical subdivisions of the state. Accordingly, forty-nine of the fifty states are divided up into senate districts that elect state senators and house districts that elect the state house of representatives (sometimes called the General Assembly or House of Delegates). These state districts can be single-member or multimember districts. In the former, the geographical district elects only one state senator or representative; in the latter, a district elects more than one senator or representative. Local representatives, such as members of a city council or county commission, can be elected by districts (whether single or multiple) or by an "at-large" election, whereby all the voters in the city or county vote for all the members of the council or commission.

How electoral district lines are drawn in district elections has an enormous impact on the value of an individual vote in determining election outcomes. As each state elects two U.S. Senators, the value of the right to vote in senatorial elections is obviously much higher in small states, such as Wyoming, with a population of 563,000, than in California, with a population of 37,254,000. This type of inequality in the value of the right to vote is built into the federal nature of the American constitutional structure. However, a comparable kind of inequality at one time also existed within states, whether in terms of districts for the House of Representatives, the state legislature, or local representative entities. For example, one district within a state might have had ten thousand residents and another one hundred thousand, with the result that the right to vote in the latter district is, mathematically speaking, one-tenth of the value of the right to vote in the former. Throughout much of the history of the United States, the different types of electoral districts within states have been "malapportioned" in this manner. The Supreme Court avoided ruling on the constitutionality of malapportioned electoral districts by claiming that the issue was a political question unsuited for judicial resolution. It was not until the 1960s that the Supreme Court, led by Chief Justice Earl Warren and often referred to as the Warren Court, confronted this highly politicized topic. In a series of decisions, the Court transformed American elections by endorsing and implementing the principle of "one person, one vote." Earl Warren called these decisions the most important ones for American democracy that the Court addressed during his tenure.

Q9. DURING THE NINETEENTH CENTURY AND THE FIRST HALF OF THE TWENTIETH, DID CONGRESS ALLOW STATE LEGISLATURES TO DETERMINE THE GEOGRAPHICAL LINES OF ELECTORAL DISTRICTS FOR ELECTIONS TO THE HOUSE OF REPRESENTATIVES?

Answer: Yes. Although in 1842 Congress did require states to use "contiguous" single-member districts in House elections, and later added that they "should" be "compact" and "equal in population," it generally did little to enforce these provisions except for the requirement of single-member districts.

The Facts: Section 2 of Article I of the Constitution commands that "Representatives . . . shall be apportioned among the several States which may be included within this Union, according to their respective Numbers, which shall be determined by adding to the whole Number of free Persons, including those bound to Service for a Term of Years, and excluding Indians not taxed, [and] three-fifths of all other Persons." At the Constitutional Convention, the northern and southern states came up with the "three-fifths clause" as a compromise to partially count slaves for congressional apportionment purposes. Section 2 added that the number of House seats assigned to each state should be recalibrated "every subsequent Term of ten Years" in such manner as Congress shall direct. Of course, as the recalibration could only be made if Congress knew how many free persons, aliens, and slaves resided in each state, this provision implicitly required a national census every ten years. Congress ordered the first census to be held in 1790, thereby initiating a process of having a national census every ten years thereafter.

The Constitution also stated that voters for House members "shall have the Qualifications requisite for Electors of the most numerous Branch of the State Legislature" (Article I, Section 2) and that state legislatures had the power to determine the "Times, Places and Manner of holding Elections for . . . Representatives, . . . but the Congress may at any time by Law make or alter such Regulations" (Article I, Section 4) (see Q2). Congress's control over the national census, its allocation of House seats to the states, and its power to regulate the "manner" of federal elections might suggest that Congress would have exercised substantial control over how states conducted federal elections within their borders, but the opposite is true.

There is considerable evidence that the framers of the Constitution preferred the model of single-member districts, a system in which the legislature establishes electoral subdivisions within the state and voters in each district vote for one candidate and the winner represents the district. For example, in *Federalist No. 56*, James Madison wrote, "Divide the largest State into ten or twelve districts and it will be found that there will be no peculiar local interests in either which will not be within the knowledge of the representative of the district." In this fashion, according to Madison, single-member districts would produce an informed and effective system of representing local state interests in the national legislature. In a similar vein, Alexander Hamilton in New York's ratifying convention claimed that the "natural and proper mode of holding elections will be to divide the state into districts in proportion to the number to be elected" (Hamilton, 1788).

Despite the framers' preference for single-member districts, they evidently thought it more important that states should have considerable latitude in how they structured their voting systems, enabling them to take into account their own unique traditions and circumstances. For example, despite his own preference for single-member districts, Madison made the following observation: "Whether the electors should vote by ballot, or viva voce, should assemble at this place or that place, should be divided into districts, or all meet at one place, should all vote for all the Representatives, or all in a district vote for a number allotted to the district, these, and many other points, would depend on the legislatures, and might materially affect the appointments" (Zagarri, 1987). Accordingly, although elections of members of the House were federal elections, the general consensus of the early republic was that states should largely control the "manner" of elections held within their borders, including whether a state would utilize single-member districts for House elections.

The Constitution's silence on this point led to a variety of early state electoral systems for House elections. Although single-member districts were popular, six states opted for "at-large" (or "general ticket") systems, in which eligible voters of the state voted for as many candidates as there were House seats apportioned to the state and the winners represented all the state's residents. However, a few states, such as New York and Pennsylvania, adopted multimember districts in which voters voted in electoral subdivisions of the state, but each district elected more than one representative to the House. Another important variation was that some states required that a candidate receive a majority of votes (which often required run-off elections) while others only required a plurality. Of course, these electoral systems were also in a constant state of flux as victorious political parties in states across the expanding country altered election rules in ways that favored them (Lampi, 2019).

As a general matter, big states with large populations and diverse interests tended to favor single-member or multimember district systems because the state legislature could draw district lines to ensure that important constituencies of the state were not underrepresented in the House of Representatives. Conversely, small states with modest, homogeneous populations tended to favor at-large voting as it increased the impact of the state's delegation on the national legislature. The representatives would presumably vote together in the House because the majority or plurality of the small states' voters elected them all into office. However, at-large voting could result in the diminution or loss of representation by an important minority interest within a state, especially if the state accepted plurality elections or if voting within a state coalesced along party lines.

This negative feature of at-large voting for members of the House was well-known in the nineteenth century. During the 1830s, the Whig Party, in particular, thought this model of voting prevented it from gaining ground in at-large southern states, such as Georgia, Mississippi, and Missouri. However, notwithstanding this alleged disadvantage, the Whigs fared well in the election of 1840; they elected their presidential candidate, William Henry Harrison, to office and took control of both the House and Senate. However, the Democrats won a majority of Alabama's legislature in 1840 and soon thereafter switched the state from a district to an at-large voting system, with the result that the Democrats won all five of the state's House seats in the next congressional election. Frustrated, many Whigs threw their support behind the following proposed amendment to the federal Apportionment Act of 1842:

> *And be it further enacted*, That in every case when a State is entitled to more than one Representative, the number to which each State shall be entitled under this apportionment shall be elected by districts, composed of contiguous territory, equal in number to the number of Representatives to which said State may be entitled; no one district electing more than one Representative. (Flores, 2000)

This proposed amendment set off a fiery debate on whether Section 4 of Article I gave Congress the power to require states to adopt single-member districts for House elections.

Defenders of state authority argued that Congress's power to control the "manner" of House elections (Article I, Section 4) was "only intended to be an ultimate power, for self-preservation," for example, if a state neglected to hold House elections. Another argued that the amendment would "plant a thorn in the bosom of many of these States that will rankle and fester there until it gangrenes the body politic" (Flores, 2000). Supporters of the amendment brushed aside such comments, arguing that "what plain, unsophisticated man" reading Article I, Section 4, ". . . would for a moment doubt the power of Congress to control the whole subject, whenever, in its discretion, it shall see fit to do so?" The language could not "be more direct, full, and explicit" (Flores, 2000).

In the end, two arguments won the day in favor of the amendment: the felt need for uniformity of House elections across the country; and, second, the moral imperative of giving minorities a fighting chance to get their candidate elected. As one representative asked, "what would become of the interests of minorities in the several States, when each state should send an entire delegation of one or other of the two great parties?" Others remarked that, "The general ticket system disfranchises the minority in a State, however near it may approach a majority, and in however so many districts it would actually constitute a majority, and be entitled to a representation in Congress," and that it was "a system so unjust, anti-republican, and so outrageous upon the rights of minorities, that it can never prevail in many States of this Union" (Flores, 2000).

Congress passed the amendment and President John Tyler signed the Apportionment Act, although he expressed reservations about the constitutionality of the single-member district provision. As an indication of the controversial nature of this requirement, it is worth noting that four states—Georgia, Mississippi, Missouri, and New Hampshire—refused to comply with the amendment in the House elections of 1842. However, a challenge to the legality of the elections in these four states ultimately proved unsuccessful as the House eventually granted the successful candidates their seats. Following the 1850 census, Congress dropped the single-member district requirement, but restored it after the 1860 census, with the same stipulation that a district should be composed of "contiguous territory." In 1872, Congress went further, insisting that districts should contain "as nearly as practicable an equal number of inhabitants" and, in 1901, mandated that House districts should be "compact" in character.

However, in terms of enforcement, it was not clear whether the requirements of an "equal number of inhabitants as practicable," "contiguity," and "compactness" were much more than admonitions. After all, Congress failed to reapportion the House following the 1910 census and its next apportionment bill in 1929 did not impose any districting requirements on the state. Later, in *Wood v. Broom* (1932), the Supreme Court held that legislative acts apportioning House seats expired with each census, which meant that the 1929 law gave states broad latitude to draw districts as they saw fit or, if they chose, to abandon single-member districts entirely. A few states, such as New York and Illinois, returned to at-large elections, but the majority preserved the more traditional model of single-member districts. It was not until 1967 that Congress once again mandated that states with more than one House representative use single-member districts (Pub. L. 90-196).

FURTHER READING

"Apportionment Act of 1842: In All Cases, By District." *Whereas: Stories from the People's House* (blog), United States House of Representatives:

History, Art, & Archive, April 16, 2019, available at https://history
.house.gov/Blog/2019/April/4-16-Apportionment-1/.
Eagles, Charles W. *Democracy Delayed: Congressional Reapportionment and Urban-Rural Conflict in the 1920s*. Athens, GA: University of Georgia Press, 2010.
Flores, Nicolas. *A History of One-Winner Districts for Congress*, Chap. 3, "The 1842 Apportionment Act," an undergraduate political science thesis, Stanford University, 2000, available at http://archive.fairvote.org/library/history/flores/apportn.htm.
Hacker, Andrew. *Congressional Districting: The Issue of Equal Representation*. 2nd ed. Washington, DC: Brookings Institution, 1966.
Hamilton, Alexander. "First Speech of June 21." Teaching American History, 1788, available at https://teachingamericanhistory.org/library/document/alexander-hamilton-speech/.
Lampi, Philip. "Mapping Early American Elections: Electing Members of Congress in the Early Republic: District vs. At-Large Elections." *Roy Rosenzweig Center for History and New Media*, 2019, available at http://earlyamericanelections.org/essays/03-lampi-election-methods.html.
Rossiter, Clinton, ed. *The Federalist Papers*. New York: Mentor, 1961.
Schmeckebier, Laurence Frederick. *Congressional Apportionment*. Washington, DC: Brookings Institution, 1941.
Tolson, Franita. "The Spectrum of Congressional Authority over Elections." *Boston University Law Review* 99 (2019): 320–393.
Zagarri, Rosemarie. *The Politics of Size*. Ithaca, NY: Cornell University Press, 1987.

Q10. DID THE REPUBLICAN GUARANTEE CLAUSE OF THE CONSTITUTION (ARTICLE IV, SECTION 4) PROVIDE THE SUPREME COURT WITH A LEGAL BASIS TO INVALIDATE HOUSE ELECTORAL DISTRICTS IF THEY CONTAINED UNEQUAL POPULATIONS?

Answer: No. Despite the connection between republican government and elections "by the People," the Supreme Court consistently held that the Republican Guarantee Clause was not a suitable basis to invalidate electoral districts that were malapportioned.

The Facts: The Republican Guarantee Clause of the Constitution (Article IV, Section 4) reads as follows: "The United States shall guarantee to every State in this Union a Republican Form of Government." At the time the Constitution was ratified, it was not clear whether this clause prohibited states from establishing electoral districts that were malapportioned by population. James Madison in *Federalist No. 39* defined "republican" government to be one which (1) "derives all its powers directly or indirectly from the great body of the people," and (2) "is administered by persons holding their offices during pleasure for a limited period, or during good behavior."

This definition, of course, did not explicitly address whether a state would lose its stature as a "republican" form of government if it established electoral districts that were malapportioned. However, in a radical case of malapportionment, for example, if a state established ten electoral districts, with 90 percent of the state's population residing in one district and ten in the remaining nine, it could be plausibly argued that the "great body of the people" were no longer appointing the "administrators" of the federal and the state government. Only a small minority of the voters would be electing the state's legislature and the federal House of Representatives and the problem would be magnified in the "indirect" elections of the U.S. Senate and the president. But even if no state was likely to adopt such an extreme form of electoral districting, at what point would malapportionment trigger the federal government's obligation to "guarantee to every State in this Union a Republican Form of Government?" A second question was whether this issue was a judicial question suitable for resolution by the Supreme Court or a political one beyond its jurisdiction.

The Supreme Court considered the nature of "political questions" in *Luther v. Borden* (1849), a case that arose during the Dorr rebellion in Rhode Island. A popularly elected government, "one established by a voluntary convention," tried to overthrow the established charter government of the state, one elected by a narrow franchise. Each government claimed to be the legitimate government of the state, but the more popular government insisted it had the better argument based on the Republican Guarantee Clause. In the end, the Supreme Court held that it was not within its power to decide which government was the legitimate government of Rhode Island. Instead, it was for Congress to decide which "senators and representatives of a State are [to be] admitted into the councils of the Union . . . as well as its republican character" and its decision "is binding on every other department of the government, and could not be questioned in a judicial tribunal."

The issue of which government of Rhode Island was legitimate was, therefore, a political question, one that was beyond the jurisdiction of the Supreme Court or any other court to answer.

The Court broadened the definition of a political question in *Taylor and Marshall v. Beckham* (1900), a case involving a decision by Kentucky's General Assembly not to seat a governor in a contested election. In the end, the Supreme Court denied that it had jurisdiction to interfere with the Assembly's authority to decide contested gubernatorial elections, holding that the Republican Guarantee Clause was not a suitable basis for jurisdiction because the dispute between the Assembly and the Governor was a political question. In a similar vein, the Supreme Court held in *Pacific States Telephone and Telegraph Company v. Oregon* (1912) that the constitutionality of permitting voters to directly enact laws through initiatives and referendums was purely a political question outside the Court's jurisdiction.

With this constitutional background, the Supreme Court finally considered whether a state violated the Republican Guarantee Clause by creating malapportioned electoral districts for House elections in *Colegrove v. Green* (1946). Three Illinois voters living in congressional districts much larger in population than others (e.g., the largest had 914,000 residents; the smallest only 112,116) claimed that the state's districting system violated the Republican Guarantee Clause, especially because Illinois had last redrawn districts in 1901. In a plurality opinion written by Justice Felix Frankfurter, the Supreme Court explained why the voters were asking the "Court what is beyond its competence to grant." The voters were not claiming a "private wrong," but rather "a wrong suffered by Illinois as a polity," and they were asking "the federal courts to reconstruct the electoral process of Illinois in order that it may be adequately represented in the councils of the Nation." According to Frankfurter, however, "no court can affirmatively re-map the Illinois districts so as to bring them more in conformity with the standards of fairness for a representative system. At best, we could only declare the existing electoral system invalid," which might result in "a statewide [at-large] ticket," a scenario that may very well be worse than a system of malapportioned districts.

In Frankfurter's view, the above possibility reflects the fact it "is hostile to a democratic system to involve the judiciary in the politics of the people." Moreover, the problem is no less "pernicious if such judicial intervention in an essentially political contest be dressed up in the abstract phrases of the law." This was not to suggest that the voters of Illinois have no remedy. The Constitution itself "has conferred upon Congress exclusive authority to secure fair representation by the States in the popular House, and left to that House determination whether States have fulfilled their responsibility." But even if Congress failed in its duty to maintain fair representation, Frankfurter thought the remedy lied not with the courts, but rather "with the people." Any judicial order mandating that Congress should fulfill its duty "would cut very deep into the very being of Congress. Courts ought not to enter this political thicket." Frankfurter concluded that any violation "of the great guaranty of a republican form of government in States cannot be challenged in the courts." Ultimately, fair representation in Congress depended "on the vigilance of the people in exercising their political rights."

Justice Hugo Black's dissent sharply disagreed with Frankfurter's reasoning that a malapportioned electoral system was outside the jurisdiction of the court because it was a "political question." First, he noted that the electoral districts of the state legislature were comparably malapportioned as the House districts, making it almost impossible for a "vigilant people" to rectify the problem. Second, although Black concedes that "voting is a part of elections, and that elections are 'political,' . . . it is a mere 'play upon words' to refer to a controversy such as this as 'political' in the sense that courts have nothing to do with protecting and vindicating the right of a voter to cast an effective ballot." It may be true that invalidating Illinois's electoral district might lead to a statewide election, with a negative effect on minority representation, but it would not "discriminate against some groups to favor others." Instead, "it gives all the people an equally effective voice in electing their representatives, as is essential under a free government, and it is constitutional." Despite Justice Black's strong dissent, *Colegrove v. Green* marked the end of any possibility of achieving equal apportionment of House electoral districts by way of judicial litigation under the Republican Guarantee Clause. The federal constitutional guarantee of a republican state government raised inherently "political questions" to be resolved by the political branches of the federal government, not the federal courts, not even the Supreme Court.

FURTHER READING

Argersinger, Peter H. *Representation and Inequality in Late Nineteenth-Century America: The Politics of Apportionment*. New York: Cambridge University Press, 2012.

Biles, Charles M. *The History of Congressional Apportionment*. Arcata, CA: Humboldt State University Press, 2017.

Celler, Emanual. "Congressional Apportionment—Past, Present, and Future." *Law and Contemporary Problems* 17 (1952): 269–275.

Elliot, Ward E. Y. *The Rise of Guardian Democracy: The Supreme Court's Role in Voting Rights Disputes, 1845–1969*. Cambridge, MA: Harvard University Press, 1974.

Grove, Tara Leigh. "The Lost History of the Political Question Doctrine." *New York University Law Review* 90 (2015): 1908–1974.
Miller, William J., and Walling, Jeremy D., eds. *The Political Battle over Congressional Redistricting*. Reprint ed. Lanham, MD: Lexington Books, 2015.
Mourtada-Sabbah, Nada, and Cain, Bruce E., eds. *The Political Question Doctrine and the Supreme Court of the United States*. Lanham, MD: Lexington Books, 2007, Chap. 4.
"Political Rights as Political Questions: The Paradox of *Luther v. Borden*." *Harvard Law Review* 100 (1987): 1125–1145.
Rossiter, Clinton, ed. *The Federalist Papers*. New York: Mentor, 1961.

Q11. IF FEDERAL COURTS WERE UNABLE TO RELY ON THE REPUBLICAN GUARANTEE CLAUSE TO REQUIRE STATES TO EQUALIZE THE POPULATIONS OF HOUSE ELECTORAL DISTRICTS, COULD THEY INVALIDATE A CHANGE IN A STATE'S ELECTORAL DISTRICT LINES BASED ON RACE OR ETHNICITY?

Answer: Yes. Although the Supreme Court was initially reluctant to authorize judicial intrusion into how a state defined a municipality's electoral district boundaries, the Warren Court ruled that the Fourteenth and Fifteenth Amendments prohibited states from purposefully drawing municipal boundaries to discriminate against voting rights of racial minorities.

The Facts: At the beginning of the twentieth century, the Supreme Court was hesitant about interfering in how a state established electoral districts within its territory, whether for state, county, or municipal elections. Regarding the boundaries of municipalities, the Court's leading case was *Hunter v. Pittsburgh* (1907), a case involving an objection by the city of Allegheny to a Pennsylvania law requiring it to unify with Pittsburgh if the majority of citizens living in the two cities voted for incorporation. As the population of Pittsburgh was larger than that of Allegheny, the latter's fear was that its interests would be subordinated to those of the former. Despite this concern, the Supreme Court invoked what it called a "settled" doctrine.

"Municipal corporations are political subdivisions of the state," the Court insisted, which means that the state may "expand or contract the territorial area, unite the whole or a part of it with another municipality, repeal the charter and destroy the corporation." In other words, the Court concluded, "the state is supreme, and its legislative body, conforming its action to the state constitution, may do as it will, unrestrained by any provision of the Constitution of the United States," which meant that the Fourteenth and Fifteenth Amendments did not restrict how states could draw municipal boundaries.

However, during the twentieth century, the Court issued a number of rulings invalidating state restrictions on the right to vote based on the Fourteenth and Fifteenth Amendments. For example, in *Nixon v. Herndon* (1927), the Court invalidated Texas's white primary, holding that it was a clear case of racial discrimination against African Americans in violation of the Fourteenth Amendment's Equal Protection Clause. Twelve years later, in *Lane v. Wilson* (1939), the Court invalidated Oklahoma's renewed attempt to establish a grandfather clause that would exempt most white voters from the state's literacy test (see Q4).

Against this background, the Court in *Gomillion v. Lightfoot* (1960) considered whether Alabama could alter the boundaries of the city of Tuskegee from a square to an irregular figure of twenty-eight sides, an alteration that would exclude all but four or five of its four hundred African American citizens from municipal elections. The law in question did not formally take away the right to vote from African Americans, but rather changed the boundaries of the district to prevent African Americans from voting in municipal elections. They could vote in county or state elections, but not in Tuskegee's.

The Court characterized the redistricting of Tuskegee as "solely concerned with segregating white and colored voters by fencing Negro citizens out of town so as to deprive them of their pre-existing municipal vote." Alabama's action was unlike the one considered in *Hunter*, the Court added, because the objection to Pennsylvania's law was not "supported by such a specific limitation upon State power as confines the States under the Fifteenth Amendment," that is, the limit prohibiting states from abridging the right to vote on account of race. Moreover, the Court continued, unlike the facts of *Colegrove v. Green* (1946):

> the Alabama Legislature has not merely redrawn the Tuskegee city limits with incidental inconvenience to the petitioners; it is more accurate to say that it has deprived the petitioners of the municipal franchise and consequent rights, and, to that end, it has incidentally changed the city's boundaries. While in form this is merely an act redefining metes and bounds, . . . the inescapable human effect of this essay in geometry and geography is to despoil colored citizens, and only colored citizens, of their theretofore enjoyed voting rights.

According to the Court, eroding the value of the right to vote of African Americans living in Tuskegee was indistinguishable from an absolute deprivation of the right to vote in violation of the Fifteenth Amendment. After all, before Alabama's change in Tuskegee's boundaries, African American residents could vote in its municipal elections; after it, all but a few could not, even if they could vote in county or state elections.

The Court also noted that Alabama did not cite "any countervailing municipal function" that the boundary change was "designed to serve." For example, in *Wright v. Rockefeller* (1964), the Warren Court reviewed a challenge to how New York had redrawn the four congressional districts of Manhattan, resulting in one district composed primarily of nonwhite and Puerto Rican citizens. The Court argued "that the District Court was not compelled to find that these districts were the product of a state contrivance to discriminate against colored or Puerto Rican voters." In fact, the Court suggested, while some minority voters living in Manhattan "would prefer a more even distribution of minority groups among the four congressional districts," "others . . . would argue strenuously that the kind of districts for which appellants contended would be undesirable, and, because based on race or place of origin, would themselves be unconstitutional." The Court's reasoning suggested the following: first, some minority voters might prefer to be concentrated in one district to ensure their candidates would win House elections; second, deliberately using race to divide a racial minority among four congressional districts might be as constitutionally questionable as concentrating most members of the racial minority into one district; and, third, it was possible for a state legislature to take account of race in electoral districting without engaging in racial discrimination.

These three points highlight the Warren Court's position that the Fifteenth Amendment only prohibited state electoral districting that qualified as purposeful discrimination against racial or ethnic minorities in voting. However, at the same time, the reasoning in *Rockefeller* suggests that the Court had abandoned its earlier view, articulated in *Gomillion*, that a dilution of the value of the right to vote had to be equivalent to an absolute deprivation of the right before it would constitute a violation of the Fifteenth Amendment. If a state drew the lines of an electoral district for a House, state, or municipal election with the purpose of discriminating against minority voters by diluting the value of their votes, that constituted a violation of the Fifteenth Amendment.

The same rule applied to a state that adopted multimember districts or at-large voting for state elections for discriminatory purposes, but here again it was the challenger who carried the burden of proof. For example, in *Fortson v. Dorsey* (1965), a case involving a challenge to Georgia's use of multimember districts for state elections, the Warren Court made it clear that such a system was not *"per se"* unconstitutional. "It might well be that, designedly or otherwise," the Court added, "a multi-member constituency apportionment scheme, under the circumstances of a particular case, would operate to minimize or cancel out the voting strength of racial or political elements of the voting population." But in this case, the challengers only made this claim "in one short paragraph" and "offered no proof to support it." They had not, therefore, carried their burden of proof; they had not established a racially discriminatory purpose and, for that reason, the Court could not find that Georgia's multimember voting system violated the Fifteenth Amendment.

In *White v. Regester* (1973), the Supreme Court applied the same standard to Texas's use of a multimember district in Bexar County for elections to the state House of Representatives. In this case, the federal district judge, who was familiar with the circumstances of Bexar County, made crucial factual findings: the multimember district "invidiously excluded Mexican-Americans from effective participation in political life, specifically in the election of representatives to the Texas House of Representatives." On appeal, the Supreme Court was "not inclined to overturn these findings, representing as they do a blend of history and an intensely local appraisal of the design and impact of the Bexar County multi-member district in the light of past and present reality, political and otherwise." Accordingly, as the Court later noted in *City of Mobile v. Bolden* (1980), the "Fifteenth Amendment does not entail the right to have Negro [or Mexican American] candidates elected" nor the candidates of any other racial or ethnic minority. All that the amendment prohibits is "purposefully discriminatory denial or abridgment by government of the freedom to vote 'on account of race, color, or previous condition of servitude.'" Of course, a separate issue is whether Congress, exercising its enforcement authority under the Fifteenth Amendment, could by a statute, such as the Voting Rights Act, render state electoral districting systems illegal if they detrimentally affected the electoral power of racial or ethnic minorities (see Q20).

FURTHER READING

Black, Merle. "Racial Composition of Congressional Districts and Support for Federal Voting Rights in the American South." *Social Science Quarterly* 59 (1978): 435–450.

Butler, Katherine I. "Constitutional and Statutory Challenges to Election Structures: Dilution and the Value of the Right to Vote." *Louisiana Law Review* 42 (1982): 851–950.

Carpeneti, W. L. "Legislative Apportionment: Multimember Districts and Fair Representation." *University of Pennsylvania Law Review* 120 (1972): 666–700.

Dixon, Robert G. *Democratic Representation: Reapportionment in Law and Politics*. New York: Oxford University Press, 1968.

Entin, Jonathan L. "Of Squares and Uncouth Twenty-Eight-Sided Figures: Reflections on *Gomillion v. Lightfoot* after Half a Century." *Washburn Law Journal* 50 (2010): 133–146.

Orsino, Roland D., and Trance, Olivia G., eds. *The House of Representatives: Apportionment and Redistricting*. Hauppauge, NY: Nova Science Publishers, 2011.

Polsby, Nelson, ed. *Reapportionment in the 1970s*. Berkeley, CA: University of California Press, 1971.

Valelly, Richard M. *The Two Reconstructions: The Struggle for Black Enfranchisement*. Chicago, IL: Chicago University Press, 2004.

Q12. AS THE SUPREME COURT REJECTED THE ARGUMENT THAT THE REPUBLICAN GUARANTEE CLAUSE WAS AN APPROPRIATE BASIS TO INVALIDATE MALAPPORTIONED HOUSE ELECTORAL DISTRICTS, WAS THERE SOME OTHER CONSTITUTIONAL PROVISION THAT THE COURT COULD UTILIZE TO INVALIDATE MALAPPORTIONED STATE ELECTORAL DISTRICTS?

Answer: Yes. Despite the Supreme Court's rejection of the Republican Guarantee Clause as a proper legal basis for invalidating malapportioned House electoral districts, the Court in *Baker v. Carr* (1962) held that the electoral districts of Tennessee's legislature violated the Equal Protection Clause of the Fourteenth Amendment.

The Facts: Even though Tennessee's Constitution required it to reapportion the state's ninety-five county-electoral districts, the state legislature refused to do so after the 1960 census. To make matters worse, Tennessee's legislature failed to reapportion these districts since 1901, resulting in radical disparities between the population of counties and the number of representatives they sent to the state legislature. Despite the large movement of people from rural to urban areas during the sixty-year hiatus, cities sent the same number of representatives to both state houses that they had sent in 1901. For example, in 1960, a single vote in rural Moore County was worth nineteen votes in Hamilton County, home of Chattanooga, while one vote in Stewart or Chester Counties was worth about eight votes in Shelby or Knox Counties, home of Memphis and Knoxville, respectively. More generally, the populations of the state's House districts varied from approximately 3,500 to 80,000, while those of the Senate districts varied from 40,000 to 240,000.

In *Baker v. Carr* (1962), the challengers argued that, even if all voters could cast their votes unimpeded, Tennessee's malapportioned electoral districts violated their rights under the Fourteenth Amendment. Their rights were violated, they claimed, because the state had diluted the value of their votes to the point that it constituted a violation of the equal protection of the laws. This argument seemed plausible, but the Court's holding in *Colegrove* was that apportionment was a political question beyond any court's jurisdiction (see Q10). How could apportionment be any less a political question simply because the challengers were attacking it under a different constitutional provision? However, it will be recalled that the Court in *Gomillion* had held that racially discriminatory apportionment was not a political question and was therefore justiciable and unconstitutional under both the Fifteenth Amendment and the Equal Protection Clause (see Q11). In *Baker*, the question was the following: which of these two precedents was applicable to Tennessee's malapportioned electoral system?

Justice William Brennan wrote the majority opinion for the Warren Court that upheld the challengers' claim that Tennessee's malapportioned electoral districts violated the Equal Protection Clause. Regarding whether apportionment of a state's legislature was a "political question," Brennan noted that the challengers' claim "neither rests upon nor implicates the Guaranty Clause, and that its justiciability is therefore not foreclosed by our decisions of cases involving that clause." As the challengers' claim was that they were being denied equal protection of the law, the case was justiciable, according to Brennan, and it did not matter that the claimed discrimination "'relates to political rights.'" In his view, the key difference between cases involving "political questions," including those based on the Guarantee Clause, was they related to "the relationship between the judiciary and the coordinate branches of the Federal Government, and not the federal judiciary's relationship to the States." In that sense, "nonjusticiability of a political question is primarily a function of the separation of powers" (the separation of the three branches of the federal government), not a function of the relationship between the Supreme Court and the fifty states.

In contrast to the judicially unmanageable standards of the Republican Guarantee Clause, Brennan wrote, the standards "under the Equal Protection Clause are well developed and familiar." For this reason, courts have the jurisdiction to decide if a state's system of apportionment "reflects no policy, but simply arbitrary and capricious action." Of course, Brennan conceded, any claim under the Equal Protection Clause must not be "so enmeshed with those political question elements which render Guarantee Clause claims nonjusticiable as actually to present a political question itself," but he concluded "that not to be the case here." The fact that issues regarding apportionment of electoral districts "touch matters of state governmental organization" could not be controlling. After all, the Court in *Gomillion* had already "applied the Fifteenth Amendment to strike down a redrafting of municipal boundaries which effected a discriminatory impairment of voting rights." Accordingly, the Court concluded, the "right asserted is within the reach of judicial protection under the Fourteenth Amendment."

Justice Felix Frankfurter, who wrote the plurality opinion in *Colegrove v. Green* and the majority opinion in *Gomillion v. Lightfoot*, dissented in *Baker v. Carr*. He began by noting that the majority had reversed "a uniform course of decision established by a dozen cases, including one by which the very claim now sustained was unanimously rejected only five years ago"—a remark that underlined the groundbreaking significance of *Baker*. Frankfurter observed further that this "impressive body of rulings thus cast aside reflected the equally uniform course of our political history regarding the relationship between population and legislative representation—a wholly different matter from denial of the franchise to individuals because of race, color, religion, or sex." In short, Frankfurter's view was that invalidating electoral districts unequal in population was vastly different from invalidating, as the Court had done in *Gomillion*, a state's invidious discrimination against a racial minority's right to vote. Accordingly, the present case "is, in effect, a Guarantee Clause claim masquerading under a different label." But if "judicial competence is wanting, it cannot," according to Frankfurter, "be created by invoking one clause of the Constitution rather than another." The complaint in this case is simply that the "basis of representation of the Tennessee Legislature hurts" the appellants, which is an attack on "the State as a State," which was, Frankfurter concluded, a clear "political question."

Frankfurter acknowledged that appellants in this case "invoke the right to vote and to have their votes counted," but he responded that "they are permitted to vote, and their votes are counted." He then added, "Talk of 'debasement' or 'dilution' is circular talk. One cannot speak of 'debasement' or 'dilution' of the value of a vote until there is first defined a standard of reference as to what a vote should be worth." Frankfurter faulted the Court for not giving lower courts any guidance on the degree to which other factors can affect the equality of population in a state's electoral districts and yet pass constitutional muster. "Room continues to be allowed for weighting," Frankfurter noted. "This, of course, implies that geography, economics, urban-rural conflict, and all the other non-legal factors which have throughout our history entered into political districting are to some extent not to be ruled out in the undefined vista now opened up by review in the federal courts of state apportionments. To some extent—aye, there's the rub." For this reason, Frankfurter concluded, "there is not under our Constitution a judicial remedy for every political mischief, for every undesirable exercise of legislative power.... In this situation, as in others of like nature, appeal for relief does not belong here. Appeal must be to an informed, civically militant electorate."

Whether Frankfurter was correct that an "informed, civically militant electorate" could convince a state legislature elected by districts that were, for sixty years, radically unequal in population to do the right thing and reapportion the state's electoral districts is uncertain. Nevertheless, he was correct that Brennan and the majority did very little in *Baker* to clarify what degree of malapportionment rendered a state's electoral system an unconstitutional violation of the Equal Protection Clause. This issue quickly resurfaced at the Warren Court, though in somewhat different contexts. For example, one year after *Baker*, the Court in *Gray v. Sanders* invalidated Georgia's county-unit system for electing candidates in the Democratic statewide primary election, a system that gave rural counties with one-third of the population of the state a majority of county-unit votes. The Court held that once "the geographical unit for which a representative is to be chosen is designated [here a statewide primary], all who participate in the election are to have an equal vote ... wherever their home may be in that geographical unit. This is required by the Equal Protection Clause of the Fourteenth Amendment." The Court added that the "conception of political equality from the Declaration of Independence, to Lincoln's Gettysburg Address, to the Fifteenth, Seventeenth, and Nineteenth Amendments can mean only one thing—one person, one vote."

In 1964, the Warren Court handed down two more apportionment decisions. First, in *Wesberry v. Sanders*, the Court held that Georgia's districts for the federal House of Representatives had to achieve "substantial equality of population" to satisfy constitutional requirements. However, as the Equal Protection Clause only restricted state action, the Court based its ruling on language contained in Article I, Section 2: members of the House were to be "chosen every second Year by the People of the several states." According to the Court, what this language meant was that "as nearly as is practicable, one man's vote in a congressional election is to be worth as much as another's. . . . To say that a vote is worth more in one district than in another would not only run counter to our fundamental ideas of democratic government, it would cast aside the principle of a House of Representatives elected 'by the People,' a principle tenaciously fought for and established at the Constitutional Convention."

That same year, in *Reynolds v. Sims* (1964) the Court returned to the issue that it had left unanswered in *Baker*: What kind of equality was required in a state legislature's electoral districts? In this case, Alabama, like Tennessee in *Baker*, had not reapportioned its electoral districts since 1901 and by 1964 they were extremely malapportioned. In its decision, the Court conceded that *Gray* and *Wesberry* were not directly controlling: *Gray* had held that "voters cannot be classified, constitutionally, on the basis of where they live, at least with respect to voting in statewide elections;" *Wesberry* was "grounded on the language of the Constitution which prescribes that members of the Federal House of Representatives are to be chosen 'by the People.'" In contrast, the Court noted, "attacks on state legislative apportionment schemes . . . are principally based on the Equal Protection Clause of the Fourteenth Amendment." Despite these differences, the Warren Court in *Reynolds* set them aside because the right to vote is "'a fundamental political right, because preservative of all rights.'" The Court explained, "Legislators represent people, not trees or acres. Legislators are elected by voters, not farms or cities or economic interests. As long as ours is a representative form of government, and our legislatures are those instruments of government elected directly by and directly representative of the people, the right to elect legislators in a free and unimpaired fashion is a bedrock of our political system."

As the right to vote is a "fundamental" political right in this sense, the Court continued, any dilution or undervaluation of the votes in one part of the state as compared to those living in another part of the same state is unconstitutional. Its effect would be equivalent to giving some voters more votes than others. It is "inconceivable," the Court argued,

> that a state law to the effect that, in counting votes for legislators, the votes of citizens in one part of the State would be multiplied by two, five, or 10, while the votes of persons in another area would be counted only at face value, could be constitutionally sustainable. Of

course, the effect of state legislative districting schemes which give the same number of representatives to unequal numbers of constituents is identical.

The Court added that any "criteria for the differentiation of citizens are insufficient to justify any discrimination, as to the weight of their votes, unless relevant to the permissible purposes of legislative apportionment" and that "an individual's right to vote for state legislators is unconstitutionally impaired when its weight is in a substantial fashion diluted when compared with votes of citizens living in other parts of the State." Accordingly, the Court would not tolerate, in any context, electoral districts that were "substantially" unequal in population; and second, that the state would bear the burden of justifying any nonsubstantial disparities in terms of "permissible purposes of legislative apportionment." If the state could not meet this latter burden, then even relatively minor "differentiations of citizens" would constitute a violation of the Equal Protection Clause. *Reynolds*, along with *Baker v. Carr*, are two milestones of the Warren Court that continue to have a profound impact on voting in the twenty-first century. The principle that everyone's vote is of equal value—a principle now widely accepted and deeply held—took root in these two Supreme Court decisions and has gradually gained more and more popular support ever since.

FURTHER READING

"*Baker v. Carr*: A Commemorative Symposium." *North Carolina Law Review* 80 (2002): 1104–1516.

"*Baker v. Carr* after 50 Years: Appraising the Reapportionment Revolution: A Symposium." *Case Western Law Review* 62 (2012): 941–1204.

Graham, Gene S. *One Man, One Vote: Baker v. Carr and the American Levellers*. Boston, MA: Little Brown, 1972.

Grofman, Bernard. *Voting Rights, Voting Wrongs: The Legacy of Baker v. Carr*. New York: Priority Press Publications, 1990.

Hamilton, Howard Devon, ed. *Legislative Apportionment: Key to Power*. New York: Harper & Row, 1964.

Mikva, Abner J. "Justice Brennan and the Political Process: Assessing the Legacy of *Baker v. Carr*." *University of Illinois Law Review* (1995): 683–698.

Van Alstyne, William W. "The Fourteenth Amendment, the 'Right' to Vote, and the Understanding of the Thirty-Ninth Congress." *The Supreme Court Review* 1965 (1965): 33–85.

Q13. WHEN THE SUPREME COURT RULED IN *REYNOLDS V. SIMS* AND *WESBERRY V. SANDERS* THAT UNEQUAL ELECTORAL DISTRICTS VIOLATED EITHER THE EQUAL PROTECTION CLAUSE OR ARTICLE I, SECTION 2, DID THE SUPREME COURT INVALIDATE THE NATURE OF REPRESENTATION UNDERLYING THE U.S. SENATE, THE ELECTORAL COLLEGE, AND THE U.S. HOUSE OF REPRESENTATIVES?

Answer: No. Despite the fact that the Supreme Court endorsed the principle of "one person, one vote" in both *Reynolds* and *Wesberry*, it did not invalidate the nature of representation of the U.S. Senate, the Electoral College, or the U.S. House of Representatives because inequalities of representation are deeply embedded in the original Constitution.

The Facts: The Supreme Court knew at the time it endorsed the principle of "one person, one vote" in *Wesberry* and *Reynolds* that it was inconsistent with the nature of representation in the U.S. Senate, the Electoral College, and the U.S. House of Representatives. The Constitution granted every state two Senate seats regardless of population and each state had Electoral College votes equal to the number of its representatives in the House, plus an additional one for each of its two senators. Representation in the Senate and the Electoral College was therefore skewed in favor of states with less population. For example, based on the 2010 census, Wyoming has approximately 560,000 people, with two senators and one representative, totaling three electoral votes, that is, one electoral vote for about 190,000 residents, while California has about thirty-seven million people, with two senators and fifty-three representatives, totaling fifty-five electoral votes, that is, one electoral vote for about 720,000 residents.

A similar problem, though one of less magnitude, arises with the House of Representatives because no House district can cross state boundaries and every state is entitled to at least one representative (Article I, Section 2). So, even if House electoral districts within a state must have "substantial equality of population," there was no conceivable way to achieve substantial equality between House electoral districts in different states (see *United States Department of Commerce v. Montana* [1992]). For example, based on the 2010 census, a House member from California represents about 750,000 people, while one from Rhode Island represents about 525,000 people because the latter, with just over a million people, is entitled to two representatives. In contrast, Montana and Delaware, both with just under a million people, are entitled to only one representative, along with South Dakota, North Dakota, Alaska, and Vermont in descending order of population. Wyoming, the state with the least population, only has 560,000 people.

The inequalities of representation in the Senate are deeply embedded in the Constitution itself. For example, Article I, Section 3, explicitly says that the "Senate of the United States shall be composed of two Senators from each State," and Article V commands "that no State, without its Consent, shall be deprived of its equal suffrage in the Senate." In addition, Article I, Section 2, requires members of the House of Representatives to be "chosen every second Year by the people *of the several States*" (emphasis added) and be "an Inhabitant of that State in which he shall be chosen." Lastly, Article II, Section 1, states that the Electoral College shall be composed of "a Number of Electors, equal to the whole Number of Senators and Representatives to which the State may be entitled in the Congress." There is little to no wiggle room in these provisions of the Constitution, with the result that the Court has no credible constitutional foothold to redress the substantial inequalities of representation embedded in the Senate, the Electoral College, and the House of Representatives.

The Warren Court in *Reynolds v. Sims* (1964) discussed the anomaly of requiring states to equalize their internal electoral districts by population while allowing huge disparities of representation in the U.S. Senate and the House of Representatives, with both types of inequalities affecting the composition of the Electoral College. The Court found it necessary to address this issue because defenders of state authority were relying on a "federal-state analogy" to justify state electoral districts not based exclusively on population. The argument was, basically, if it is okay for the federal government to have unequal electoral districts for the Senate and the House of Representatives, it must be okay for states to have them for their legislatures. The Court responded that the "system of representation in the two Houses of the Federal Congress is one ingrained in our Constitution," that it "is one conceived out of compromise and concession indispensable to the establishment of our federal republic" because "a group of formerly independent States bound themselves together under one national government." It did not matter, in the Court's view, "that almost three-fourths of our present States were never, in fact, independently sovereign." States admitted into the Union were on an equal par with the original thirteen even if they had never been independent or fully sovereign at any time.

According to the Warren Court, the key dispositive fact was that "at the time of the inception of the system of representation in the Federal Congress, a compromise [the Great Compromise] between the larger and smaller States on this matter averted a deadlock in the Constitutional Convention which had threatened to abort the birth of our Nation." In contrast, the "[p]olitical subdivisions of the States—counties, cities, or whatever—never were and never have been considered as sovereign entities. Rather, they have been traditionally regarded as subordinate governmental instrumentalities created by the State to assist in the carrying out of state governmental functions." For this reason, even though the Court had characterized voting as a "fundamental political right," the Equal Protection Clause did not require the U.S. Senate, the Electoral College, or the U.S. House of Representatives to honor the principle of "one person, one vote."

The Court also addressed why it would be problematic to require states to base representation of the lower house of the legislature on equal electoral districts, but allow them to structure representation in the state's upper house in a way that would permit them to place significant weight on factors other than population, such as traditional political subdivisions (county or city boundaries) or geographical and economic interests. The Court reasoned that if Senate districts could be constitutionally unequal, "an individual citizen's ability to exercise an effective voice in the only instrument of state government directly representative of the people might be almost as effectively thwarted as if neither house were apportioned on a population basis." This was so because "in all too many cases, the more probable result would be frustration of the majority will through minority veto in the house not apportioned on a population basis, stemming directly from the failure to accord adequate overall legislative representation to all of the State's citizens on a nondiscriminatory basis."

The Warren Court did not address why this objection did not also apply to the U.S. Senate, probably because there was arguably no remedy for the problem. The inequalities of representation at the federal level were so deeply embedded in the constitutional structure that only a constitutional amendment could remedy them. Of course, any such amendment was highly unlikely because three-fourths of the states (today thirty-eight of fifty) would have to ratify it. Perhaps at some point in the future, thirty-eight states might eliminate the Electoral College in favor of a popular presidential election (see Q34), but it is difficult to imagine that the thirteen least populous states would ever give up their right to two senators or the right to elect one of their own citizens to the House of Representatives.

The main point, however, is to appreciate the reality and significance of this disjunction between the federal government's system of representation as it is reflected in the U.S. Senate, the Electoral College, and the House of Representatives, and the system of representation that operates at the state level. The Supreme Court has more or less equalized the value of the right to vote in terms of population at the state level, but not at the federal. The effects of this disjunction are real, pervasive, and long-lasting. For example, in the last seven presidential elections, two candidates won the majority of votes in the Electoral College, but they lost the popular vote. The impact on the representative character of the Senate is also troubling. In 1810, approximately 33 percent of the population, those living in a majority of the least populated states, could elect a majority of senators. Ever since, the overall trend has been downward, with about 20 percent able to elect a majority of senators in 1900 and 17 percent today (Lee, 1999). Representational inequality has less of an impact in the House of Representatives, but it is not negligible. Recall that Rhode Island has two representatives with just over a million people, while Montana and Delaware has one each with just under a million.

FURTHER READING

Badger, Emily. "As American as Apple Pie? The Rural Vote's Disproportionate Slice of Power." *The New York Times*, November 20, 2016, available at https://www.nytimes.com/2016/11/21/upshot/as-american-as-apple-pie-the-rural-votes-disproportionate-slice-of-power.html?_r=1%20%E2%80%A6.

Dahl, Robert A. *How Democratic Is the American Constitution?* 2nd ed. New Haven, CT: Yale University Press, 2003.

Goldberg, Arthur L. "The Statistics of Malapportionment." *Yale Law Journal* 72 (1962): 90–106.

Lee, Frances E., and Oppenheimer, Bruce I. *Sizing Up the Senate: The Unequal Consequences of Equal Representation*. Chicago, IL: University of Chicago Press, 1999.

Levinson, Sanford. *Our Undemocratic Constitution: Where the Constitution Goes Wrong (And How We the People Can Correct It)*. New York: Oxford University Press, 2006.

McKay, Robert B. "The Federal Analogy and State Apportionment Standards." *Notre Dame Law Review* 38 (1963): 487–498.

Q14. DID THE WARREN COURT PERMIT A STATE TO MAINTAIN UNEQUAL ELECTORAL DISTRICTS IF THE STATE'S VOTERS OVERWHELMINGLY APPROVED THIS TYPE OF INEQUALITY VIA REFERENDUM OR INITIATIVE?

Answer: No. The Warren Court ruled that states could not maintain unequal electoral districts even if its voters overwhelmingly approved of them because the right to an equal vote was a personal, individual right.

The Facts: In its general election of November 1962, the Colorado electorate rejected by a vote of 311,749–149,822 a constitutional amendment that would have required both houses of its legislature to be based only on population. At the same time, it adopted (by a vote of 305,700–172,725) a state constitutional amendment that provided for the apportionment of the Colorado House of Representatives on the basis of population, but allowed other factors, such as geography, compactness, contiguity, natural boundaries, and county lines, to significantly shape representation in the Senate. To implement this amendment, the Colorado legislature enacted a law that made it possible for approximately one-third of the state's voters to elect a majority of the Senate. A number of residents of the Denver metropolitan area filed suit in federal court, claiming that the state senate's system of apportionment violated the Equal Protection Clause of the Fourteenth Amendment because it was arbitrary, irrational, and discriminatory.

The district court, in *Lucas v. Forty-Fourth General Assembly of Colorado* (1963), rejected the plaintiffs' argument, holding that the "contention that the voters have discriminated against themselves appalls, rather than convinces" and that "a proper recognition of the judicial function precludes a court from holding that the free choice of the voters between two conflicting theories of apportionment is irrational or the result arbitrary." The "people are free," the Court noted, "to establish the governmental forms which they desire, and, when they have acted, the courts should not enter the political wars to determine the rationality of such action." To buttress this argument, the district court pointed out that all the plaintiffs were from counties that overwhelmingly preferred an unequal system of representation for the state's senate. In these circumstances, the court claimed, "it is difficult to comprehend how the plaintiffs can sue to vindicate a public right. At most they present a political issue which they lost" and the court declined "to act as a superelectorate to weigh the rationality of a method of legislative apportionment adopted by a decisive vote of the people." In conclusion, the district judge pointed out that the Colorado amendment had been approved in accordance with the "full operation of the one-man, one-vote principle." In his opinion, it only made sense to respect the result of the operation of this principle, even if the result departed somewhat from the principle itself.

The plaintiffs appealed and the Supreme Court handed down its decision on June 15, 1964, the same day it decided *Reynolds v. Sims*, the decision upholding the principle of "one person, one vote" (see Q12). Chief Justice Earl Warren wrote the majority opinion, which rejected the significance of the fact that Colorado's apportionment plan was "adopted in a popular referendum," calling it "insufficient to sustain its constitutionality." Citing *West Virginia State Board of Education v. Barnette* (1943), Warren affirmed that "'[o]ne's right to life, liberty, and property . . . and *other fundamental rights* may not be submitted to vote; they depend on the outcome of no elections [emphasis added],'" adding that a "citizen's constitutional rights can hardly be infringed simply because a majority of the people choose that it be." Accordingly, the fact that the "apportionment plan was approved by the electorate is without federal constitutional significance if the scheme adopted fails to satisfy the basic requirements of the Equal Protection Clause." Nor can the plan be deemed "rational," as the district judge found, simply "because it takes into account a variety of geographical, historical, topographic and economic considerations," at least not if the plan "fails to provide an adequate justification for the substantial disparities from population-based representation in the allocation of Senate seats to the disfavored populous areas." As Colorado had not provided such a justification, its appropriation system violated the Equal Protection Clause.

The implication of Warren's opinion was that the principle of "one person, one vote" was constitutionally more sacrosanct than any result of the operation of the principle itself. Although Justices Stewart and Clark concurred with the majority's decision to invalidate Alabama's system of apportionment in *Reynolds v. Sims*, both dissented in *Lucas*. Stewart refused to join "the fabrication of a constitutional mandate which imports and forever freezes one theory of political thought into our Constitution, and forever denies to every State any opportunity for enlightened and progressive innovation in the design of its democratic institutions." Freezing the "one-person, one-vote" principle into the Constitution, according to Stewart, was a mistake because representative government "is a process of accommodating group interests through democratic institutional arrangements. Its function is to channel the numerous opinions, interests, and abilities of the people of a State into the making of the State's public policy." As these opinions and interests evolve, a state's system of representation should not be forever subject to an "uncritical, simplistic, and heavy-handed application of sixth-grade arithmetic," but rather should be flexible enough to adjust through "a realistic accommodation of the diverse and often conflicting political forces operating within a State."

In the end, Stewart adopted a two-part test to decide if a state's apportionment system met the requirements of the Equal Protection Clause. First, "in the light of the State's own characteristics and needs, the plan must be a rational one;" second, "the plan must be such as not to permit the systematic frustration of the will of a majority of the electorate of the State." Applying this test to the Colorado system, Stewart concluded that it was "entirely rational" and "under the liberal initiative provisions of the Colorado Constitution," the majority of Colorado's voters "retains the power to reverse its decision to do so. Therefore, there can be no question of frustration of the basic principle of majority rule." Stewart's view of the right to an equally weighted vote was one that respected a majority's decision to protect the rights of the minority, even if that protection was achieved by a "reasonable" departure from the principle of "one person, one vote."

Justice Clark joined Stewart's dissent, but added a few observations as to why Colorado's system of apportionment should be upheld. First, the apportionment in the House of Representatives was "within 4.9% of being perfect." Second, the appropriation of Colorado's Senate was approved "by a majority vote of every political subdivision in the State." Third, "the Senate's majority is elected by 33.2% of the population," which is "a much higher percentage than that which elects a majority of the Senate of the United States." Fourth, "Colorado enjoys the initiative and referendum system" and the "State Assembly has been reapportioned eight times since 1881," implying that the people of Colorado have "complete awareness" of the importance of apportionment. Fifth, Colorado "has mountainous areas which divide it into four regions," along with "some depressed areas, diversified industry, and varied climate, as well as enormous recreational regions and difficulties in transportation," all of which "give rise to problems indigenous to Colorado, which only its people can intelligently solve." Sixth, in Clark's view, "if one house is fairly apportioned by population (as is admitted here), then the people should have some latitude in providing, on a rational basis, for representation in the other house." In the end, Clark found that Colorado's apportionment system did not violate equal protection because it was "not arbitrary," but instead rested "on reasonable grounds which . . . are peculiar to that State."

The key issue raised by *Lucas* was whether the Court should strictly enforce the "one person, one vote" principle across all elected offices of a state. Certainly, Alabama's system of apportionment that the Court invalidated in *Reynolds*, one that had not been adjusted in sixty years, was clearly invidious, irrational, and discriminatory. But Colorado's situation was very different from Alabama's. Citizens of Colorado were not trapped by a recalcitrant legislature that refused to reapportion its electoral districts. The voters of Colorado exercised their power to pass a state constitutional amendment that gave the minorities of the state, those that lived in the state's less populous counties, more electoral power in one branch of the state legislature than the principle of "one person, one vote" would have granted them. Was such a concession unconstitutional because it did not sufficiently respect numbers or did the Equal Protection Clause only require a reasonable allocation of seats in Colorado's senate, not one based on arithmetical equality? *Lucas* helps us consider this question in a context where voters have exercised their right to an equally weighted vote in a way to permit what they believed was a reasonable departure from the principle of "one person, one vote."

FURTHER READING

Bickel, Alexander. "The Durability of *Colegrove v. Green*." *Yale Law Journal* 72 (1962): 39–45.

Dahl, Robert. *A Preface to Democratic Theory*. Expanded ed. Chicago, IL: University of Chicago Press, 2006.

Dunbar, Duke W., and Ginsberg, Charles. *Forty-Fourth General Assembly of Colo. v. Lucas: U.S. Supreme Court Transcript of Record with Supporting Pleadings*. Boston, MA: Gale ECCO, 2011.

Freund, Paul A. "New Vistas in Constitutional Law." *University of Pennsylvania Law Review* 112 (1964): 631–646.

Israel, Jerold. "Nonpopulation Factors Relevant to an Acceptable Standard of Apportionment." *Notre Dame Law Review* 38 (1963): 499–517.

McKay, Robert B. "Political Thickets and Crazy Quilts: Reapportionment and Equal Protection." *Michigan Law Review* 61 (1963): 645–710.

Neal, Phil C. "*Baker v. Carr*: Politics in Search of Law." *The Supreme Court Review* 1962 (1962): 252–327.

"Reapportionment." *Harvard Law Review* 79 (1966): 1226–1287.

Sturtevant, Josh. "Missed Opportunities in Lucas v. The Forty-Fourth General Assembly of the State of Colorado." *BlawgConomics*, January 22, 2010, available at https://blawgconomics.blogspot.com/2010/01/missed-opportunities-in-lucas-v-forty.html.

Q15. DID THE WARREN COURT APPLY THE PRINCIPLE OF "ONE PERSON, ONE VOTE" FLEXIBLY, ALLOWING RELATIVELY SMALL VARIATIONS IN POPULATION BETWEEN ELECTORAL DISTRICTS WITHOUT REQUIRING THE STATE TO EXPLAIN OR JUSTIFY THEM?

Answer: No. Although the Warren Court permitted states a bit more discretion in how they drew their own electoral districts—as opposed to federal House districts—the Court insisted that states must justify even minor variations of population between their own electoral districts.

The Facts: It might seem obvious that the principle of "one person, one vote" is self-explanatory and that it would have the same meaning wherever it was applied. However, the Warren Court knew that states could not possibly draw electoral districts within their border with "mathematical precision," that is, with exactly the same number of people living in each district. For example, in *Reynolds v. Sims* (1964), the Court wrote, "it is a practical impossibility to arrange legislative districts so that each one has an identical number of residents, or citizens, or voters. Mathematical exactness or precision is hardly a workable constitutional requirement." The Court even conceded that "more flexibility may . . . be constitutionally permissible with respect to state legislative apportionment than in congressional districting." One reason why this was so, in the Court's view, was that "almost invariably, there is a significantly larger number of seats in state legislative bodies to be distributed within a State than congressional seats." For this reason, it might be constitutional for a state "to use political subdivision lines to a greater extent in establishing state legislative districts than in congressional districting while still affording adequate representation to all parts of the State."

In the same vein, the Court added, "a consideration that appears to be of more substance in justifying some deviations from population-based representation in state legislatures is that of insuring some voice to political subdivisions, as political subdivisions." The Warren Court, therefore, knew early on that the principle of "one person, one vote" might have different meanings depending on context. However, despite this concession, the Court nonetheless insisted that "the Equal Protection Clause requires that a State make an honest and good faith effort to construct districts, in both houses of its legislature, as nearly of equal population as is practicable." Deviations in population, therefore, may be permissible under the principle of "one person, one vote," but not deviations without a credible justification.

At first, a number of states overestimated the degree of constitutional flexibility they had in drawing up state electoral districts. For example, in *Swann v. Adams* (1967), the Warren Court reviewed Florida's apportionment plan that utilized multimember districts for each house, but the districts varied in population, some significantly. The senate districts ranged from 87,595 to 114,053, the smallest in population overrepresented by 15.09 percent and the largest in population underrepresented by 10.56 percent. Similarly, the house multimember districts ranged from 34,584 to 48,785, which meant that the least populated district was 18.28 percent overrepresented and the most populated district was 15.27 percent underrepresented. However, despite these relatively large disparities, under Florida's plan, a majority of state senators could not be elected unless they had the support of districts with 48.38 percent of the population, while a majority of the state house needed the support of districts with 47.79 percent of the population. The implication was that most of the state electoral districts were roughly equal in population, but there were several outliers. Florida, therefore, argued that the population variance among the districts were inconsequential and consistent with the Equal Protection Clause.

Notwithstanding the overall rough equality of Florida's apportionment system, the Court invalidated it because Florida failed "to articulate acceptable reasons for the variations among the populations of the various legislative districts with respect to both the senate and house of representatives." Moreover, the Court argued that "variations of 30% among senate districts and 40% among house districts can hardly be deemed *de minimis*," at least not for persons living in the largest senate and house districts. The Court noted, "none of our cases suggests that differences of this magnitude will be approved without a satisfactory explanation grounded on acceptable state policy." Such explanations could include "the integrity of political subdivisions, the maintenance of compactness and contiguity in legislative districts, or the recognition of natural or historical boundary lines." If Florida had linked the population variances among its electoral districts to explanations of this sort, then perhaps the principle of "one person, one vote" would be satisfied. Accordingly, a population variance of electoral districts "approved in one State has little bearing on the validity of a similar variation in another State." The implication was that the principle of "one person, one vote" meant different things in different states, depending on whether the state can justify the population variances based on the "particular circumstances" of the state (see also *Kilgarlin v. Hill* [1967]).

One year later, in *Avery v. Midland County* (1968), the Warren Court considered whether districts in elections for the Commissioners Court of Midland County, Texas, were subject to the principle of "one person, one vote." In this local election, there were only four electoral districts in the county, but one was radically unequal to the other three, having a population of 67,906 while the others had populations, respectively, of 852, 414, and 828. The Commissioners Court was the general governing body of the county, with broad responsibilities. The Court quickly concluded, "a State's political subdivisions must comply with the Fourteenth Amendment" because the "actions of local government are the actions of the State." Accordingly, "when the State delegates lawmaking power to local government and provides for the election of local officials from districts specified by statute, ordinance, or local charter, it must insure that those qualified to vote have the right to an equally effective voice in the election process."

The Court acknowledged that if the Commissioners Court were "a special purpose unit of government assigned the performance of functions affecting definable groups of constituents more than other constituents, we would have to confront the question whether such a body may be apportioned in ways which give greater influence to the citizens most affected by the organization's functions." This conclusion once again implied that "one person, one vote" could mean different things depending on context. As the Court explained, the Constitution was not "a uniform straitjacket [that] bind[s] citizens in devising mechanisms of local government suitable for local needs and efficient in solving local problems." However, this degree of flexibility could not be granted to the Commissioners Court because it made "a substantial number of decisions that affect all citizens," not just a subset of them.

Two years later, in *Hadley v. Junior College District* (1970), the Court extended the principle of "one person, one vote" to all local elections open to a popular vote, not just to those that elected public officials exercising general authority. As the Court concluded, "we think the decision of the State to select that official by popular vote is a strong enough indication that the choice is an important one." Accordingly, any local elections open to a popular vote were subject to the principle of "one person, one vote."

In *Kirkpatrick v. Preisler* (1969), the Court considered whether Missouri's apportionment of House congressional districts met the standard of "one person, one vote." Based on the 1960 census, Missouri had ten congressional districts, which meant, by dividing its total population by ten, that each district ideally should have 431,981 persons. However, Missouri's legislature in 1967 passed an apportionment law that created one district with a population 12,260 less than the ideal average (2.84 percent) and another with 13,542 (3.13 percent) above it. Missouri argued, first, that these variations were "so small that they should be considered *de minimis*, and, for that reason, to satisfy the 'nearly as practicable' limitation and not to require independent justification." However, if the Court found these variances not to be *de minimis*, Missouri argued that they were nonetheless justified based on "such factors as the representation of distinct interest groups, the integrity of county lines, the compactness of districts, the population trends within the State, the high proportion of military personnel, college students, and other nonvoters in some districts, and the political realities of 'legislative interplay.'"

The Court rejected both of Missouri's arguments. The Court would not adopt "fixed numerical standards which excuse population variances without regard to the circumstances of each particular case." While the degree of equality of House districts that "may practicably be achieved may differ from State to State and from district to district," every "State must justify each variance, no matter how small." Moreover, Missouri's justifications for its variations, in the Court's view, were inadequate. First, "to create districts with specific interest orientations is antithetical to the basic premise of the constitutional command to provide equal representation for equal numbers of people." Second, problems "*created by partisan politics cannot justify an apportionment which does not otherwise pass constitutional muster.*" Third, variances are not justified "if they necessarily result from a State's attempt to avoid fragmenting political subdivisions by drawing congressional district lines along existing county, municipal, or other political subdivision boundaries." Lastly, the Court dismissed Missouri's commitment to compact electoral districts, concluding that a "State's preference for pleasingly shaped districts can hardly justify population variances." Clearly, the Warren Court in the late 1960s scrutinized population variances between a state's congressional districts with a very skeptical eye (see also *Wells v. Rockefeller* [1969]).

Four years after Chief Justice Earl Warren retired in 1969, the Supreme Court finally upheld population variances in state legislative electoral districts in *Mahan v. Howell* (1973), a case evaluating Virginia's apportionment plan for its lower house. The districts varied in population, with one district overrepresented by 6.8 percent and another underrepresented by 9.6 percent. Virginia justified the variations based on "the integrity of traditional county and city boundaries, and that it was impossible to draft district lines to overcome unconstitutional disparities and still maintain such integrity." The Court found this justification persuasive, noting that "whereas population alone has been the sole criterion of constitutionality in congressional redistricting under Article I, Section 2, broader latitude has been afforded the States under the Equal Protection Clause in state legislative redistricting." Despite the variances in the house districts noted above, Virginia satisfied the principle of "one person, one vote" because it had conducted "an honest and good faith effort to construct districts . . . as nearly of equal population as is practicable." That was all that the Constitution required (see also *White v. Regester* [1973] and *Gaffney v. Cummings* [1973]).

In contrast, the Court that same year in *White v. Weiser* (1973) required a higher standard for the congressional districts of Texas. The state of Texas had created districts that were on average above and below the ideal population by, respectively, 2.43 percent and 1.7 percent, with a maximum of 4.13 percent. The Court invalidated the plan because the variances, despite their relatively small nature, "were not 'unavoidable,' and the districts were not as mathematically equal as reasonably possible." Here again, as in *Kirkpatrick*, the state was not permitted to justify these variations based on a desire to avoid "fragmenting political subdivisions," maintain "existing relationships between incumbent congressmen and their constituents," or preserve "the seniority the members of the State's delegation have achieved in the United States House of Representatives." Accordingly, the principle of "one person, one vote" has a different meaning depending upon whether it is applied to congressional, state, or local districts. In every case, any population variance must be justified, but the weight of the requisite justification varies with the nature of the electoral district. Accordingly, the principle of "one person, one vote" does not mean the same thing everywhere and everyplace. Such justified variations in the size of electoral districts, especially at the state level, continue to exist in today's voting system.

FURTHER READING

Ansolabehere, Stephen, and Snyder, James M., Jr. *The End of Inequality: One Person, One Vote and the Transformation of American Politics*. New York: W. W. Norton & Company, 2008.

Auerbach, Carl A. "The Reapportionment Cases: One Person, One Vote-One Vote, One Value." *The Supreme Court Review* 1964 (1964): 1–87.

Ball, Howard. *Warren Court's Conceptions of Democracy: An Evaluation of the Supreme Court's Apportionment Opinions*. Vancouver, BC: Fairleigh Dickinson University Press, 1975.

Briffault, Richard. "Who Rules at Home?: One Person/One Vote and Local Governments." *University of Chicago Law Review* 60 (1993): 339–424.

Hayden, Grant M. "The False Promise of One Person, One Vote." *Michigan Law Review* 102 (2003): 213–267.

Phillips, Barbara Y. "Reconsidering *Reynolds v. Sims*: The Relevance of Its Basic Standard of Equality to Other Vote Dilution Claims." *Howard Law Journal* 38 (1995): 561–585.

Smith, J. Douglas. *On Democracy's Doorstep: The Inside Story of How the Supreme Court Brought "One Person, One Vote" to the United States.* New York: Hill and Wang, 2014.

Q16. DID THE WARREN COURT HAND DOWN ANY MAJOR DECISIONS ON THE RIGHT TO VOTE BESIDES THOSE RELATED TO APPORTIONMENT AND ELECTORAL DISTRICTING?

Answer: Yes. The Warren Court invalidated poll taxes in state and federal elections, upheld Congress's Voting Rights Act of 1965 and extended the right to vote in local school district elections to all eligible voters.

The Facts: The Supreme Court upheld the constitutionality of poll taxes in *Breedlove v. Suttles* (1937), but the Twenty-Fourth Amendment of the Constitution, ratified in 1964, prohibited denials or abridgments of the right to vote in federal elections based on a "failure to pay any poll tax or other tax" (see Q8). Virginia, which had an annual poll tax of $1.50 for both federal and state elections, required voters to pay three years of the poll tax before he or she could vote in an election. To comply with the new amendment, Virginia changed its law so that a voter in a federal election could either pay the poll tax or file a "witnessed or notarized certificate of residence" each election year. Virginia argued that its new law was consistent with the amendment because the voter was no longer "required" to pay the poll tax as a precondition for voting in a federal election. Each voter had the choice of paying the poll tax or going through the bother of filing the requisite certificate.

In *Harman v. Forssenius* (1965), the Court rejected Virginia's argument, noting that the Twenty-Fourth Amendment "expressly guarantees that the right to vote shall not be 'denied or abridged' [by reason of failure to pay a poll tax]. . . . Thus, like the Fifteenth Amendment, the Twenty-fourth 'nullifies sophisticated, as well as simple-minded modes' of impairing the right guaranteed." As Virginia "imposes a material requirement solely upon those who refuse to surrender their constitutional right to vote in federal elections without paying a poll tax," the law "unquestionably erects a real obstacle to voting in federal elections for those who assert their constitutional exemption from the poll tax." In the Court's view, filing the "witnessed" or "notarized" certificate of residence "is plainly a cumbersome procedure," but even a "less onerous" alternative to paying the poll tax would be unconstitutional. "For federal elections, the poll tax is abolished absolutely as a prerequisite to voting, and no equivalent or milder substitute may be imposed."

The following year, in *Harper v. Virginia Board of Elections* (1966), the Court addressed whether Virginia could continue to enforce its $1.50 annual poll tax in state elections. The Court began its analysis with the following quotation from *Reynolds v. Sim* (1964): "'A citizen, a qualified voter, is no more nor no less so because he lives in the city or on the farm. This is the clear and strong command of our Constitution's Equal Protection Clause.'" Relying on this premise, the Court continued, "We say the same whether the citizen, otherwise qualified to vote, has $1.50 in his pocket or nothing at all, pays the fee or fails to pay it." The Court elaborated further: the "principle that denies the State the right to dilute a citizen's vote on account of his economic status or other such factors, by analogy, bars a system which excludes those unable to pay a fee to vote or who fail to pay." Poor people who cannot or will not pay the poll tax have a federal right to vote in a state election.

A key premise of the Court's reasoning was that wealth, unlike the ability to read and write, has no bearing on the intelligent use of the ballot. The Court had upheld the constitutionality of literacy tests in *Lassiter v. Northampton County Board of Elections* (1959), but it had done so with the "warning that the result would be different if a literacy test, fair on its face, were used to discriminate against a class." In the Court's view, poll taxes were different from literacy tests because voting has "no relation to wealth nor to paying or not paying this or any other tax." It is true, the Court conceded, that states often charge fees for all kinds of licenses, such as a driver's license, but the difference is that Virginia's poll tax is a precondition for voting. "Wealth, like race, creed, or color, is not germane to one's ability to participate intelligently in the electoral process." A tax as a precondition for voting introduces "a capricious or irrelevant factor" and is, for that reason, a form of "invidious" discrimination. It is a violation of the Equal Protection Clause because "the right to vote is too precious, too fundamental to be so burdened or conditioned." By this reasoning, the Court abolished all poll taxes in state elections.

Also in 1966, the Court decided two cases upholding the constitutionality of the Voting Rights Act of 1965: *South Carolina v. Katzenbach* and *Katzenbach v. Morgan*. The former case, which will be discussed in chapter 3, upheld the validity of the law's general provisions based on Congress's power to enforce the Fifteenth Amendment's prohibition of racial discrimination in voting. The latter case considered a specific provision of Section 4 of the law, one that prohibited states from requiring literacy tests for persons who had completed six years of education in Puerto Rico, even if the language of instruction was not English. New York required its Puerto Rican citizens to take a literacy test and argued that Congress's power to enforce the Fourteenth Amendment only permitted it to prohibit voting qualifications that the courts had already ruled unconstitutional. As the Court in *Lassiter v. Northampton County Board of Elections* (1959) had ruled that literacy tests were constitutional, New York claimed that the ban in Section 4 was unconstitutional. The Warren Court rejected New York's reasoning in *Morgan*, arguing that it "would depreciate both congressional resourcefulness and congressional responsibility for implementing the Amendment" by confining its power "to the insignificant role of abrogating only those state laws that the judicial branch was prepared to adjudge unconstitutional." *Lassiter* had only held that literacy tests were not unconstitutional "in all circumstances," the Court noted, and therefore it was "inapposite" to whether Section 4 was "appropriate legislation to enforce the Equal Protection Clause."

To decide this latter question, the Court assumed that the enforcement provision of the Fourteenth Amendment gave Congress "the same broad powers expressed in the Necessary and Proper Clause." Accordingly, the constitutional test for the former was the same as that of the latter: "'Let the end be legitimate, let it be within the scope of the constitution, and all means which are appropriate, which are plainly adapted to that end, which are not prohibited, but consist with the letter and spirit of the constitution, are constitutional.'" With this broad understanding of the Fourteenth Amendment's enforcement clause, the Court had no difficulty concluding that Section 4 "may be viewed as a measure to secure for the Puerto Rican community residing in New York nondiscriminatory treatment by government," not just in the "imposition of voting qualifications" but also in the "administration of governmental services, such as public schools, public housing and law enforcement." After all, the enhanced electoral power will clearly "be helpful in gaining nondiscriminatory treatment in public services for the entire Puerto Rican community." It was for Congress to judge whether the "need of the Puerto Rican minority for the vote warranted federal intrusion upon any state interests served by the English literacy requirement." It was not for the Court to second-guess Congress's appraisal of the relevant factors. All that the Court had to find was that there was "a basis upon which the Congress might resolve the conflict as it did."

One last major decision by the Warren Court on voting rights was *Kramer v. Union Free School District No. 15* (1969), which considered the constitutionality of a New York law that excluded otherwise eligible voters from school district elections if they did not own or lease taxable property in the district or were not parents or custodians of children enrolled in the district's schools. An otherwise eligible voter who lived with his parents objected, claiming that the law's additional requirements for voting in school district elections violated the Equal Protection Clause. The Court began its review with the assumption that the law must be "carefully" and "meticulously" scrutinized because (1) the right to vote "'in a free and unimpaired manner is preservative of other basic civil and political rights;'" and (2) "[a]ny unjustified discrimination in determining who may participate in political affairs or in the selection of public officials undermines the legitimacy of representative government." For these reasons, the Court insisted that any exclusion of an otherwise eligible voter must be "necessary to promote a compelling state interest."

The goal of New York's law was to limit school district elections to those who are "primarily interested" or "primarily affected" by these elections, that is, to those who pay the taxes (either directly or through rent) that finance the school district or who have primary care of the students in school. The Court declined to address whether such a goal was "compelling" as, in its opinion, the exclusion of otherwise eligible voters was hardly a "necessary" means to this end. In fact, according to the Court, New York's law permitted many persons to vote "who have, at best, a remote and indirect interest in school affairs and, on the other hand, exclude others who have a distinct and direct interest in the school meeting decisions." Accordingly, the law was "not sufficiently tailored to limiting the franchise to those 'primarily interested' in school affairs to justify the denial of the franchise to appellant and members of his class." The fit between the class of voters that were excluded from the franchise and the purpose of the law was simply too tenuous to pass the "strict scrutiny" required by the Equal Protection Clause for laws that impaired the right to vote.

One year after the retirement of Chief Justice Earl Warren, the Supreme Court upheld in *Oregon v. Mitchell* (1970) the constitutionality of an amendment to the Voting Rights Act of 1965 that prohibited the use of all literacy tests in both federal and state elections. Congress argued that it had the authority to enact the amendment on the basis of its power to enforce the Fourteenth and Fifteenth Amendments. The justices issued a number of opinions in this case, but they were unanimous in their judgment that the ban was within Congress's power to prevent racial discrimination in voting. Two years later, in *Dunn v. Blumstein* (1972), the Court carried on the tradition of the Warren Court by placing constitutional limits on state residency requirements for voter registration. It held that Tennessee's requirements of (1) one year in state and (2) three months in county violated the Equal Protection Clause because it furthered no compelling state interest. In its opinion, the Court suggested that thirty days would be an ample amount of time for the state to prevent voter fraud. The short residency requirements familiar to today's voter are the result of the spirit that animated the Warren Court's understanding of the fundamental nature of the right to vote.

FURTHER READING

Ackerman, Bruce, and Nou, Jennifer. "Canonizing the Civil Rights Revolution: The People and the Poll Tax." *Northwestern Law Review* 103 (2009): 63–148.

Berman, Ari. *Give Us the Ballot: The Modern Struggle for Voting Rights in America.* New York: Farrar, Straus, and Giroux, 2015.

Lawson, Steven F. *Black Ballots: Voting Rights in the South, 1944–1969.* Lanham, MD: Lexington Books, 1999.

Ogden, Frederic D. *The Poll Tax in the South.* Tuscaloosa, AL: University of Alabama Press, 1958.

Podolefsky, Ronnie L. "The Illusion of Suffrage: Female Voting Rights and the Women's Poll Tax Repeal Movement after the Nineteenth Amendment." *Columbia Journal of Gender and Law* 7 (1998): 185–237.

Soltero, Carlos R. "*Katzenbach v. Morgan* (1966) and Voting Rights of Puerto Ricans with Limited English Proficiency." In *Latinos and American Law: Landmark Supreme Court Cases.* Austin, TX: University of Texas Press, 2006, Chap. 4.

Tokaji, Daniel P. "Intent and Its Alternatives: Defending the New Voting Rights Act." *Alabama Law Review* 58 (2006): 349–375.

3

The Voting Rights Act in the Twenty-First Century

As discussed in chapter 1, the original Constitution delegated the authority to decide who can vote in federal elections to state legislatures, reserving for Congress the power to alter the "Regulations" states imposed on the "Times, Places, and Manner" of federal elections. Of course, important amendments to the Constitution have restricted state control over the federal right to vote by prohibiting any denial or abridgment of the right on grounds of race, sex, age, or ability to pay a tax. These amendments, however, were negative rather than positive in form. By telling states what they *cannot* do regarding the right to vote, not what they *must* do, the Constitution established a constitutional floor—a minimal set of requirements that state governments must respect. In contrast, the Voting Rights Act of 1965 (VRA) extended and broadened the American right to vote in a positive sense beyond the constitutional minimum. In doing so, the significance of the VRA is monumental. Many commentators have argued that the VRA is the most effective civil rights law Congress has ever enacted.

The VRA is also important because it granted the executive branch of the federal government the authority to enforce the expanded right to vote. Such federal enforcement of statutory voting rights can, in some ways, be far more effective than judicial decisions protecting the right to vote in individual lawsuits. Whereas executive enforcement can be applied across jurisdictions, a lawsuit is typically reactive to a specific wrong and limited to the specific circumstances of a particular case within a single jurisdiction. Moreover, the VRA authorized the federal government to require states to take positive steps to empower voters and prevent states from violating the right to vote, whether the right was rooted in the Constitution or in the VRA. Lastly, the VRA gave courts another foundation, other than the Constitution, on which to base their decisions regarding the right to vote. Of course, courts might interpret a provision of the VRA in a narrow way, but if so, then Congress could amend the law, pushing courts to expand the statutory right to vote. For the above reasons, the passage of the VRA set the stage for a transformation of the American right to vote, making it more meaningful and robust for millions of American citizens. However, in *Shelby County v. Holder* (2013), the Supreme Court invalidated a crucial provision of the VRA that enabled the federal government to protect the right to vote from state infringements (see Q23). Accordingly, though there is no question that the VRA has had a huge and positive impact on the right to vote, its future role may be more circumscribed, depending upon whether Congress enacts any revisions of the VRA and, if so, how the Court reacts to them. The VRA's future is, therefore, uncertain.

Q17. WAS THE VOTING RIGHTS ACT OF 1965 POLITICALLY UNCONTROVERSIAL AS IT PASSED BY LARGE MARGINS IN BOTH THE SENATE (77–19) AND THE HOUSE OF REPRESENTATIVES (333–85)?

Answer: No. The VRA was a highly controversial law, especially in southern states, because it authorized an unprecedented degree of federal control and supervision of state electoral practices.

The Facts: Although both houses of Congress enacted the VRA by wide margins, in reality, it was the culmination of a long-fought and bitterly contested campaign led by the African American civil rights movement. This movement's first major success was its victory in *Brown v. Board of Education* (1954), which ended legally mandated racial segregation in public education. Three years later, Congress passed the Civil Rights Act of 1957, which created the Civil Rights Division of the Department of Justice (DOJ) and the Commission on Civil Rights, two administrative entities committed to the enforcement of the Fifteenth Amendment's prohibition of racial discrimination in voting. Another step forward was the Civil Rights Act of 1960, which granted federal courts the power to oversee voter registration in jurisdictions found to have engaged in racial discrimination. The Civil Rights Act of 1964, which prohibited racial discrimination in privately owned public accommodations such as hotels, theaters, and restaurants, was the movement's second major achievement. Amid sit-in demonstrations by civil rights activists at white-only lunch counters in a number of southern cities, President John F. Kennedy proposed this legislation to Congress in June 1963, but conservative southern Democrats blocked the bill. Kennedy's assassination on November 22, 1963, presented a tragic opportunity: his successor, President Lyndon B. Johnson, called on Congress to pass the bill as a legacy to Kennedy's memory. Eighteen senators, mostly southern Democrats led by Richard Russell (D-GA) and Strom Thurmond (D-SC), filibustered the bill for months, but the Senate ultimately passed it on June 19, 1964. A House-Senate conference committee adopted the bill and Johnson signed it into law on July 2, 1964.

The Civil Rights Act was controversial for a number of reasons, including the question of whether Congress had the constitutional authority to require the owners of privately owned businesses to serve African Americans. Many years earlier, in the *Civil Rights Cases* (1883), the Supreme Court had invalidated a similar law on the ground that Congress did not have the authority to pass such legislation as a means of enforcing the Thirteenth and Fourteenth Amendments. In 1964, Congress circumvented this earlier ruling by not basing its authority to enact the Civil Rights Act only on its power to enforce these amendments but also on its power to "regulate commerce . . . among the several States" (Article I, Section 8). The controversial claim was that racial discrimination against African Americans by hotels, restaurants, theaters, and other public accommodations had a depressing effect upon interstate commerce by discouraging interstate travel and other commercial transactions. The Court endorsed the validity of this argument in *Heart of Atlanta Motel, Inc. v. United States* (1964). This decision, handed down on December 14, 1964, increased the turmoil brought on by the implementation of the Civil Rights Act itself and by ongoing protests by the civil rights movement, including protests centered on the right to vote.

The *Heart of Atlanta Motel* decision came only a month after Lyndon Johnson won reelection and the Democratic Party won large majorities in both houses of Congress. Johnson, from Texas, knew all about the subtle and not-so-subtle means by which southern states disfranchised African Americans. Accordingly, despite the recent passage of the Civil Rights Act of 1964, he supported moving forward with a voting rights bill even if doing so risked losing the support of conservative southern Democrats.

Johnson's administration began working on such a bill in late 1964 at the same time that two leading civil rights organizations, the Student Nonviolent Coordinating Committee and the Southern Christian Leadership Conference, led by Dr. Martin Luther King Jr., ramped up a protest campaign in Alabama. This campaign focused on the injustice of white suppression of voting rights in Selma, the seat of Dallas County. Selma had a long history of resistance to black voting and Alabama Governor George Wallace, a fervent opponent of the civil rights movement, strongly supported the status quo.

The key problem in Alabama was not explicit forms of racial discrimination, which the Fifteenth Amendment explicitly prohibited, but rather that local officials were able to keep African Americans off voting rolls by applying nonracial qualifications for voting (such as literacy tests, poll taxes, or registration requirements) in a racially discriminatory manner. In addition, white racists threatened potential black voters with violence, loss of employment, or other types of reprisals.

These methods of suppressing the black vote were very effective in Dallas County. During the early 1960s, the county's population was approximately 57 percent black, but only 156 of approximately 15,000 black residents were registered to vote (about 1 percent), and only 14 blacks had been added to the county's voting rolls since 1954. The passage of the Civil Rights Act in early July of 1964 was thus widely seen by the civil rights groups as a tool that could be used to tear down these practices in Dallas County. A group of fifty black activists tried to register to vote at the county courthouse on July 6, including John Lewis, who later became a prominent member of the House of Representatives (D-GA). They were stopped by Sheriff Jim Clark and his deputies. Notorious for their violent tendencies, Clark and his men used cattle prods to arrest the men and incarcerate them in the county jail. Three days later, Alabama Judge James Hare issued an injunction against black organizations, ordering them not to sponsor any political gatherings of more than three people (Garrow, 1978).

In defiance of Judge Hare's injunction, King initiated the voting rights campaign in Selma by addressing a rally of several hundred people at a black church on January 2, 1965. "Today marks the beginning of a determined, organized, mobilized campaign to get the right to vote everywhere in Alabama," he said. "We must be ready to go to jail by the thousands. . . . Our cry to the state of Alabama is a simple one. Give us the ballot!" (Cannon, 2018). In the following weeks, a number of voter registration marches to the county courthouse took place in Selma. At first, these marches were relatively peaceful, but they turned violent on January 22 when Clark's police officers used nightsticks to attack a hundred black teachers protesting on the courthouse steps. More such incidents followed, many of which were memorialized by front-page photographs in national newspapers. These photographs of white police officers beating African Americans, including women, who were trying to register to vote had a major impact on northern public opinion, increasing sympathy for the civil rights activists. On February 18, in the nearby town of Marion, Alabama, state troopers attacked a group of demonstrators. One of the demonstrators, Jimmie Lee Jackson, was shot by a state trooper and later died of his injuries. A group of white vigilantes in attendance beat up national newspaper reporters who were covering the demonstration. Predictably, press assessments in northern papers were harsh.

In response to Jackson's death, King announced a protest march from Selma to Montgomery, the state's capitol, a distance of fifty-one miles. A group of six hundred marchers, led by John Lewis, gathered for this event on Sunday, March 7, but a large number of state troopers and local police blocked the march at Edmund Pettus Bridge, which spanned the Alabama River. After the marchers refused to turn around, the police beat them with their nightsticks. Over fifty people suffered injuries requiring hospitalization. Filmed by TV cameramen, the spectacle known as "Bloody Sunday" was broadcast across the nation. A March 9th *Washington Post* editorial titled "Outrage at Selma" captured the national sentiment:

> The news from Selma, Alabama, where police beat and mauled and gassed unarmed, helpless and unoffending citizens will shock and alarm the whole nation. It is simply inconceivable that in this day and age, the police who have sworn to uphold the law and protect the citizenry could resort, instead, to violent attacks upon them.
>
> Decent citizens will weep . . . [and] recoil in horror from the spectacle of sadism. . . . This brutality is the inevitable result of the intolerance fostered by an infamous state government that is without conscience or morals.
>
> [Congress] . . . must promptly pass legislation that will put into federal hands the registration of voters that the Alabama authorities will continue to obstruct as long as they have any discretion. (Garrow, 1978)

On the same day this editorial was published, King led a march across the bridge in violation of an injunction issued by a federal judge, but police blocked it once again and the marchers returned to Selma.

That night violence once again erupted. White vigilantes attacked three white clergymen, including James J. Reeb, a Unitarian minister from Boston, who died of his injuries a few days later. As the situation continued to deteriorate, President Johnson addressed a joint session of Congress on Monday, March 15. In this nationally broadcast address, Johnson called the events in Selma a "turning point in man's unending search for freedom." He pointed to the "harsh fact . . . that in many places in this country men and women are kept from voting simply because they are Negroes." How was this done? Johnson answered as follows:

> Every device of which human ingenuity is capable has been used to deny this right. The Negro citizen may go to register only to be told that the day is wrong, or the hour is late, or the official in charge is absent. And if he persists, and if he manages to present himself to the registrar, he may be disqualified because he did not spell out his middle name or because he abbreviated a word on the application.
>
> And if he manages to fill out an application he is given a test. The registrar is the sole judge of whether he passes this test. He may be asked to recite the entire Constitution, or explain the most complex provisions of State law. And even a college degree cannot be used to prove that he can read and write.
>
> For the fact is that the only way to pass these barriers is to show a white skin. (Johnson, 1965a)

Johnson reminded his audience that the Constitution clearly prohibited any denial of the right to vote because of "race or color" and that all the members of Congress had "sworn an oath before God to support and defend that Constitution" and indicated that he would soon send to Congress a bill "designed to eliminate illegal barriers to the right to vote." Johnson closed his speech with the observation that what happened in Selma was part of an "effort of American Negroes to secure for themselves the full blessings of American life" and that their cause "must be our cause too. Because it is not just Negroes, but really it is all of us, who must overcome the crippling legacy of bigotry and injustice. And we shall overcome" (Johnson, 1965a).

The VRA was introduced into Congress two days later, on Wednesday, March 17—the same day federal judge Frank Johnson issued an injunction ordering state and Dallas County officials not to interfere with an upcoming protest march from Selma to Montgomery. On Sunday, March 21, over three thousand marchers began the trek, led by Reverend King, under the protection of the watchful eyes of national guardsmen and federal officials. Thousands of supporters greeted the arrival of the marchers at the state capitol in Montgomery on March 25. In a powerful speech,

King argued that the "confrontation of good and evil compressed in the tiny community of Selma generated the massive power to turn the whole nation to a new course. A president born in the South had the sensitivity to feel the will of the country," to pledge the "might of the federal government to cast off the centuries-old blight," and to praise "the courage of the Negro for awakening the conscience of the nation" (King, 1965). Only federal protection of the right of African Americans to vote would achieve meaningful racial equality.

Opposed by Senator James Eastland (D-MS), Chair of the Senate Judiciary Committee, Johnson's Voting Rights Bill languished in committee, but Senate Majority Leader Mike Mansfield (D-MT) won a vote that brought the bill to the full Senate. The debate on the Senate floor began on April 22 and ended on May 25 with a cloture vote of 70–30, three votes more than was needed to end the filibuster by southern Democrats. The following day, the Senate passed the bill 77–19, with seven additional senators jumping on the bandwagon of protecting African Americans' right to vote. In the House, the Judiciary Committee tangled over the bill from March 19 until July 6, at which point the full House debated the measure, voting in favor of it on July 9 by a margin of 338–85. A conference committee resolved the differences between the two bills and President Johnson signed the bill into law on August 6, calling it "a triumph for freedom as huge as any victory that has ever been won on any battlefield." He thought it was a victory of this proportion because "the vote is the most powerful instrument ever devised by man for breaking down injustice and destroying the terrible walls which imprison men because they are different from other men" (Johnson, 1965b). In effect, Congress had enacted an unprecedented voting rights law within five months, an achievement made possible only because of the brutality African Americans endured in and around Selma, Alabama, earlier that year. But for this sacrifice in life and blood, it is highly unlikely that Congress would have had the courage and determination to enact the VRA. Accordingly, one measure of the controversial nature of this law is the degree of the sacrifice that made it possible.

Fifty years later, in a speech on August 6, 2015, President Barack Obama delivered remarks heralding the importance of the VRA. As the first African American elected to the highest office of the land—in 2008, in an election that marked the law's extraordinary impact on American society—Obama recognized that it was "one of our nation's most influential pieces of legislation." Obama noted, however, that Congress did not enact the VRA simply because "it was the right thing to do." In his view, the VRA was the legacy of the men and women who marched for the right to vote in Selma, Alabama in 1965—men and women who were "willing to sacrifice their own bodies in order to help bring America closer to its ideals of equality and justice for all." We "owe" those citizens "a great debt," he said, adding, "I am certain I wouldn't be where I am today without their sacrifices." In light of these sacrifices, Obama concluded that those who choose not to exercise the right to vote in today's world "dishonor those who fought so hard to give us" this "fundamental" right "in the first place." His words were a reminder that the VRA has not only transformed American society but still plays an important inspirational role in making "this union a little more perfect for the next generation" (Obama, 2015).

FURTHER READING

"Bloody Sunday—Selma, Alabama." *YouTube Video*, available at https://www.youtube.com/watch?v=P7vrrYVyN3g.

Branch, Taylor. *At Canaan's Edge: American in the King Years, 1965–68*. Reprint ed. New York: Simon & Schuster, 2007.

Cannon, Carl M. "From Detroit to Selma: Viola Liuzzo's Sacrifice." *Real Clear Politics*, January 2, 2018, available at https://www.realclearpolitics.com/articles/2018/01/02/from_detroit_to_selma_viola_liuzzos_sacrifice_135894.html.

Finkelman, Paul. "The Necessity of the Voting Rights Act of 1965 and the Difficulty of Overcoming Almost a Century of Voting Discrimination." *Louisiana Law Review* 76 (2015): 181–223.

Garrow, David J. *Protest at Selma: Martin Luther King, Jr., and the Voting Rights Act of 1965*. New Haven, CT: Yale University Press, 1978.

Johnson, Lyndon B. "President Johnson's Special Message to the Congress: The American Promise." *LBJ Presidential Library*, March 15, 1965a, available at http://www.lbjlibrary.org/lyndon-baines-johnson/speeches-films/president-johnsons-special-message-to-the-congress-the-american-promise/.

Johnson, Lyndon B. "Remarks on the Signing of the Voting Rights Act." August 6, 1965b, available at https://millercenter.org/the-presidency/presidential-speeches/august-6-1965-remarks-signing-voting-rights-act.

King, Martin Luther, Jr. "Our God Is Marching On!" March 25, 1965, available at https://kinginstitute.stanford.edu/our-god-marching.

Landsberg, Brian K. *Free at Last to Vote: The Alabama Origins of the 1965 Voting Rights Act*. Lawrence, KS: University of Kansas Press, 2007.

Obama, Barack. "50 Years After the Voting Rights Act, We Still Have Work to Do." August 6, 2015, available at https://obamawhitehouse.archives.gov/blog/2015/08/06/50-years-after-voting-rights-act-we-still-have-work-do.

Q18. AS THE VOTING RIGHTS ACT OF 1965 AUTHORIZED AN UNPRECEDENTED DEGREE OF FEDERAL CONTROL AND SUPERVISION OVER STATE ELECTORAL PRACTICES, WAS ITS CONSTITUTIONALITY IN DOUBT WHEN IT WAS ENACTED?

Answer: Yes. The constitutionality of the VRA was in doubt when it was enacted, but the Supreme Court upheld the law in *South Carolina v. Katzenbach* (1966), expressing the hope that the VRA would finally end a century of racial discrimination against African Americans' right to vote.

The Facts: Soon after President Johnson signed the VRA into law in August 1965, South Carolina invoked the Supreme Court's original jurisdiction and challenged the law's constitutionality on two general grounds. First, the state claimed the VRA exceeded the powers Congress had under Section 2 of the Fifteenth Amendment to enforce it by "appropriate legislation." In its view, Congress's power to enforce the Fifteenth Amendment was triggered only if a state denied or abridged the right to vote on the basis of race or color by law or an official policy. If a state electoral procedure was merely racially discriminatory in its effect, South Carolina's position was that Congress could not act unless a court had earlier found that the purpose of the practice was to discriminate on the basis of race. To allow Congress to act before a judicial finding, South Carolina argued, "would be to rob the courts of their rightful constitutional role." Second, because it had not engaged in any formal denial or abridgment of the right to vote based on race or color and no court had found that South Carolina had engaged in racial discrimination, the VRA necessarily encroached on the reserved powers of the states protected by the Tenth Amendment.

The Court flatly rejected South Carolina's understanding of Congress's enforcement power under the Fifteenth Amendment in *South Carolina v. Katzenbach* (1966). In particular, the Court rejected South Carolina's claim that Congress could not act prior to a judicial finding of racial discrimination. To the contrary, the Court argued, Congress and the judicial branch both have "full remedial powers to effectuate the constitutional prohibition against racial discrimination in voting." Regarding the breadth of Congress's remedial power, the test to be applied was the one Chief Justice Marshall had announced in *McCulloch v. Maryland* (1819):

> Let the end be legitimate, let it be within the scope of the constitution, and all means which are appropriate, which are plainly adapted to that end, which are not prohibited, but consistent with the letter and spirit of the constitution, are constitutional.

Accordingly, the Court rejected South Carolina's argument that Congress's remedial powers were limited to forbidding "violations of the Fifteenth Amendment in general terms—that the task of fashioning specific remedies or of applying them to particular localities must necessarily be left entirely to the courts." Congress could provide remedies for any sort of electoral practice that it considered violations of the right to vote protected by the Fifteenth Amendment. Moreover, because the VRA was within the remedial powers that the Congress had under Section 2 of the Fifteenth Amendment, it logically could not constitute a violation of South Carolina's reserved powers under the Tenth Amendment.

According to the Court, Congress enacted the VRA prior to any judicial finding because it had found that "case-by-case litigation was inadequate to combat widespread and persistent discrimination in voting." The "inordinate amount of time and energy required to overcome the obstructionist tactics invariably encountered in these lawsuits" was simply too much for the great majority of black citizens to overcome. In such circumstances, there was nothing wrong with shifting "the advantage of time and inertia from the perpetrators of the evil to its victims." Second, although Congress applied a few "general" provisions of the VRA to the entire country, it had decided to apply certain "special" provisions only "to a small number of States and political subdivisions." The trigger for this "special coverage" was twofold: First, the state or political subdivision had to use a "test or device" that discriminated on the basis of race or color; second, less than 50 percent of eligible voters in the jurisdiction were registered to vote in November 1964 or had cast votes in the presidential election of 1964. A "test or device" could be a literacy test, an educational credential, some sort of proof of good moral character, or the recommendation of a third person. Applying these criteria in 1964, the Attorney General had determined that Alabama, Louisiana, Mississippi, Georgia, South Carolina, and Virginia were subject to the "special provisions" of the VRA, as well as parts of North Carolina and one county in

Arizona. South Carolina claimed that this provision violated the equality of states, but the Court brushed this objection aside, holding that the Constitution only required that states be admitted into the Union on an equal basis, not that "remedies for local evils which have subsequently appeared" must be nationally applied.

"Special coverage" under Section 5 of the VRA meant that the above states and political subdivisions could not deny a person the right to vote based on any new "qualification, prerequisite, standard, practice, or procedure" without first obtaining "preclearance" from the Attorney General or a three-judge DC District Court that the new standard neither had the "purpose" nor the "effect" of denying a person the right to vote on account of race or color. This "preclearance" procedure extended to electoral districting, voter qualifications, and the conversion of elective offices to appointive ones. The Court argued that this "uncommon exercise of congressional power" was appropriate because states in the past "had resorted to the extraordinary stratagem of contriving new rules of various kinds for the purpose of perpetuating voting discrimination in the face of adverse federal court decrees." Congress, therefore, "had reason to suppose that these States might try similar maneuvers in the future in order to evade the remedies for voting discrimination contained in the Act itself." As earlier precedents supported the view "that exceptional conditions can justify legislative measures not otherwise appropriate," the Court concluded that, under "the compulsion of these unique circumstances, Congress responded in a permissibly decisive manner."

The "preclearance" requirement and procedure remained in effect until the covered state or political subdivision convinced the three-judge district court that it had not engaged in any racial discrimination in its voting practices for five years. South Carolina argued that these termination procedures were a "nullity" as it would be near impossible for state officials to prove that not a single instance of racial discrimination occurred within its many political subdivisions for a five-year period. The Court dismissed this concern, holding that a state "need not disprove each isolated instance of voting discrimination in order to obtain relief in the termination proceedings." In the Court's view, the burden of proof was "quite bearable, particularly since the relevant facts relating to the conduct of voting officials are peculiarly within the knowledge of the States and political subdivisions themselves."

South Carolina noted that a provision of the VRA suspended all literacy tests in federal elections in covered jurisdictions and argued that it was inconsistent with the Court's ruling that literacy tests were constitutional in *Lassiter v. Northampton County Board of Elections* (1959). In response, the Court observed that the "record shows that, in most States covered by the Act, including South Carolina, various tests and devices have been instituted with the purpose of disenfranchising Negroes, have been framed in such a way as to facilitate this aim, and have been administered in a discriminatory fashion for many years." After all, the Court noted, if the Act had simply required that literacy tests be fairly administered in the future, Congress knew that this option "would freeze the effect of past discrimination in favor of unqualified white registrants." This was so because covered states "had been allowing white illiterates to vote for years."

The VRA also authorized the Attorney General to appoint federal examiners or observers to monitor voter registration and voting in covered jurisdictions. This provision brought employees of the federal government directly into the day-to-day voting operations of a state. Examiners were authorized, in effect, to register voters, review the jurisdiction's voter registration procedures, and maintain their own list of eligible voters, while observers monitored how poll workers functioned in local polling places and how voting officials tabulated the ballots. The Court rejected the claim that the law gave too much arbitrary discretion to the Attorney General, pointing out that the law directed him or her "to calculate the registration ratio of nonwhites to whites [in the jurisdiction], and to weigh evidence of good faith efforts to avoid possible voting discrimination." Moreover, the VRA permitted covered jurisdictions affected by this provision to seek judicial review, thereby "assuring the withdrawal of federal examiners from areas where they are clearly not needed." Even if the standard for judicial withdrawal of federal examiners or observers appointed by the Attorney General was high, the Court asserted that it was still possible for a state or political subdivision to meet it. The state simply had to show that there was "no longer reasonable cause to believe that persons will be deprived of or denied the right to vote on account of race or color."

In closing, the Court noted that Congress had observed "nearly a century of widespread resistance to the Fifteenth Amendment." By enacting the VRA, Congress had finally marshaled "an array of potent weapons against the evil, with authority in the Attorney General to employ them effectively." The key to the VRA's effectiveness, the Court recognized, was that remedial measures enforced by the executive branch of the federal government would supplement the judicial remedies of the past—remedies that had proven to be inadequate. The Court welcomed its new partner in the effort to make the Fifteenth Amendment a reality, perhaps implicitly acknowledging that the judicial branch could not achieve this goal alone. Holding that the provisions of the VRA discussed above were "valid means for carrying out the commands of the Fifteenth Amendment," the Court concluded its opinion with the following wish: "Hopefully, millions of non-white Americans will now be able to participate for the first time on an equal basis in the government under which they live. We may finally look forward to the day when truly '[t]he right of citizens of the United States to vote shall not be denied or abridged by the United States or by any State on account of race, color, or previous condition of servitude.'"

South Carolina v. Katzenbach was indisputably a milestone. By recognizing Congress's wide-ranging constitutional authority to enforce the Fifteenth Amendment, the Court enabled Congress to renew and amend the VRA in 1970, 1975, 1982, 1992, and 2006. These exertions of congressional authority significantly broadened and deepened the scope of voting rights of racial and ethnic minorities, fundamentally reshaping the voting practices of Americans in the twenty-first century. For example, Congress increased the number of electoral districts subject to the special provisions of the VRA in 1968 and 1972. It gave more protection to the voting rights of language-based minorities in 1975, and in 1982 it permanently prohibited all states from adopting voting practices that had a discriminatory "effect," regardless of whether a state enacted or implemented the practice for a discriminatory "purpose." In 2006, Congress renewed the VRA for twenty-five years, till 2031, as well as prohibited states subject to the VRA's "special provision" from engaging in all forms of racial discrimination in voting, not just those that had a "retrogressive" discriminatory purpose. All these laws were constitutionally rooted in the remedial power that Congress has under Section 2 of the Fifteenth Amendment. It was the Supreme Court's interpretation of this constitutional provision in *South Carolina v. Katzenbach* that made all this possible. This case, therefore, remains the underlying legal foundation for racial and ethnic minorities experiencing racial discrimination in voting to seek redress from Congress in the twenty-first century.

FURTHER READING

Bickel, Alexander M. "The Voting Rights Cases." *The Supreme Court Review* 1966 (1966): 79–102.

Derfner, Armand. "Racial Discrimination and the Right to Vote." *Vanderbilt Law Review* 26 (1973): 523–543.

Fuentes-Rohwer, Luis E. "Understanding the Paradoxical Case of the Voting Rights Act." *Florida State University Law Review* 36 (2009): 697–763.

Katz, Ellen D. "South Carolina's 'Evolutionary Process.'" *Columbia Law Review Sidebar* 113 (2013): 55–65.

May, Gary. *Bending Toward Justice: The Voting Rights Act and the Transformation of American Democracy*. New York: Basic Books, 2013.

"Transcript of Voting Rights Act (1965)." n.d., available at https://www.ourdocuments.gov/doc.php?flash=true&doc=100&page=transcript.

"Voting Rights Act of 1965." *Duke Law Journal* 1966 (1966): 463–483.

Q19. DO FEDERAL "EXAMINERS" AND "OBSERVERS" OF ELECTIONS CONTINUE TO PLAY AN IMPORTANT ROLE IN STATES SUBJECT TO THE "SPECIAL PROVISIONS" OF SECTION 5 OF THE VOTING RIGHTS ACT?

Answer: No. Although federal "examiners" and "observers" of elections played a crucial role in the protection of the voting rights of racial minorities during the 1960s and 1970s, the need for them began to decline during the 1980s, and today their role is fulfilled primarily by volunteers.

The Facts: Federal voting "examiners" and "observers" were literally the eyes and ears of the federal government that ensured compliance with the VRA during the 1960s and 1970s. Under Section 3, a federal district court may authorize the use of examiners or observers as a remedy in a lawsuit alleging a violation of voting rights. The judge could authorize them on an interim basis or "as part of any final judgment if the court finds that violations of the fifteenth amendment . . . have occurred." In contrast, under Section 6 of the VRA, the Attorney General can appoint examiners and observers to a jurisdiction subject to Section 5's "special provisions" of the VRA under two conditions: on the receipt of twenty "meritorious" written complaints from residents of a covered jurisdiction alleging racial discrimination; or, if the ratio of nonwhite persons to white persons registered to vote within a covered jurisdiction appears to be "reasonably attributable" to violations of the right to vote. In the latter case, however, the Attorney General must also consider whether there is "substantial evidence" that the jurisdiction is making "bona fide" efforts to comply with the Fifteenth Amendment. After this appraisal, the Attorney General decides if the appointment of examiners/observers is "necessary" to enforce the Fifteenth Amendment. The Attorney General, therefore, had broad discretion to appoint federal examiners in jurisdictions subject to the "special provisions" of the VRA, and federal courts could do the same for uncovered jurisdictions if they discriminated in the electoral process on the basis of race or, after 1975, against language minorities ("Transcript of Voting Rights Act (1965)," n.d.).

Section 7 of the VRA authorized federal examiners to review the qualifications of voter applicants and place them on a list of eligible voters if they met all the State's voter qualifications that were "not inconsistent with the Constitution and laws of the United States." In the early years of the VRA's enforcement, federal examiners were ultimately responsible for the registration of a large percentage of black voters, especially in southern states. The examiners issued a certificate to each African American they identified as an eligible voter; added that name to a list of eligible voters; and sent this list of eligible voters to responsible state officials, who were legally required to place the names on the state's official voter registration list. If state officials challenged the eligibility of any person on the list, a hearing officer from the federal Civil Service Commission would issue a final determination, which only would be subject to the review of a federal appellate court. The bottom line was that federal, not state, officials would ultimately decide if African Americans were entitled to vote in any jurisdiction if either a federal court or the Attorney General had decided that federal examiners were necessary or appropriate.

In any jurisdiction where a federal examiner was registering black voters, Section 8 of the VRA authorized the Attorney General to request the Civil Service Commission to send federal observers to that same jurisdiction. The function of the federal observer was twofold: first, to observe any election in the jurisdiction to determine "whether persons who are entitled to vote are being permitted to vote," and second, to observe any location in the jurisdiction where votes were counted to determine "whether votes cast by persons entitled to vote are being properly tabulated." These observers reported their findings to the federal examiner and to either the Attorney General or the district court.

There is no doubt that both examiners and observers deterred voting officials from engaging in racial discrimination. They were trained to contemporaneously write down everything they saw or heard during the registration and election process. Obviously, their later testimony in a civil lawsuit or criminal case, backed up as it were with their written notes, would be highly credible. Southern voting officials who were responsible for voter registration, the election, and the tabulation of the results knew that it would be very difficult to challenge their testimony in a lawsuit or a review by the Attorney General. Criminal penalties for violating the VRA were as high as a $10,000 fine or five years of imprisonment, or both. Under these circumstances, local voting officials had little choice but to respect the right of racial minorities to vote, in particular, African Americans in southern states.

The deterrent impact of federal examiners and observers is correlated to the preventative purpose of the VRA. Rather than trying to remedy individual violations of the Fifteenth Amendment after they had happened, whether by litigation or prosecution on a case-by-case basis, the VRA's purpose was to prevent the violation in the first place. Accordingly, the effectiveness of the VRA can be gauged somewhat by the extent of the role that examiners and observers played, especially in the early years when opposition to the VRA was widespread. In that vein, the Voter Education Project reported that the percentage of voting-age African Americans registered in Georgia counties by federal examiners had reached 69.5 percent in 1966, far higher than the 10.3 percent registered in 1960. By December 31, 1967, the Attorney General had assigned examiners to fifty-eight counties in five southern states and they registered 150,767 nonwhites. The federal observer program had a similar impact. In November 1966, there were approximately six hundred observers in southern polling places and more than nine hundred the following year. Although these observers had no immediate enforcement authority, they could easily report what they saw to DOJ attorneys. For this reason, "their presence often deters local election officials from engaging in discriminatory practices" (USCCR, 2006).

Any jurisdiction subject to monitoring by federal examiners and observers could attempt to terminate it under Section 13 in two alternative ways. First, a jurisdiction covered by Section 5 could petition the Attorney General for an end to both programs. If he or she felt it was warranted, the Attorney General could then ask the Census Bureau to determine if 50 percent of the nonwhite persons of voting age residing in the jurisdiction were registered to vote. If 50 percent were registered, then the Attorney General could release the jurisdiction from coverage (1) if the names of all persons identified as eligible to vote by the federal examiner were on the jurisdiction's official voter registration list; and (2) there was no longer "reasonable cause" to believe that the jurisdiction would deny the right to vote on account of race or color. The latter criterion, obviously, gave the Attorney General considerable discretion.

Second, if a court appointed the examiners/observers, then the jurisdiction could seek from the judge a declaratory judgment releasing it from coverage. In such an instance, the court was empowered to order the Census Bureau to determine if 50 percent of nonwhite persons of voting age were registered. The court was also granted the authority to require such a determination by the Census Bureau if it found that the

Attorney General's refusal to request such a determination was "arbitrary" or "unreasonable."

Following Congress's extension of the VRA's "special provisions" to "language minorities" in 1975 (see Q22), the role of federal examiners and observers expanded accordingly. The Comptroller General reported in 1978 that the Attorney General and district courts had assigned federal examiners to sixty-one jurisdictions across "covered" states and over ten thousand observers to polling sites in ninety-one elections (CG, 1978). However, the need for federal examiners began to decline during the late 1970s. By 1983, examiners were assigned to only eight counties, two in Georgia and six in Mississippi, each spending no more than a few days in each jurisdiction.

After 1983, neither the Attorney General nor a federal court sent an examiner to any jurisdiction to help register African Americans or members of "language minorities." Legislative developments further eroded the need for federal examiners. For example, in 1993, Congress enacted the National Voter Registration Act, which required states to register voters at all departments of motor vehicles, all armed forces recruitment centers, and all state or county public assistance offices (e.g., offices handling applications for food stamps). The law also required states to register any person that filled out a federal voter registration and sent it to local officials. In 2002, Congress also enacted the Help America Vote Act, which required states to maintain a statewide voter registration list and compelled state election officials to supply voters whose eligibility to vote was uncertain with a provisional ballot. This ballot would be counted within days of an election if the local board of elections determined that the voter was in fact registered and eligible to vote. With these reforms, it became apparent that the federal voting examiner program was no longer necessary. Congress repealed it in 2006.

However, throughout this time period, the observer program continued to play an important role in federal efforts to enforce the VRA, both to prevent racial discrimination and to secure compliance with the VRA's bilingual election requirement. From 1965 to 2007, approximately twenty-two thousand federal observers were sent to certified jurisdictions to monitor elections. In 2005, "a record of 1,463 federal observers and 533 Department personnel were sent to monitor 163 elections in 105 jurisdictions in 29 states." However, following 2005, the number of observers assigned to "certified" jurisdictions began to decline, presumably because the Attorney General no longer thought they were necessary to ensure compliance with the VRA. In 2006, it sent observers only to eighteen counties in five states (Tucker, 2007).

In 2012, observers monitored activities at polling places in only seventeen jurisdictions (DOJ, 2012).

Following the Supreme Court's invalidation of the coverage formula of Section 4 of the VRA in *Shelby County v. Holder* (2013) (see Q23), the DOJ revised its webpage titled "About Federal Observers and Election Monitoring" to make it clear that it would no longer rely on certifications by the Attorney General "to identify jurisdictions for election monitoring." It would continue, however, to send federal election observers "where there is a relevant court order" requiring such monitoring as a remedy for a VRA violation. These federal observers are specially recruited and trained by the Office of Personnel Management (OPM). In addition to these OPM observers, the revised webpage noted, the DOJ would send its own personnel to watch the voting process in jurisdictions suspected of illicit voting practices. These observers could be DOJ attorneys or staff members from the Civil Rights Division who are in close contact with state and local election officials. Any citizen can request DOJ monitoring of a jurisdiction's election activity by providing specific and detailed information regarding the need for it, such as incidents of voter discrimination, names and addresses of victims, and locations. These federal observers, whether OPM-trained or DOJ employees, are still important, the webpage continued, because they "have a unique ability to help deter wrongdoing, defuse tension, promote compliance with the law and bolster public confidence in the electoral process." However, notwithstanding the effectiveness of federal election observers, the webpage concluded that the DOJ would not be able to send as many observers after *Shelby County* as it had "in similar past elections." Accordingly, despite all that federal election observers have done in the past to secure the right to vote of racial and language minorities, their role in future elections is uncertain.

FURTHER READING

Comptroller General of the United States (CG). *Voting Rights Act—Enforcement Needs Strengthening: A Report*. Washington, DC: General Accounting Office, 1978, available at https://www.gao.gov/assets/130/121337.pdf.

Davidson, Chandler, and Grofman, Bernard, eds. *Quiet Revolution in the South: The Impact of the Voting Rights Act, 1965–1990*. Princeton, NJ: Princeton University Press, 1994.

Department of Justice (DOJ). "'About Federal Observers and Election Monitoring' and 'Fact Sheet on Justice Department's Enforcement

Efforts Following *Shelby County* Decision.'" n.d., available at https://www.justice.gov/crt/about-federal-observers-and-election-monitoring.

Department of Justice (DOJ). "Press Release: Justice Department to Monitor Polls in 23 States on Election Day." November 2, 2012, available at https://www.justice.gov/opa/pr/justice-department-monitor-polls-23-states-election-day.

"Transcript of Voting Rights Act (1965)." n.d., available at https://www.ourdocuments.gov/doc.php?flash=true&doc=100&page=transcript.

Tucker, James Thomas. "The Power of Observation: The Role of Federal Observers under the Voting Rights Act." *Michigan Journal of Race & Law* 13 (2007): 227–276.

United States Commission on Civil Rights (USCCR). *Political Participation: A Report*. Washington, DC: United States Government Printing Office, 1968.

United States Commission on Civil Rights (USCCR). *Voting Rights Enforcement & Reauthorization*. Washington, DC: United States Government Printing Office, 2006.

"Voting Rights Act of 1965." New Haven, CT: Yale Law School (The Avalon Project): Documents in Law, History and Diplomacy, available at https://avalon.law.yale.edu/20th_century/voting_rights_1965.asp.

Q20. WAS SECTION 2 OF THE VOTING RIGHTS ACT REDUNDANT BECAUSE IT ONLY BANNED WHAT THE FIFTEENTH AMENDMENT ALREADY PROHIBITED?

Answer: No. Although the breadth of ban on racial discrimination in voting found in Section 2 was initially unclear, Congress amended the provision in 1982 to confirm that the statutory ban on racial discrimination was broader than the Fifteenth Amendment's language.

The Facts: Section 2 of the VRA is a "general" provision applicable to the entire nation, not just to "covered" jurisdictions subject to Section 5's "special provisions." Its language is as follows:

No voting qualification or prerequisite to voting, or standard, practice, or procedure shall be imposed or applied by any State or political subdivision to deny or abridge the right of any citizen of the United States to vote on account of race or color.

In *Allen v. State Board of Elections* (1969), the Supreme Court held that Section 5 prohibited any change, such as a change of an electoral district's boundaries, that had "the effect of denying citizens their right to vote because of their race." Plaintiffs, therefore, did not have to prove a state's unlawful intent to block federal preclearance of such a change. At the time, it was not clear whether Section 2 had the same scope, but the Court resolved this ambiguity in *Mobile v. Bolden* (1980), a case involving an African American challenge to Mobile, Alabama's at-large voting system for its three-member municipal commission, which exercised all legislative, executive, and administrative power in the city. This method meant that a majority of white voters could easily elect an all-white commission, while it was impossible for the black minority to elect any commissioners. Mobile had adopted this form of selection in 1911, which meant that the at-large method of electing the commissioners was not a new change subject to the preclearance requirement of Section 5 of the VRA. The African American challengers claimed that Mobile's system violated not just the Equal Protection Clause and the Fifteenth Amendment but also Section 2 of the VRA. Accordingly, the Court had to consider whether to extend the "effects test" of Section 5 to both the constitutional right to vote and Section 2's nationwide ban on racial discrimination in voting.

In a 6–3 decision, the Court upheld the legality of Mobile's at-large voting system. A four-justice plurality set aside the constitutional objections, remarking that the Equal Protection Clause is violated "only if there is purposeful discrimination," and that a state's electoral practice that was "racially neutral on its face violates the Fifteenth Amendment only if motivated by a discriminatory purpose" (see also *Rogers v. Lodge* [1982]). That only left Section 2 of the VRA. Regarding this statutory claim, the plurality argued that "the sparse legislative history of § 2 makes clear that it was intended to have an effect no different from that of the Fifteenth Amendment." Accordingly, the African American challengers had the burden of proving that city officials in 1911 established the at-large system for the purpose of racial discrimination or that current officials were operating it with this unlawful purpose. A couple of justices thought the challengers had met this burden or that proof of unlawful intent was not necessary to establish a constitutional violation, but a majority of the justices agreed that a constitutional violation of the Fifteenth Amendment required proof of a state's unlawful intent and that Section 2 of the VRA added no additional protection.

Unhappy with the Court's decision in *Mobile*, Congress amended the VRA in the Voting Rights Act Amendments of 1982 by prohibiting any state from imposing or applying any voting qualification or other prerequisite "in a manner which results in a denial or abridgement" of the right to vote "on account of race or color." In Section 3 of the law, it defined "denial or abridgement" as follows:

> A violation of . . . is established if, based on the totality of circumstances, it is shown that the political processes leading to nomination or election in the State or political subdivision are not equally open to participation by members of a class of citizens protected by [Section 2] . . . in that its members have less opportunity than other members of the electorate to participate in the political process and to elect representatives of their choice. The extent to which members of a protected class have been elected to office in the State or political subdivision is one circumstance which may be considered: *Provided*, That nothing in this section establishes a right to have members of a protected class elected in numbers equal to their proportion in the population.

Congress's extension of Section 2 beyond the requirements of either the Fourteenth or Fifteenth Amendment had a large impact on how courts later evaluated the legality of at-large or multimember elections. Such elections might not violate the Constitution because there was no unlawful intent, but they could nonetheless violate the VRA.

In *Thornburg v. Gingles* (1986), a case involving North Carolina's use of multimember districts in state legislative elections, the Supreme Court considered which factors were relevant to assessing whether elections were "equally open to participation" by African Americans in the "totality of circumstances." Citing the Senate majority report that accompanied the Voting Rights Act Amendments of 1982, the Court noted a number of "typical factors," including "the extent of any history of official discrimination," the extent to which voting "is racially polarized," and the extent to which "political campaigns have been characterized by overt or subtle racial appeals." The Court agreed that these factors were relevant to establishing "a claim of vote dilution through submergence in multimember districts," but ruled that they were not sufficient. A minority group must also demonstrate (1) "that it is sufficiently large and geographically compact to constitute a majority in a single-member district;" (2) "that it is politically cohesive;" and (3) "that the white majority votes sufficiently as a bloc to enable it . . . usually to defeat the minority's preferred candidate." Accordingly, not all at-large elections violated Section 2 but those that satisfied this three-part test (which became known as the *Gingles* test) did violate the VRA, even if they did not violate either the Fourteenth or the

Fifteenth Amendment. Applying these criteria, the Court found that all of North Carolina's multimember districts violated Section 2.

In *Growe v. Emison* (1993) and *Voinovich v. Quilter* (1993), the Court considered whether to apply the *Gingles* test to single-member electoral districts if states were concentrating many minority voters into a few single-member districts ("packing") or dispersing them among many such districts ("cracking"). Of course, both "packing" and "cracking" negatively affected the electoral influence of racial minorities: the former by limiting the possible number of minority representatives; the latter by making it impossible for the racial minority to elect a minority candidate. However, in *Growe*, the Supreme Court refused to provide any relief because the challengers had not shown that the minority group was politically cohesive; and in *Voinovich*, the Court ruled that the challengers had failed to establish that whites voted as a bloc. These two cases made it clear that racial or language-based minorities had the burden of proving that the state's electoral practice met the *Gingles* test. The state was under no obligation to prove that it did not.

A year later, in *Johnson v. De Grandy* (1994), the Court reviewed a Hispanic challenge to Florida's use of single-member districts for both houses of the state legislature. Florida's plan created nine House and three Senate districts in Dade County that were majority Hispanic, rather than eleven and four districts, respectively. In the end, the Court rejected the Hispanic challenge to Florida's districting plan, holding that a successful challenge required plaintiffs to satisfy not just the three criteria of the *Gingles* test but also one additional condition. Courts "must also examine other evidence in the totality of circumstances, including the extent of the opportunities minority voters enjoy to participate in the political processes." In that regard, the Court found that Florida's plan created a number of "majorityminority districts in substantial proportion to the minority's share of voting-age population." For example, Hispanics were 50 percent of the voting-age population of Dade County and under the state's plan would have "supermajorities in 9 of the 18 House districts located primarily within the county." What must be avoided, the Court concluded, was a reading of Section 2 that defined vote dilution "as a failure to maximize" the number of majority-minority districts. Any such interpretation "tends to obscure the very object of the statute and to run counter to its textually stated purpose. One may suspect vote dilution from political famine, but one is not entitled to suspect (much less infer) dilution from mere failure to guarantee a political feast."

In *Bartlett v. Strickland* (2009), the Court addressed whether North Carolina could invoke Section 2 to justify a violation of the state

Constitution for the purpose of creating not a majority-minority district but a minority district that included crossover white voters who were more likely to vote for minority candidates than the average white voter. The Supreme Court had already held in *League of United Latin American Citizens v. Perry* (2006) that Section 2 did not require a state to create a "minority-influence" district, that is, one "in which a minority group can influence the outcome of an election even if its preferred candidate cannot be elected." But North Carolina, the Court conceded, was attempting to create a "crossover district," that is, one in which "the minority population, at least potentially, is large enough to elect the candidate of its choice with help from voters who are members of the majority and who cross over to support the minority's preferred candidate."

In the end, the Court's majority ruled that North Carolina's effort to establish so-called "effective minority districts" was "contrary" to the mandate of Section 2 because it "would grant minority voters 'a right to preserve their strength for the purposes of forging an advantageous political alliance,'" not to prevent dilution of the racial minority's vote. The Court also observed that it was "difficult to see how the majority-bloc voting requirement [the third criterion of the *Gingles* test] could be met in a district where, by definition, white voters join in sufficient numbers with minority voters to elect the minority's preferred candidate." In addition, the Court added, only "when a geographically compact group of minority voters could form a majority in a single-member district has the first *Gingles* requirement been met." Any reading of Section 2 to require "crossover districts" beyond those narrow conditions would, in the Court's view, raise "serious constitutional concerns under the Equal Protection Clause." With this conclusion, the Court was highlighting that Section 2 of the VRA, one of Congress's remedial measures under the Fifteenth Amendment, could come into tension with the requirements of the Equal Protection Clause of the Fourteenth Amendment.

This tension between Section 2 and the Equal Protection Fourteenth Amendment is a major controversy regarding racial discrimination and the right to vote in the twenty-first century. For example, the Court held in *Alabama Legislative Black Caucus v. Alabama* (2015) that, if a state invokes Section 2 to justify race-based districting, it can meet the "strict scrutiny" standard of the Equal Protection Clause only if it has "a strong basis in evidence" that the VRA required this type of action. In *Cooper v. Harris* (2017), the Court elaborated on what it meant by "a strong basis in evidence." A state using race-based districting must have "'good reasons' to think it would transgress the Act if it did *not* draw race-based district lines." The Court added that, if "a State has good reason to think that all the '*Gingles* preconditions' are met, then so too it has good reason to believe that § 2 requires drawing a majority-minority district. But if not, then not." Applying these criteria, the Court concluded that the state of North Carolina did not have "good reason" for racial districting because it had not scrutinized whether the white majority engaged in bloc voting—the third *Gingles* criterion.

However, the following year, in *Abbott v. Perez* (2018), the Court ruled that even if the *Gingles* criteria were met, the minority challenger yet had the burden of proving that, "under the totality of circumstances, the district lines dilute the votes of the members of the minority group." Those who challenged a state's districting, the Court insisted, had the burden of proving that a racial/ethnic minority was geographically compact enough to constitute a majority in a district; that it was politically cohesive; that the white majority tended to vote as a bloc; and that the state's districting plan diluted the votes of the racial minority. Under this criteria, proving that the state's racial districting could have benefited the political interests of racial minorities was insufficient; challengers had to prove a negative impact on their electoral influence, not a less than perfect impact. This relatively high standard became even more important after the Supreme Court invalidated the VRA's coverage formula (Section 4) in *Shelby County v. Holder* (2013) (see Q23), a decision that rendered the "special provisions" of Section 5 inoperative. The effect of this ruling was to make Section 2 the primary means by which racial/ethnic minorities could challenge a state's voting practices.

FURTHER READING

Adams, Ross J. "Whose Vote Counts? Minority Vote Dilution and Election Rights." *Washington University Journal of Urban and Contemporary Law* 35 (1989): 219–235.

Boyd, Thomas M., and Markman, Stephen J. "The 1982 Amendments to the Voting Rights Act: A Legislative History." *Washington and Lee Law Review* 40 (1983): 1347–1428.

Bullock, Charles S., III, and Dunn, Richard E. "The Demise of Racial Redistricting and the Future of Black Representation." *Emory Law Journal* 48 (1999): 1209–1253.

Clegg, Roger, and von Spakovsky, Hans A. "Disparate Impact and Section 2 of the Voting Rights Act." *Mississippi Law Journal* 85 (2017): 1357–1372.

Pildes, Richard H. "Is Voting-Rights Law Now at War with Itself? Social Science and Voting Rights in the 2000s." *North Carolina Law Review* 80 (2002): 1517–1573.

Tokaji, Daniel P. "The New Vote Denial: Where Election Reform Meets the Voting Rights Act." *South Carolina Law Review* 57 (2006): 689–731.

"Voting Rights Act of 1965." New Haven, CT: Yale Law School (The Avalon Project): Documents in Law, History and Diplomacy, available at https://avalon.law.yale.edu/20th_century/voting_rights_1965.asp.

Williamson, Richard A. "The 1982 Amendments to the Voting Rights Act: A Statutory Analysis of the Revised Bailout Provisions." *Washington University Law Review* 62 (1984): 1–77.

Q21. COULD A STATE USE RACE AS A FACTOR IN DRAWING ELECTORAL DISTRICT LINES TO COMPLY WITH SECTION 5 OF THE VOTING RIGHTS ACT TO SUCH AN EXTENT THAT IT VIOLATED THE EQUAL PROTECTION CLAUSE OF THE FOURTEENTH AMENDMENT?

Answer: Yes. Although the Supreme Court was initially more flexible, it eventually ruled that if the use of race became the "predominant" factor in drawing electoral district lines to satisfy preclearance requirements under Section 5, it would constitute a violation of the Equal Protection Clause of the Fourteenth Amendment.

The Facts: Under the preclearance requirement of Section 5 of the VRA, a covered state has the burden of proving that any change in its electoral system does not have the "purpose" or "effect" of discriminating on the basis of race or color. While the statutory "purpose" standard under Section 5 was the same as the constitutional standard under the Fifteenth Amendment, each requiring a finding of a racially discriminatory purpose, the "effect" standard was solely a statutory one. Regarding the meaning of the latter requirement, the Supreme Court in *Beer v. United States* (1976) held that a change in a state's electoral practices had a discriminatory "effect" only if the change constituted a "retrogression," that is, only if it produced more of a discriminatory impact than what existed prior to the change. Accordingly, an electoral reform that produced a racially discriminatory impact "equal to" or "less than" what had existed before the change did not violate Section 5.

In *United Jewish Organization of Williamsburg, Inc. v. Carey* (1977) (*UJO*), the Supreme Court reviewed a New York districting plan that split the Hasidic Jewish community of Brooklyn's Williamsburg area (about thirty thousand people) into two state senate and two assembly districts. New York redrew these districts, not for the purpose of creating more nonwhite majority districts, but to increase the size of the nonwhite majority in each district to some point between 65 and 75 percent. Objecting to the change, members of the Hasidic community claimed the plan would dilute the value of their votes "solely for the purpose of achieving a racial quota . . . in violation of the Fourteenth Amendment," as well as assign them to districts "solely on the basis of race" in violation of the Fifteenth Amendment.

The Court responded that "New York adopted the 1974 plan because it sought to comply with [§ 5 of] the Voting Rights Act." This purpose, in the Court's view, was enough to conclude that the plan did not violate the Equal Protection Clause of the Fourteenth Amendment even if the state used "specific numerical quotas in establishing a certain number of black majority districts." The Court added that the plan "represented no racial slur or stigma with respect to whites or any other race, and we [therefore] discern no discrimination violative of the Fourteenth Amendment, nor any abridgment of the right to vote on account of race within the meaning of the Fifteenth Amendment." New York had not acted with any illicit racial "purpose" because Brooklyn's Hasidic Jews, in the Court's view, were members of the white race and the plan did not dilute or negatively affect the white majority's vote.

The year after *UJO*, the Court addressed the constitutionality of affirmative action in *Regents of the University of California v. Bakke* (1978), a case involving a state medical school that annually set aside sixteen admission slots for members of identified racial minorities, including African Americans. Despite the "benign" purpose of the program, Justice Lewis Powell's pivotal opinion applied "strict scrutiny" to the program, which is the highest standard of the Equal Protection Clause. This stringent test meant that the medical school was in compliance with the Equal Protection Clause only if the program was "narrowly tailored" to achieve a "compelling interest." Powell concluded that the program was not "narrowly tailored" because the school used a "quota" to admit minority students, rather than a "goal."

More than a decade later, the Court in *City of Richmond v. J. A. Croson Co.* (1989) applied strict scrutiny and invalidated a program requiring city contractors to subcontract 30 percent of construction contracts to minority-owned business enterprises. The Court explained that "strict scrutiny" was the appropriate standard because "[a]bsent searching judicial inquiry into the justification for such race-based measures, there is simply no way of determining what [racial] classifications are 'benign' or 'remedial' and what classifications are in fact motivated by illegitimate notions of racial inferiority or simple racial politics." The Court added,

"Indeed the purpose of strict scrutiny is to 'smoke out' illegitimate uses of race by assuring that the legislative body is pursuing a goal important enough to warrant use of a highly suspect tool."

In *Shaw v. Reno* (1993), the Supreme Court considered if these affirmative action decisions had a bearing on whether a state's electoral districting plan under Section 5 of the VRA came into tension with the Equal Protection Clause of the Fourteenth Amendment. The case involved North Carolina's effort to obtain the Attorney General's approval for a redistricting plan under Section 5. The plan created a second majority-black district that ran for approximately 160 miles along the corridor of Interstate 85. Five residents objected, claiming that the state had concentrated black voters "arbitrarily," without regard to the traditional districting principles of compactness, contiguity, and respect for political subdivisions. In its decision, the Court conceded two important points: first, "the legislature always is *aware* of race when it draws district lines, just as it is aware of age, economic status, religious and political persuasion, and a variety of other demographic factors," and, second, the "Court never has held that race-conscious state decisionmaking is impermissible in *all* circumstances." A state subject to Section 5's preclearance requirement, for example, must obviously take race into account to ensure that its districting plan comports with Section 5's "nonretrogression" principle. However, the Court insisted, if a state uses race as a factor in electoral districting more extensively than what the "nonretrogression" principle requires, that additional amount would be consistent with the Equal Protection Clause only if it passed strict scrutiny, that is, only if it was "narrowly tailored" to achieve a "compelling purpose."

According to the Court, North Carolina's "snake-like" African American district did not meet this test because its shape was irrational and in no way a narrowly tailored means to comply with Section 5. In fact, the district was "so highly irregular that, on its face, it rationally cannot be understood as anything other" than an effort to segregate voters "on the basis of race." North Carolina has grouped into "one district individuals who belong to the same race, but who are otherwise widely separated by geographical and political boundaries, and who may have little in common with one another but the color of their skin," which, the Court noted sharply, "bears an uncomfortable resemblance to political apartheid." Moreover, even if North Carolina's goal was not political apartheid, "reapportionment is one area in which appearances do matter" because where district lines are drawn can "reinforce the belief . . . that individuals should be judged by the color of their skin" and, for that reason, "balkanize us into competing racial factions."

Two years later, in *Miller v. Johnson* (1995), the Court broadened the prohibition against using race to satisfy preclearance obligations under Section 5 by rejecting a claim that a district had to have a "bizarre" shape to violate the Equal Protection Clause: "Shape [of the district] is relevant not because bizarreness is a necessary element of the constitutional wrong or a threshold requirement of proof, but because it may be persuasive circumstantial evidence that race for its own sake, and not [for] other districting principles, was the legislature's dominant and controlling rationale in drawing its district lines." For this reason, citizens objecting to Georgia's districting plan approved by the Attorney General under Section 5 "may rely on evidence other than bizarreness to establish racebased districting." Of course, the Court admitted, "redistricting by definition involves racial considerations," but Georgia impermissibly allowed race to become "the predominant, overriding factor." The Court refused to accept Georgia's contention that it had "a compelling interest in complying with whatever preclearance mandates the Justice Department issues." According to the Court, "the judiciary retains an independent obligation in adjudicating consequent equal protection challenges to ensure that the State's actions are narrowly tailored to achieve a compelling interest" (See also *Bush v. Vera* [1996]).

North Carolina returned to the Court with its second effort to comply with the Justice Department's Section 5 preclearance mandate in *Shaw v. Hunt* (1996), but the Court quickly threw out the "serpentine district" that had been "dubbed the least geographically compact district in the Nation." However, the Court found that North Carolina's third effort to meet the demands of Section 5 was consistent with the Equal Protection Clause in *Hunt v. Cromartie* (2001). Although the contested district still had an unusual shape, it split many towns and counties into separate districts, and it yet had a high African American voting population, the Court found this evidence was insufficient to establish that the legislature's purpose was "predominantly" based on race. It was true that many white registered Democrats were excluded from the district while many black registered Democrats were included, but the key fact was that "white voters registered as Democrats 'cross-over' to vote for a Republican candidate more often than do African-Americans, who register and vote Democratic between 95% and 97% of the time." This fact, according to the Court, made it possible that the state was drawing electoral lines on the basis of voter reliability to vote for a particular party, rather than on race.

The Court reasoned as follows: if the goal of North Carolina's districting plan was to create a safe Democratic seat, reliable voting behavior would have been more important than voter registration. Accordingly, as African Americans in the Democratic Party vote Democratic more reliably, it would have made sense for North Carolina to keep white Democrats out of the district and black Democrats in. In this fashion, "a legislature may, by placing reliable Democratic precincts within a district without regard to race, end up with a district containing more heavily African-American precincts, but the reasons would be political rather than racial." Because a partisan/political rationale for the plan was consistent with the evidence, the Court concluded that the plaintiffs had not shown "that a facially neutral law" was "'unexplainable on grounds other than race.'" And so, if a state legislature was trying to satisfy its obligations under Section 5 not to engage in the dilution of the voting power of racial minorities, it could do so without violating the Equal Protection Clause by using race as a proxy for partisan voter reliability. Regardless of the degree of reliance, the Court was implying that using race as a proxy in this fashion precluded it from becoming the "predominant" factor of the legislature's districting plan.

After the 2000 census, the Supreme Court considered the constitutionality of Georgia's new apportionment plan for the state senate in *Ashcroft v. Georgia* (2003), a case that once again highlighted the continuing tension between Section 5 and the Equal Protection Clause in the twenty-first century. The Democratic majority in the General Assembly decided "to maintain the number of majorityminority districts, but to increase the number of so-called 'influence' districts, where black voters would be able to exert a significant—if not decisive—force in the election process." To make this happen, the plan "'unpacked' the most heavily concentrated majority-minority districts . . . and created a number of new influence districts." The result was that thirteen districts had "a majority-black voting age population," thirteen other districts had "a black voting age population of between 30% and 50%," and four had "a black voting age population of between 25% and 30%." However, the black voting-age population in three majority-minority districts dropped from 60.58 percent to 50.31 percent, from 55.43 percent to 50.66 percent, and from 62.45 percent to 50.80 percent. The DC District Court refused to "pre-clear" this plan because it diluted the African American vote in these three districts and Georgia had not established that this "retrogression" would be compensated by gains in other districts. After all, there was no guarantee that the districts with less than a 51 percent black majority would be able to elect candidates sympathetic to black interests.

The Supreme Court began its analysis of the case with the assumption that a state may pursue different strategies to comply with Section 5's requirement of maintaining a racial minority's "effective exercise of the electoral franchise." A state "may choose to create a certain number of 'safe' districts, in which it is highly likely that minority voters will be able to elect the candidate of their choice," or it "may choose to create a greater number of [influence] districts in which it is [only] likely . . . that minority voters will be able to elect candidates of their choice." If a state opts for the latter option, it will not violate Section 5 simply because it prefers "to risk having fewer minority representatives in order to achieve greater overall representation of a minority group by increasing the number of representatives sympathetic to the interests of minority voters." The Court concluded, "Section 5 gives States the flexibility to implement the type of plan that Georgia has submitted for preclearance—a plan that increases the number of districts with a majority-black voting age population, even if it means that in some of those districts, minority voters will face a somewhat reduced opportunity to elect a candidate of their choice."

Ashcroft reveals that in the twenty-first century the Supreme Court has had to confront complex trade-offs between the requirements of Section 5 of the VRA and the Equal Protection Clause of the Fourteenth Amendment. However, a great deal of this tension dissipated when the Court took the huge step of invalidating the coverage formula of Section 4 of the VRA in *Shelby County v. Holder* (2013). The coverage formula identified the electoral districts—whether states, counties, cities, or precincts—that the Attorney General could subject to the "special provisions" of Section 5. Without the coverage formula, Section 5 became inoperative unless a federal judge found that an electoral district had engaged in racial discrimination (see Q23). Accordingly, *Shelby County* has significantly narrowed the scope of Section 5 and has, for this reason, substantially eroded its importance. It will languish in this state until Congress enacts a new coverage formula based on current voting patterns and practices, an unlikely event in today's intensely partisan and polarized political climate.

FURTHER READING

Bositis, David A., ed. *Redistricting and Minority Representation: Learning from the Past, Preparing for the Future*. Lanham, MD: University Press of America, 1998.

Burke, Christopher M. *The Appearance of Equality: Racial Gerrymandering, Redistricting, and the Supreme Court*. Santa Barbara, CA: Praeger, 1999.

Grofman, Bernard, Handley, Lisa, and Lublin, David. "Drawing Effective Minority Districts: A Conceptual Framework and Some Empirical Evidence." *North Carolina Law Review* 79 (2001): 1383–1430.

Lublin, David. *The Paradox of Representation: Racial Gerrymandering and Minority Interests in Congress.* Princeton, NJ: Princeton University Press, 1999.

Pitts, Michael J. "What Has Twenty-Five Years of Racial Gerrymandering Doctrine Achieved?" *UC Irvine Law Review* 9 (2018): 229–273.

Rush, Mark E., and Engstrom, Richard L. *Fair and Effective Representation?: Debating Electoral Reform and Minority Rights.* Lanham, MD: Rowman & Littlefield, 2001.

Yarbrough, Tinsley E. *Race and Redistricting: The Shaw-Cromartie Cases.* Lawrence, KS: University Press of Kansas, 2002.

Q22. DID CONGRESS EVER BROADEN THE VOTING RIGHTS ACT TO PROHIBIT DISCRIMINATION AGAINST NONRACIAL MINORITIES, AND TO REQUIRE STATES AND POLITICAL SUBDIVISIONS TO PROVIDE ASSISTANCE TO THESE MINORITIES IN EXERCISING THEIR VOTING RIGHTS?

Answer: Yes. In 1975, Congress broadened the coverage formula of Section 4 to apply Section 5's "special" provisions to "language minorities" and enacted a new provision that required states and political subdivisions to conduct bilingual elections if a percentage of a "language minority" was not proficient in the English language.

The Facts: The central focus of the VRA was to prohibit states from denying the right to vote on the basis of race or color. However, Section 4(e) of the VRA also made it illegal for a state to deny any person the right to vote if he or she completed a sixth-grade education in a school in the United States, regardless if class instruction was in a language other than English. This provision was of particular benefit to Puerto Ricans in New York City who could not pass the state's literacy test and had attended school in the U.S. commonwealth of Puerto Rico. However, in 1970, Congress broadened the ban on literacy tests from those states subject to the "special provisions" of the VRA to all states across the nation. This extension of the ban removed a major barrier to the right to vote confronting members of language minorities who were somewhat literate in English. However, banning literacy tests did not do much to enfranchise those citizens who could neither read nor write English, at least not those who resided in jurisdictions that conducted "English-only" elections.

It was not until 1975 that the House Subcommittee on Civil and Political Rights held a hearing on the problems "language minorities" had exercising their voting rights in the United States. A number of Puerto Rican and Mexican American voters complained that voter registration forms were very difficult for them to fill out in English. They also stated that it was challenging to understand the meaning of proposed constitutional amendments or referenda if they were written only in English. In response to these criticisms, Congress expanded the scope of the "special provisions" of the VRA to include the following "language minorities": Native Americans, Asian Americans, Alaskan Natives, and those of "Spanish heritage." Congress explained why this amendment to the VRA was necessary in Title II of the amendment:

> The Congress finds that voting discrimination against citizens of language minorities is pervasive and national in scope. Such minority citizens are from environments in which the dominant language is other than English. In addition they have been denied equal educational opportunities by State and local governments, resulting in severe disabilities and continuing illiteracy in the English language. The Congress further finds that, where State and local officials conduct elections only in English, language minority citizens are excluded from participating in the electoral process. In many areas of the country, this exclusion is aggravated by acts of physical, economic, and political intimidation. The Congress declares that, in order to enforce the guarantees of the fourteenth and fifteenth amendments to the United States Constitution, it is necessary to eliminate such discrimination by prohibiting English-only elections, and by prescribing other remedial devices.

Relying on this rationale, the 1975 amendment broadened the "special provisions" of the VRA to apply to a "language minority" if the following three conditions were satisfied: (1) if election materials were not available in the language of the minority; (2) if the "language minority" was more than 5 percent of the voting-age population of the jurisdiction; and (3) if less than 50 percent of the voting-age citizens had registered for or voted in the 1972 presidential election.

If a "language minority" satisfied these three criteria, the minority gained the protection of the "special provisions" of the VRA on an equal basis with members of racial minorities. Accordingly, these jurisdictions could not use any "test or device" for voter registration that discriminated against the language minority; the Attorney General could send federal election examiners to conduct voter registrations and observers to monitor elections; any changes to election law had to be "precleared" by the Attorney General or the DC District Court. These preclearances would not be granted if the "purpose" or "effect" of the change was to deny or abridge the right to vote of language minorities. The new states that became subject to Section 5's "special provisions" included Alaska, Arizona, Texas, and parts (typically counties) of California, Colorado, Florida, Hawaii, Michigan, New York, North Carolina, and South Carolina.

The 1975 amendment to the VRA also imposed a duty on all jurisdictions to require bilingual elections for ten years if (1) more than 5 percent of the voting-age population was composed of one of the four "language minorities" identified above; and (2) the English illiteracy rate of the minority, defined as failure to finish the fifth grade, was greater than the national rate. For this requirement, there was no need to determine that less than 50 percent of the voting-age citizens had registered for or voted in the 1972 presidential election. Accordingly, states that qualified had to provide election materials and oral assistance to the minority in its own language, but they were not subject to Section 5's more onerous "special provisions."

One interesting question regarding the bilingual provision was how to apply it to language minorities if their language was oral or unwritten, such as Alaskan Natives and Native American Indians. The 1975 law resolved this issue by requiring states to provide such language minorities with "oral instructions, assistance, or other information relating to registration and voting." Another issue concerned language minorities that included "subgroups," such as "Asian Americans," or those that used a distinctive dialect of the language of the minority, such as Chinese subgroups. Regarding this question, the DOJ split the difference, requiring states to satisfy the bilingual language requirement for subgroups of Asian Americans, but permitting them to provide written voting materials to Chinese citizens in the dialect that was generally used (Tucker, 2006). Despite this small concession, it is clear that the 1975 amendments to the VRA broadened the scope of the VRA considerably and thereby significantly expanded federal supervision of state and federal elections.

In the 1982 VRA Amendments Act, Congress adopted an "effects test" for Section 2 of the VRA (see Q20) and extended the bilingual language requirement for seven additional years (from 1985 until 1992). However, it amended the latter so that the Census Bureau would not count members of a language minority who could speak English well enough to participate in the electoral process to determine whether the minority constituted 5 percent of the voting-age population. This change reduced the number of counties across the nation subject to the bilingual requirement, as well as introduced an incongruity into the VRA. While members of a language minority who spoke English well were counted to determine if a jurisdiction was subject to the onerous "special provisions" of the VRA, they were not counted to determine if a state was subject to the less-onerous bilingual election requirement (Laney, 2008).

In 1982, Congress also added a provision to the VRA that applied across the nation, not just to jurisdictions with a sizable language minority. The provision stated that "[a]ny voter who requires assistance to vote by reason of blindness, disability, *or inability to read or write* may be given assistance by a person of the voter's choice, other than the voter's employer or agent of that employer or officer or agent of the voter's union" (emphasis added). The provision's purpose was to prevent discrimination against voters who needed assistance and whose vote was, for that reason, more likely to be unduly influenced or manipulated. Accordingly, all states had to respect the right of citizens with "limited English proficiency" to bring with them an interpreter to give them assistance throughout the voting process, from registering to vote to casting a ballot. Although this provision generally focused on disabled voters, its impact on "limited-English-proficiency" (LEP) voters was substantial. The U.S. Census Bureau defines LEP persons as anyone who reports on the census that they speak English "not at all," "not well," or "well," rather than "very well," and it currently estimates that approximately 8.3 percent of the population five years old and over are LEP. This means that the number of LEP voters is substantial, but of course not all LEP persons invoke their right to an interpreter when they register to vote or cast their ballot (Census Bureau, 2020).

In the Voting Rights Language Assistance Act of 1992, Congress extended the bilingual requirement until 2007. It did so over the general objection that the requirement discouraged immigrant citizens from learning English and therefore exacerbated linguistic and cultural divisions in American society. The main rationale for this extension was that the percentage of Hispanic, Asian American, and Native American citizens who registered and voted lagged significantly behind the registration and voting percentage of white citizens. Another common problem was that language minorities tended to live in very large metropolitan areas, making it impossible for them to reach the 5 percent trigger despite large absolute numbers. This was especially a problem with Asian Americans because each "subgroup," such as the Vietnamese, had to meet the trigger independently. Native Americans had difficulty reaching the trigger because reservations often crossed county or state lines, thereby splitting their numbers into two or more electoral subdivisions. In its 1992 amendment of the VRA, Congress responded to these complaints in two ways. First, it added a numerical trigger to the bilingual requirement: if more than ten thousand citizens of a language minority were illiterate in English and the illiteracy rate of the group is higher than the national rate, then a jurisdiction must provide bilingual assistance. Second, regarding Native American or Alaskan Native citizens, a jurisdiction must provide assistance if it contained all or *any part* of a reservation with a language minority if the English-illiterate members were more than 5 percent of the jurisdiction's voting-age population.

Following the highly controversial 2000 election, the U.S. Commission on Civil Rights found that there was extensive disfranchisement of members of Florida's African American, Hispanic, and Haitian communities (see USCCR, 2001). The Commission's report encouraged debate in Congress and a number of bills were introduced, but none of them were enacted until the Voting Rights Act of 2006. This law extended the bilingual requirement, as amended, for an additional twenty-five years to 2031. It also switched the evidentiary basis for deciding if the trigger for the requirement was met from "census data" to a new national survey called the American Community Survey. This new survey is ongoing and collects more recent data than the census on demographic changes across the United States, including data on English proficiency. These provisions of the Voting Rights Act of 2006 reflect Congress's continuing commitment to the voting rights of language minorities. As of 2016, parts of twenty-nine states are subject to the bilingual requirement of the VRA. The DOJ will continue to file cases to vindicate these rights until at least 2031. A recent case, described on the Department's webpage titled "Cases Raising Claims Under the Language Minority Provisions of the Voting Rights Act," involved New York's Orange County's alleged failure to provide election-related information and language assistance in Spanish to thousands of LED Puerto Rican voters.

FURTHER READING

Boyd, Thomas M., and Markman, Stephen J. "The 1982 Amendments to the Voting Rights Act: A Legislative History." *Washington and Lee Law Review* 40 (1983): 1347–1428.

Cartagena, Juan. "Latinos and Section 5 of the Voting Rights Act: Beyond Black and White." *National Black Law Journal* 18 (2005): 201–233.

Census Bureau. "People That Speak English Less Than 'Very Well' in the United States," April 8, 2020, available at https://www.census.gov

/library/visualizations/interactive/people-that-speak-english-less-than-very-well.html.

Hunter, David H. "The 1975 Voting Rights Act and Language Minorities." *Catholic University Law Review* 25 (1976): 250–270.

Laney, Garrine P. "The Voting Rights Act of 1965, As Amended: Its History and Current Issues." *CRS Report for Congress:* 95-896, June 12, 2008, available at https://www.everycrsreport.com/files/20080612 _95-896_301af1b9828fb8e5201323a94ee64e4b93eff65a.pdf.

Marmolejos, Poli A. "Requirements of the Voting Rights Language Assistance Act of 1992." *Berkeley La Raza Law Journal* 6 (1993): 148–155.

Saunders, Morgan E. "Digital-Age Discrimination: The Voting Rights Act, Language-Minorities, and Online Voter Registration." *Columbia Journal of Law and Social Problems* 50 (2017): 449–505.

Tucker, James Thomas. "Enfranchising Language Minority Citizens: The Bilingual Election Provisions of the Voting Rights Act." *New York University Journal of Legislation and Public Policy* 10 (2006): 195–260.

United States Commission on Civil Rights (USCCR). "Voting Irregularities in Florida during the 2000 Presidential Election." Approved June 8, 2001, available at https://www.usccr.gov/pubs/vote2000/report /appendix/exsum.htm.

Q23. HAS THE CONSTITUTIONALITY OF ALL THE PROVISIONS OF THE VOTING RIGHTS ACT REGARDING ITS SCOPE AND COVERAGE BEEN CONSISTENTLY UPHELD BY THE SUPREME COURT?

Answer: No. Although the Supreme Court repeatedly upheld the constitutionality of the VRA for almost fifty years, it invalidated the coverage formula of Section 4 in *Shelby County v. Holder* (2013), a groundbreaking decision that rendered the "special provisions" of Section 5 inoperative, thereby sharply reducing the federal government's ability to monitor state electoral practices.

The Facts: The VRA was composed of nationwide permanent provisions, such as Section 2's ban on denying or abridging the right to vote on account of race or color, and "special temporary provisions," which were applicable only to a limited number of "covered jurisdictions," such as Section 5's requirement that they obtain the approval of the Attorney General or a three-judge DC District Court before enforcing any change in electoral law. The Attorney General decided if a state or political subdivision was a covered jurisdiction based on the following criteria established by Section 4: (1) if the jurisdiction used a racially discriminatory "test or device" as a prerequisite for voting; and (2) if less than 50 percent of the voting-age population in the jurisdiction were registered to vote or voted in the 1964 presidential election. In 1965, the jurisdictions that qualified under this "coverage formula" were Alabama, Georgia, Louisiana, Mississippi, South Carolina, Virginia, and parts of North Carolina and one county in Arizona. Initially authorized for five years, Congress extended the "special provisions" of the VRA, in 1970 (for five years), 1975 (for seven years), 1982 (for twenty-five years), and 2006 (for twenty-five years).

In 1970 and 1975, Congress shifted the second criterion of Section 4's coverage formula from registration and voter turnout in the 1964 election to the 1968 and 1972 elections, respectively. Congress also identified English-only elections as a "test or device" and applied Section 5's "special provisions" to jurisdictions of this type if 5 percent of the voting-age population spoke a language other than English (see Q22). With these changes, Alaska, Arizona, Texas, and counties in California, Florida, Michigan, New York, North Carolina, and South Dakota became "covered jurisdictions." In 1982, Congress tightened the VRA's "bailout" provision, making it more difficult for covered jurisdictions to escape the reach of the "special provisions." The original VRA only required the jurisdiction to prove that it had not used a "test or device" in a racially discriminatory manner for a five-year period, while the 1982 amendment installed a ten-year period and required the jurisdiction to prove additional facts, such as, that it had never failed to get preclearance for changes in its election laws, that it never lost a voting discrimination lawsuit, and that it had made good-faith efforts to eliminate "intimidation" and "harassment" of voters. In this fashion, Congress broadened Section 4's coverage formula, making it easier for the Attorney General to identify states and their political subdivisions as covered jurisdictions, while it narrowed the "bailout" provision, making it harder for covered jurisdictions to get out from under the "special provisions," including the burdensome preclearance requirement.

Although the Supreme Court upheld the coverage formula and the preclearance requirement in *South Carolina v. Katzenbach* (see Q18) and later cases, it expressed reservations about Sections 4 and 5 in *Northwest Austin Municipal Utility District No. One v. Holder* (2009), decided three years after Congress reauthorized the VRA in 2006. The case from Texas involved the elected board of a small utility district that wanted to bail out of the VRA's preclearance requirement. The utility district lost in the district court on the ground that it was ineligible to invoke the bailout provision because it did not register voters. The Supreme Court described the case as "a small utility district raising a big question—the constitutionality of Section 5 of the Voting Rights Act." Despite this dramatic description, the Court in the end decided the case on statutory grounds without reaching the constitutional question. In the Court's view, the VRA permitted any type of political subdivision to exercise the bailout provision, including elected entities that did not register voters. By deciding the case on this basis, the Court remarked, it was simply following its "usual practice" of avoiding "the unnecessary resolution of constitutional questions."

Despite the Court's unwillingness in *Northwest Austin* to consider the constitutionality of Section 5, the majority in this 8–1 decision expressed its concerns about both it and Section 4. In the Court's view, Section 5 has "substantial 'federalism costs'" because it "goes beyond the prohibition of the Fifteenth Amendment by suspending *all* changes to state election law—however innocuous—until they have been precleared by federal authorities in Washington, D.C." In the Court's view, this requirement offends the principle that "States enjoy 'equal sovereignty.'" Any departure from this principle requires a strong showing why it is needed, but the VRA's coverage formula "is based on data that is now more than 35 years old, and there is considerable evidence that it fails to account for current political conditions." Whether current conditions can continue to justify Section 5, the Court conceded, was "a difficult constitutional question," but one that the Court need "not answer today" because "the Voting Rights Act permits all political subdivisions, including the [utility] district in this case, to seek relief from its preclearance requirements." This interpretation of the VRA allowed the Court to avoid what it called the "big" constitutional question in *Northwest Austin*.

Following this decision, Congress did not amend the VRA to alleviate the constitutional concerns expressed by the Court about Section 5, but Shelby County, Georgia, sensed an opportunity and filed a lawsuit challenging the constitutionality of both Sections 4 and 5. The district court and the DC Circuit upheld the VRA in its entirety, but the Supreme Court reversed in *Shelby County v. Holder* (2013), a 5–4 decision. Rarely has the vote of one justice had such an enormous impact on the right to vote in the United States. Chief Justice Roberts's majority opinion largely focused on the coverage formula of Section 4, highlighting that Congress had not updated it since 1975, which meant that the data the Attorney General used to decide if a jurisdiction was covered by Section 5 was over forty years old. Conceding that the formula was "rational" when Congress enacted the VRA, "things have changed dramatically," Roberts argued.

Congress itself had noted these improvements when it reauthorized the VRA in 2006, "writing that '[s]ignificant progress has been made in eliminating first generation barriers experienced by minority voters, including increased numbers of registered minority voters, minority voter turnout, and minority representation in Congress, State legislatures, and local elected offices.'" Drawing on the statistics gathered by the House and the Senate in 2006, Roberts underlined the fact that in 2004 "African-American voter turnout exceeded white voter turnout in five of the six [southern] States originally covered by Section 5, with a gap in the sixth State of less than one half of one percent." Of course, these improvements, the Court admitted, "are in large part *because* of the Voting Rights Act," but "there is no denying that, due to the Voting Rights Act, our Nation has made great strides."

Turning to the issue of the constitutionality of Section 4's coverage formula, Roberts argued that it needed a strong justification for two reasons: first, under the Tenth Amendment, "States retain broad autonomy in structuring their governments" and the framers "'intended the States to keep for themselves . . . the power to regulate elections'" and "'determine the conditions under which the right of suffrage may be exercised.'" Second, there is a "'fundamental principle of *equal* sovereignty' among the States," such that each state is "'equal in power, dignity and authority.'" Equal state sovereignty, in the Court's view, "'is essential to the harmonious operation of the scheme upon which the Republic was organized.'" Despite the intrinsic importance of each of these principles, the VRA, Roberts points out, "sharply departs" from both of them. States that meet the coverage formula of Section 4 "must beseech the Federal Government for permission to implement laws that they would otherwise have the right to enact and execute on their own."

It is true, Roberts admitted, that in *Katzenbach* the Court found these departures from the basic features of our system of government justified because "[a]t the time, the coverage formula—the means of linking the exercise of the unprecedented authority with the problem that warranted it—made sense," but in 2013, almost fifty years later, it "no longer does so." It is based "on decades-old data relevant to decades-old problems, rather than current data reflecting current needs." For that reason, the coverage formula is not within Congress's power to enforce the Fifteenth Amendment because this power "is not designed to punish for the past; its purpose is to ensure a better future." Accordingly, the Court concluded, if Congress is "to divide the States" into two groups, it "must identify those jurisdictions to be singled out on a basis that makes sense in light of current conditions. It cannot rely simply on the past."

Justice Ginsburg's dissent rested on the premise that it was "well established that Congress's judgment regarding exercise of its power to enforce the Fourteenth and Fifteenth Amendments warrants substantial [judicial] deference" based on both "constitutional text and precedent." The "stated purpose" of these amendments "was to arm Congress with the power and authority to protect all persons within the Nation from violations of their rights by the States." Echoing the language of *Katzenbach* (see Q18), Ginsburg insisted that in exercising this power "Congress may use 'all means which are appropriate, which are plainly adapted' to the constitutional ends declared by these Amendments." The "surest way" to confirm that the reauthorization of Sections 4 and 5 met this standard was that Congress explicitly found that the preclearance procedure was "still effectively preventing discriminatory changes to voting law." In fact, when Congress reauthorized the VRA in 2006, it found that "there were *more* DOJ objections [to voting changes] between 1982 and 2004 (626) than there were between 1965 and the 1982 reauthorization (490)." In addition, there was evidence that litigation "was an inadequate substitute for preclearance in the covered jurisdictions" because it "occurs only after the fact" and is expensive, placing "a heavy financial burden on minority voters."

In light of this evidence, according to Ginsburg, Congress concluded that "conditions in the South have impressively improved" and that "the VRA was the driving force behind it" but also that "voting discrimination had evolved into subtler second-generation barriers, and that eliminating preclearance would risk loss of the gains that had been made." The principle of "equal sovereignty" cannot properly be used to prevent Congress from remedying these "subtler" forms of voting discrimination because that principle only applies to "the admission of new States," not to federal laws that treat states differently because constitutional violations are more likely in some than in others. It is true, Ginsburg conceded, that the VRA was "extraordinary," not "ordinary" legislation, "but the evidence supporting the 2006 reauthorization of the VRA was "also extraordinary." Congress's crucial finding was that "'40 years has not been a sufficient amount of time to eliminate the vestiges of discrimination following nearly 100 years of disregard for the dictates of the 15th Amendment.'" As Congress was explicitly empowered to enforce the Fifteenth Amendment, the Court should, in Ginsburg's view, defer to its assessment that Section 4's coverage formula was a "rational" and "appropriate" method to root out the remaining "vestiges" of voting discrimination.

The Court did not explicitly strike down Section 5's preclearance requirement in *Shelby County*, but it made this provision inoperative because the Attorney General could no longer use the formula of Section 4 to identify covered jurisdictions. However, the decision left untouched Section 2 of the VRA, which means that the DOJ can still initiate lawsuits in federal court to protect racial and language minorities from voting discrimination. If a district judge finds that discrimination has occurred, the preclearance requirement under the "bail in" provision of Section 3 of the VRA continues to be a viable remedy. However, judicial imposition of the preclearance requirement in individual voting discrimination lawsuits is not an equivalent remedy to the discretionary authority that the Attorney General had previously exercised under Section 4.

The Court's decision in *Shelby County* was arguably a turning point in the history of voting rights and, for that reason, reaction to it was intense, in both negative and positive characterizations. A "deeply disappointed" President Barack Obama claimed the decision "upsets decades of well-established practices that help make sure voting is fair, especially in places where voting discrimination has been historically prevalent." In contrast, Senator Charles E. Grassley (R-IA), ranking Republican on the Judiciary Committee remarked, "What it tells me is after 45 years, the Voting Rights Act worked, and that's the best I can say. It just proves that it worked" (Calmes, 2013). Whether it eliminated all discrimination in voting or not, Texas officials announced within hours of the decision that they would reintroduce a voter identification law that the Attorney General had blocked under Section 5's preclearance provision the year before. Of course, states not within Section 4's coverage formula had already instituted such voter identification laws, which arguably raises the question why Texas cannot enact such a law.

One general reaction to the Court's decision in *Shelby County* was that it was very unlikely that Congress would adopt a new coverage formula, which of course heightens the seismic nature of the decision (Calmes, 2013). On one of its webpages titled "Jurisdictions Previously Covered by Section 5," the DOJ lists nine states (Alabama, Alaska, Arizona, Georgia, Louisiana, Mississippi, South Carolina, Texas, and Virginia), fifty-six counties of six other states that were partially covered by Section 5, and two townships in Michigan. All of these jurisdictions now have more latitude to experiment with their voting laws in ways that will undoubtedly affect the right to vote for years to come. For example, Alabama (2014), South Carolina (2014), and Mississippi (2014) followed Texas's lead and implemented strict voter ID laws that the DOJ had previously disallowed (see Q30); Arizona consolidated their polling places and placed limits on mail-in ballots (2016); and Georgia required exact matches to voter registration lists (2017) (Weiser, 2018).

Of course, during this same period, states that were not previously covered by Section 5 have also enacted such laws. The key issue in any evaluation *of Shelby County* is the trade-off between the value of federalism (equal state sovereignty) versus the value of easy access to the ballot for eligible voters. In this context, the Democratic House of Representatives passed the Voting Rights Advancement Act on December 6, 2019, by a vote of 228–187, with one Republican voting in favor. The bill included a new coverage formula for Section 5: federal preclearance would be required if fifteen or more voting rights violations occurred in a state during the last twenty-five years or ten or more such violations if the state itself, rather than a political subdivision, was responsible for one of the violations. President Donald Trump immediately threatened to veto any such legislation, but his threat will more than likely prove unnecessary as there is little to no chance that the bill will ever make it to the floor of the Republican-controlled Senate (Stolberg, 2019). *Shelby County's* impact on racial and language-based minorities to effectively exercise their right to vote will likely be felt for years if not generations.

FURTHER READING

Blacksher, James, and Guinier, Lani. "Free at Last: Rejecting Equal Sovereignty and Restoring the Constitutional Right to Vote: *Shelby County v. Holder*." *Harvard Law & Policy Review* 8 (2014): 39–69.

Blum, Edward, and Campbell, Lauren. *Assessment of Voting Rights Progress in Jurisdictions Covered Under Section Five of the Voting Rights Act.* Washington, DC: American Enterprise Institute, 2006, available at https://bdgrdemocracy.files.wordpress.com/2012/02/20060515_blumcampbellreport-vra-gaddie.pdf.

Bullock, Charles S., III, Gaddie, Ronald Keith, and Wert, Justin J. *The Rise and Fall of the Voting Rights Act*. Norman, OK: University of Oklahoma Press, 2016.

Calmes, Jackie, Brown, Robbie, and Robertson, Campbell. "On Voting Case, Reaction from 'Deeply Disappointed' to 'It's about Time.'" *The New York Times*, June 25, 2013, available at https://www.nytimes.com/2013/06/26/us/politics/on-voting-case-reaction-from-deeply-disappointed-to-its-about-time.html.

Consovoy, William S., and McCarthy, Thomas R. "*Shelby County v. Holder*: The Restoration of Constitutional Order." *Cato Supreme Court Review* 2012–2013 (2012–2013): 31–62.

Stolberg, Sheryl Gay, and Cochrane, Emily. "House Passes Voting Rights Bill Despite Near Unanimous Republican Opposition." *The New*

York Times, December 6, 2019, available at https://www.nytimes.com/2019/12/06/us/politics/house-voting-rights.html.

Weiser, Wendy, and Feldman, Max. *The State of Voting 2018*. New York: Brennan Center for Justice, 2018, available at https://www.brennancenter.org/sites/default/files/2019-08/Report_State_of_Voting_2018.pdf.

4

Partisan Gerrymandering

As discussed in previous chapters, electoral districting can significantly impact the value of an American citizen's right to vote. Chapter 2 explained that electoral districts unequal in population can erode the voting power of those in heavily populated districts, while chapter 3 considered how electoral district lines could be drawn to diminish or increase the voting power of racial, ethnic, or language minorities. This chapter addresses the degree to which a state can undermine the value of the right to vote if it draws electoral district lines on the basis of partisanship, a practice known as "gerrymandering."

The namesake of this partisan practice is one of its first practitioners, Elridge Gerry, the Massachusetts governor who signed a bill in 1812 that created a long, thin, oddly shaped state senate district that, in the eyes of its critics, resembled a "salamander." The obvious strategy behind this districting law was to split Federalist Party strongholds into separate districts and thereby ensure victory for Gerry's Democratic-Republican Party. Although the 1812 law was not the first time that partisan considerations shaped how American electoral districts were drawn, the Federalist Party's heated attack on the bill, including the following satirical cartoon that appeared in the *Boston Gazette* on March 26, 1812 (see figure 4.1), increased its notoriety.

The original caption under the cartoon called the district a "horrid Monster" that had appeared during the last session of the state legislature. In the aftermath of the 1812 election, the term "gerry-mander" quickly

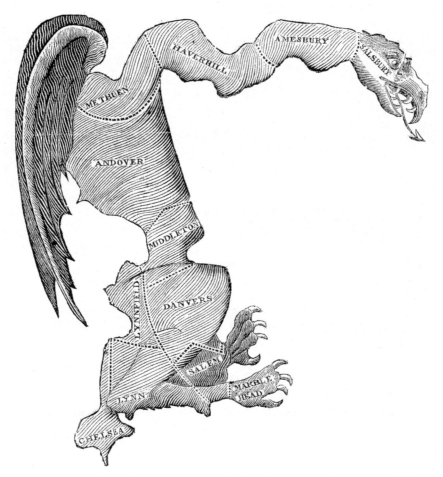

Figure 4.1 A broadside printing of the Gerry-mander map of Essex County in Salem, Massachusets in 1812. (Library of Congress)

became the catch-term to both designate and denigrate this technique of maximizing a political party's electoral influence. Accordingly, the origin of the term reflects the long and somewhat unsavory role that partisan gerrymandering has played in the political history of the United States.

It is important to appreciate the degree to which partisan gerrymandering is a direct attack by one party on the other party's ideology and influence. Other forms of electoral districting, such as malapportionment or racial/ethnic districting, may inflate or deflate the electoral influence of citizens based on the place of their residence or their minority status.

Often the effect of such districting is to indirectly augment or burden a political party because most people who live in certain areas, such as the inner cities, the suburbs, or who are of a certain racial or ethnic minority, belong to the affected party. But such an indirect effect often has an uncertain impact on a party's chances to win an election.

The difference with partisan gerrymandering is that it strikes directly at the political ideology of the opposite party by one of two basic methods: "packing" or "cracking." Packing consists of concentrating likely supporters of the opposite party into a few electoral districts, thereby ensuring many wasted votes in the supermajorities of the opposite party. Cracking, in contrast, consists of spreading likely supporters of the opposite party into many electoral districts. This dilution of their voting power ensures that the party to which they belong is a minority in each district, thus greatly reducing their prospects for winning district-wide elections. These techniques obviously violate the spirit of democratic principles, but they are both effective means by which a political party can insulate and entrench its electoral dominance by undermining the value of the right to vote by members of the opposing party.

Q24. HAS PARTISAN GERRYMANDERING EVOLVED SIGNIFICANTLY THROUGHOUT AMERICAN POLITICAL ELECTORAL HISTORY?

Answer: Yes, although the underlying principles of partisan gerrymandering have remained the same, the sophisticated computer techniques that have recently come into use have arguably made partisan gerrymandering qualitatively more effective and therefore far more controversial.

The Facts: Partisan gerrymandering may have arisen in the Philadelphia area as early as 1705, but it certainly was widely practiced by the end of the eighteenth century. The new Constitution itself broadened the field for partisan gerrymandering because states had the option of creating districts for congressional elections. By 1840, "the gerrymander was a recognized force in party politics and was generally attempted in all legislation enacted for the formation of election districts" (Griffith, 1907). In 1842 Congress expanded the field for gerrymandering by requiring states to use single-member districts in congressional elections. Congress attempted to temper the effects of gerrymandering by insisting that districts be compact and contiguous, but many state legislatures either did not respect these principles or figured out ways to draw compact and contiguous districts that were nonetheless gerrymandered. Redistricting occurred not after each decennial census but whenever a party's electoral victory gave it a chance to gain advantage. Around the turn of the twentieth century, Congress declined to renew the requirements of compactness and contiguity, granting state legislatures greater freedom to engage in more extreme forms of partisan gerrymandering.

Ironically, such extreme forms of gerrymandering led to less party competition and one-party dominance in many state legislatures, which, in turn, led to less redistricting and less active gerrymandering. As one commentator has noted, "Where one party dominated a state legislature the incentives to gerrymander dissipated" (Engstrom, 2013). During the first half of the twentieth century, state legislatures were also lawfully able to malapportion electoral districts, that is, create districts with unequal populations, which considerably magnified the effects of partisan gerrymanders. The dominant party in a state could not only draw electoral district lines with partisanship in mind but also carve a sparsely populated area of the state inhabited primarily by its members into several districts, while packing a disproportionate large number of the opposite party's members into one district (often centered around a specific population center). In other words, malapportionment combined with party gerrymandering tended to create a relatively "locked" electoral system, such as the solid Democratic South. One example is Louisiana. Democrats in Louisiana won every seat in the state legislature from 1900 through 1964. The Democrat-controlled state legislature thus had little incentive to change the shape of any of the state's disticts. In fact, Louisiana's congressional electoral lines remained unchanged from 1912 to 1966.

During the 1950s, the Republican Party was able to achieve comparable advantages in the North and Midwest. "Throughout the North, Republicans held a substantial edge in the number of districts that were drawn by Republican redistricting regimes after 1940" (Engstrom, 2013). Of course, the more durable and rigid a gerrymander, the more insidious it became in terms of democratic principles and values. The electoral system was "stacked" or, if you will, "rigged" against a party that was powerless to change it.

Two fundamental developments during the 1960s dismantled the malapportioned and gerrymandered system described above: first, the Supreme Court ruled that malapportioned electoral districts violated the Constitution and that state legislatures must reapportion after each decennial census (see Q12); second, the Democratic Party's support of federal civil rights legislation led Republican Richard Nixon to adopt a "southern strategy" that persuaded many white southerners to switch their allegiance to the Republican Party in the 1968 elections. These developments made elections more competitive in the 1970s, which paradoxically elevated the significance of gerrymandering: if a single party controlled a state legislature, it was the one tool that it could yet lawfully use to maintain partisan advantage. At the same time, the new constitutional requirement that electoral districts have equal populations made it more challenging for the architects of redistricting to create effective partisan gerrymanders. The data, technology, expertise, and resources to draw effective gerrymandered districts with equal populations were simply not available. As John Ryder, chair of the Republican Redistricting Committee explains, "When I started doing this in the mid-70s, we were using handheld calculators, paper maps, pencils, and really big erasers. It was pretty primitive" and, for that reason, the resulting gerrymanders were neither reliable nor effective (Newkirk, 2017).

Things changed during the 1990s with the development of powerful computers, suitable mapmaking software, and the digitization of vast amounts of social, economic, and political information. For example, the U.S. Census Bureau developed TIGER/Line files, a digital database of geographic features, such as roads, railroads, rivers, lakes, and legal boundaries. Also during the 1990s, the Caliper Corporation developed and marketed *Maptitude for Redistricting*, a software specifically designed for drawing electoral district maps. By this point, computing power had increased dramatically to the point that districting maps could be drawn on PCs, rather than mainframes. More accessible computing power lowered the costs of drawing new redistricting maps and broadened the amount of data that went into them, down to the voting precinct and urban-block level. The types of data also expanded from census information, party affiliations, and racial/ethnic demographics of local political subdivisions to voting results from previous elections and consumer data suggesting likely voting predispositions. All of these trends made partisan gerrymandering less expensive, but at the same time, more effective and reliable. Rather than hunches, intuitions, and pencils determining the shape of electoral district, now it was technology, mathematics, and mountains of relevant data.

After a surge of statehouse victories in the 2000 elections, the Republican Party took advantage of this new technology and expertise in the redistricting cycle that followed, establishing gerrymandered electoral systems in Florida, Michigan, Pennsylvania, and Texas. In the latter case, Democratic legislators at first tried to block the state's 2003 gerrymander by fleeing the state, depriving the state legislature of a quorum needed to pass the new districting plan, but eventually Democratic resolve eroded and the legislature adopted the new gerrymandered map (Toobin, 2003). The Republicans redoubled their efforts to control statehouses for redistricting purposes after Democratic candidate Barack Obama won the 2008 presidential election. In a meeting on June 8, 2009, Thomas Hofeller, a Republican strategist deeply involved in partisan gerrymandering around the country, gave a presentation to the Republican Legislative Campaign Committee entitled "Redistricting 2010: Preparing for Success." Hofeller underlined the significance of the 2010 state elections, explaining that they should "target control of state legislative chambers that either party held by five or fewer seats." If the Republicans won those state elections in 2010, they could gerrymander them to such a degree that they would be in the "red" column for the long term and give the Republican Party better odds of retaining control of the House of Representatives for years to come (Daley, 2018).

In 2010, the Republican State Leadership Committee (RSLC) established the Redistricting Majority Project (REDMAP) to implement Hofeller's strategy. The project recruited and trained Republican candidates in targeted swing states, financed advertising that helped these candidates win elections, and provided Republican state legislatures with experienced redistricting lawyers to defend against Democratic legal challenges to new gerrymandered electoral maps. The Republicans calculated that they could control twenty-five congressional seats if they won 107 races in sixteen swing states. In part because Republican donors contributed $30 million to finance the project, the strategy worked well. Before the 2010 election, the Democratic Party controlled both houses of the state legislature and the governorship (often referred to as a "trifecta") in sixteen states, while the Republican Party did the same in eight states, but afterward the Republicans were in control of twenty states, while Democratic control dropped to eleven. In addition, as the House of Representatives's webpage titled "Majority Changes in the House of Representatives, 1856 to the Present" reports, the Democrats lost sixty-four seats to the Republicans in the 2010 election. As one critic of REDMAP claimed, the plan "proved more effective than any Republican dared dream. Republicans held the U.S. House in 2012, despite earning 1.4 *million fewer votes* than Democratic congressional candidates, and won large GOP majorities in the Ohio, Wisconsin, Michigan and North Carolina state legislatures even when more voters backed Democrats" (Daley, 2018).

These results, of course, were possible only because Republicans engaged in extreme partisan gerrymandering. That is not to say, however, that Democrats did not do the same thing in the states they controlled. Maryland was a case in point. Prior to the 2010 election, its congressional delegation was 6–2 in favor of Democrats. Not satisfied with this clear majority, Maryland Democrats post-2010 drew up a districting plan that was known as "the 7-1 map," a plan that knocked out of office a ten-year Republican incumbent. The 7-1 map was challenged in court and eventually wound up at the Supreme Court (see Q25), but the key point is that Democrats had no more scruples about engaging in extreme forms of partisan gerrymandering than the Republicans; they simply had less opportunity to implement this strategy after the string of Republican victories in the 2010 state elections. The degree of Republican success is reflected in a 2017 AP study that concluded there were "four times as many states with Republican-skewed state House or Assembly districts than Democratic ones" (Lieb, 2017).

Computers, data, and expertise, along with increasing political polarization, are largely responsible for today's extreme partisan gerrymanders. "Today, partisan lawmakers can use algorithms to design thousands of hypothetical district maps nearly instantaneously. With relatively few resources, they can then carefully predict how each layout might tip the scales in their favor, even adjusting house by house as needed" (Matsakis, 2019). However, the same factors that have made partisan gerrymanders more reliable and effective have also arguably made them easier to detect and to remedy. Journalists, researchers, and civil rights groups can quickly evaluate the partisan consequences of one electoral map over another and publish their findings for all to see. This is one reason why there is overwhelming popular support to put an end to extreme gerrymanders and return to the time when voters chose their representatives, rather than vice versa.

In this effort to expose gerrymandered districts, experts have produced a number of tests that assess, purportedly in a neutral manner, the degree to which any particular electoral map is a partisan gerrymander. For example, the "lopsided-averages test" compares the average vote a party receives in the elections prior to and after redistricting. If the difference between the averages is beyond what is typical, the new map is classified as a gerrymander. There is also an "efficiency gap test," which measures how many votes a party wasted compared to the other party. For example, if Party A wasted 21 percent of votes on average (losing by small margins in many districts, but winning by huge margins in a small number of districts), while Party B wasted only 6 percent of votes on average (winning by small margins in many districts and losing by as little as possible in the others), then the electoral map is a gerrymander. Lastly, the "partisan bias" test determines how many seats in the legislative house a party would win if both parties received exactly 50 percent of the statewide vote. If one party would win only 20 percent of the seats, then the map was biased against it. The argument, explained one elections scholar, is that "computer-based techniques can show beyond a statistical doubt that a district-boundary map favoring one party over another did not arise by geographic accident" (Wang, 2019).

Whether these tests are politically "neutral" in an absolute sense in all contexts may be doubted, but they do provide a means to measure the degree to which partisanship has shaped one electoral map compared to another. However, even if such tests have a considerable degree of validity, it is still not clear whether Congress has the authority to compel their use, whether federal courts or state courts have the authority to provide remedies based on them, or whether voters may amend their state constitutions to shift the power of redistricting from state legislatures to nonpartisan redistricting commissions. If none of these options are feasible, then state legislatures may be the only governmental entity that can fix the problem of extreme partisan gerrymandering. The irony is that many of the current members of state legislatures are the direct beneficiaries of partisan gerrymandering, making it very unlikely that they will ever do anything to fix the problem. Indeed, many of these members do not recognize extreme gerrymanders as a problem at all.

FURTHER READING

Daley, David. "How the Republicans Rigged Congress—New Documents Reveal an Untold Story." *Salon*, February 6, 2018, available at https://www.salon.com/2018/02/06/how-the-republicans-rigged-congress-and-poisoned-our-politics/.

Draper, Robert. "The League of Dangerous Mapmakers." *The Atlantic*, October 2012, available at https://www.theatlantic.com/magazine/archive/2012/10/the-league-of/309084/.

Engstrom, Erik J. *Partisan Gerrymandering and the Construction of American Democracy*. Ann Arbor, MI: University of Michigan Press, 2013.

Griffith, Elmer C. *The Rise and Development of the Gerrymander*. Chicago, IL: Scott, Foresman and Company, 1907.

Hunter, Thomas Rogers. "The First Gerrymander? Patrick Henry, James Madison, James Monroe, and Virginia's 1788 Congressional Districting." *Early American Studies* 9 (2011): 781–820.

Lieb, David A. "AP Analysis Shows How Gerrymandering Benefited GOP in 2016." *PBS Newshour*, June 25, 2017, available at https://www.pbs.org/newshour/politics/ap-analysis-shows-gerrymandering-benefited-gop-2016.

Matsakis, Louise. "Big Data Supercharged Gerrymandering. It Could Help Stop It Too." *Wired*, June 28, 2019, available at https://www.wired.com/story/big-data-supercharged-gerrymandering-supreme-court/.

Newkirk, Vann R., II. "How Redistricting Became a Technological Arms Race." *The Atlantic*, October 28, 2017, available at https://www.theatlantic.com/politics/archive/2017/10/gerrymandering-technology-redmap-2020/543888/.

Toobin, Jeffrey. "The Great Election Grab." *The New Yorker*, November 30, 2003, available at https://www.newyorker.com/magazine/2003/12/08/the-great-election-grab.

Wang, Sam. "Gerrymandering, or Geography." *The Atlantic*, March 26, 2019, available at https://www.theatlantic.com/ideas/archive/2019/03/how-courts-can-objectively-measure-gerrymandering/585574/.

Q25. HAS THE SUPREME COURT EVER INVALIDATED AN EXTREME PARTISAN GERRYMANDER ON CONSTITUTIONAL GROUNDS?

Answer: No. Although the Court at one point seriously contemplated holding extreme forms of partisan gerrymandering unconstitutional, it has never done so. In fact, it has firmly endorsed the position that partisan gerrymandering is a "political" and "nonjusticiable" question outside the jurisdiction of the federal judiciary.

The Facts: The Supreme Court first confronted the role of partisanship in electoral districting in *Gaffney v. Cummings* (1973), a case addressing whether Connecticut's 1971 reapportionment plan was constitutional under the "one person, one vote" standard established by *Reynolds v. Sims* (1964) (see Q12). The state's redistricting plan permitted deviations in the populations of state Senate and House districts by 1.81 percent and 7.83 percent, respectively. One goal of the plan was "political fairness," which meant that the boundary lines of districts were drawn so that both Houses would reflect each party's statewide voting strength. To achieve this goal of rough proportional representation, the basis of the plan was not party registration, but the actual voting results for the preceding three statewide elections. As the statewide count in these three elections favored the Republican Party, the plan placed Democratic candidates at a disadvantage in many of the state's electoral districts. Accordingly, the plaintiffs charged that the plan was an unconstitutional gerrymander because it did not respect the "one person, one vote" principle of *Reynolds*.

Responding to these claims, the Supreme Court concluded, first, that the deviations in population between the electoral districts "fail in size and quality to amount to "invidious discrimination" under the Fourteenth Amendment," partly because the *average* variations of Senate and House districts were only 0.45 percent and 1.90 percent, respectively. Second, the Court rejected the plaintiff's characterization of the plan "as nothing less than a gigantic political gerrymander" because electoral districting inevitably has and is intended to have substantial political consequences. Intentionally drawing an electoral map that has substantial political consequences, in the Court's view, was insufficient to constitute an unconstitutional gerrymander. On the other hand, the Court observed, electoral districting "is not wholly exempt from judicial scrutiny." If a political group has "been *fenced out* of the political process and their voting strength *invidiously* minimized [emphasis added]," the Court did not rule out the possibility of judicial relief. However, the Court concluded, the Republican effort in Connecticut to achieve "a rough sort of proportional representation" between the two major parties was hardly "invidious" in nature.

In *Davis v. Bandemer* (1986), the Court returned to the issue of partisan gerrymandering. In a sharply divided decision, three justices argued that such claims raised nonjusticiable political questions that the judiciary "should leave to the legislative branch as the Framers of the Constitution unquestionably intended," adding that apportionment is "a political question in the truest sense of the term" because it would "inject the courts into the most heated partisan issues." The other six justices insisted that partisan gerrymandering was a "justiciable" issue, but four of the six held that Indiana's reapportionment plan, even if it was intended to discriminate against the Democratic Party, did not have a "sufficiently adverse effect" to constitute a violation of the Equal Protection Clause. This was true even if Democratic candidates received 51.9 percent of the statewide vote for the House in the 1982 elections and won only 43 of 100 seats and 53.1 percent of the vote statewide for the Senate and won only thirteen of the twenty-five seats that were up for reelection. This result was not "sufficiently adverse" to Democratic candidates, according to the four-justices, because the Constitution does not require "that legislatures in reapportioning must draw district lines to come as near as possible to allocating seats to the contending parties in proportion to what their anticipated statewide vote will be." In addition, a reapportionment plan is not unconstitutional simply because it intentionally "makes winning elections more difficult" for one major political party in comparison to the other. Instead, the plan must "consistently degrade a voter's or a group of voter's influence on the political process as a whole" based on "evidence of continued frustration of the will of a majority of the voters or effective denial to a minority of voters of a fair chance to influence the political process." The plaintiffs in *Bandemer*, in the view of the plurality of the justices, had not shown this level of electoral degradation, frustration, or unfairness.

Eighteen years after *Bandemer* the Court once again addressed the question of whether partisan gerrymandering was a "political question" in *Vieth v. Jubelirer* (2004). In this case, the Democratic plaintiffs claimed that Pennsylvania's 2002 plan for congressional elections created electoral districts that were "meandering and irregular" in character and "ignor[ed] all traditional redistricting criteria, including the preservation of local government boundaries, solely for the sake of [Republican] partisan advantage." Writing for a four-justice plurality, Justice Antonin Scalia concluded that the case should be summarily dismissed because electoral districting was a "political question" outside the jurisdiction of federal courts because there were no "judicially manageable standards" to decide which gerrymanders were constitutionally acceptable and which were not. Unlike Congress, which can enact "inconsistent, illogical, and ad hoc" laws, the "law pronounced by the courts," Scalia insisted, "must be principled, rational, and based upon reasoned distinctions." In the eighteen years since *Bandemer*, it would be a "fantasy," according to Scalia, to believe that lower federal courts have discovered "judicially discernible and manageable standards" to distinguish constitutional partisan gerrymanders from unconstitutional ones. The proposed standards, such as "fair" or "competitive" districts, were in reality subjective political standards, not legal ones. The Court, therefore, had no choice but to "conclude that political gerrymandering claims are nonjusticiable and that *Bandemer* was wrongly decided."

Justice Kennedy agreed with the plurality that the case had to be summarily dismissed, but he refused to foreclose all possibility of judicial relief if a limited and precise rationale for invalidating an extreme partisan gerrymander could be found. Kennedy acknowledged the plurality was correct that in 2004 no "substantive definition of fairness in districting seems to command general assent" and no principle has evolved that would "confine judicial intervention." Accordingly, by invalidating a partisan gerrymander, judges would necessarily "risk assuming political, not legal, responsibility for a process that often produces ill will and distrust." He also granted that there were "weighty arguments" in favor of the position that no such definition will ever emerge. He added, though, that it was not "in our tradition to foreclose the judicial process from the attempt to define standards and remedies where it is alleged that a constitutional right is burdened or denied" and contended that the fact that "no such standard has emerged in this case should not be taken to prove that none will emerge in the future." Accordingly, Justice Kennedy found the case justiciable, but agreed with the plurality that the case must be dismissed because the allegations of the complaint, even if true, would not constitute a violation of the Equal Protection Clause.

Justices Stevens, Souter, Ginsburg, and Breyer dissented in *Jubelirer*, implying that there was still support on the Court for the position that partisan gerrymandering was a justiciable constitutional issue. However, there was no longer a decisive majority on the Court in favor of finding partisan gerrymandering either justiciable or not justiciable. This stalemate reappeared in later cases, including *League of United Latin American Citizens (LULAC) v. Perry* (2006) and *Gill v. Whitford* (2018).

Justice Kennedy's retirement in 2018 marked a turning point. His replacement—Brett Kavanaugh—joined four other justices in *Rucho v. Common Cause* (2019) to form a majority holding that partisan gerrymandering was a nonjusticiable political question outside the jurisdiction of the federal courts. The decision, which dealt with North Carolina's map for congressional elections, was clear and decisive. For the foreseeable future, voters of whatever political party living in electoral districts gerrymandered by the opposing political party will not be able to seek relief in federal courts.

In his majority opinion in *Rucho*, Chief Justice John Roberts identified what he thought were two insurmountable obstacles to recognizing partisan gerrymandering as a justiciable issue: (1) there was no legal standard of "fairness" and (2) there was no way for judges to measure how much of a departure from "fairness" was necessary to render a gerrymander unconstitutional. Regarding the first obstacle, Roberts wrote that any "judicial decision on what is 'fair' in this context would be an 'unmoored determination' of the sort characteristic of a political question beyond the competence of the federal courts." And regarding the second obstacle, Roberts remarked that, "it is only after determining how to define fairness that you can even begin to answer the determinative question: 'How much is too much?'"

In Robert's view, these two obstacles highlight the difference between partisan gerrymandering and both malapportionment and districting for the purpose of suppressing a racial minority. Electoral districts of equal size is a clear legal standard; absolute equality may not be obtainable, but the standard is clear; it is "a matter of math." And, unlike partisan gerrymandering, "a racial gerrymandering claim does not ask for a fair share of political power and influence" but rather for "the elimination of a racial classification." A claim of partisan gerrymandering, in contrast, "cannot ask for the elimination of partisanship" because the Constitution entrusts districting to political entities.

Roberts highlighted the fact that the majority was not condoning partisan gerrymandering. "Excessive partisanship in districting," he conceded, "leads to results that reasonably seem unjust" and that "such gerrymandering is 'incompatible with democratic principles.'" However, the unjustness and undemocratic character of excessive gerrymandering, in Roberts's view, "does not mean that the solution lies with the federal judiciary." Instead, voters and candidates frustrated and stymied by partisan gerrymandered electoral systems must seek relief in legislatures (whether Congress or the individual state legislatures) or state courts. Roberts comes to this conclusion because, in his mind, to do otherwise would lead to "an unprecedented expansion of [federal] judicial power.

> The expansion of judicial authority would not be into just any area of controversy, but into one of the most intensely partisan aspects of American political life. That intervention would be unlimited in scope and duration—it would recur over and over again around the country with each new round of districting, for state as well as federal representatives. Consideration of the impact of today's ruling on democratic principles cannot ignore the effect of the unelected and politically unaccountable branch of the Federal Government assuming such an extraordinary and unprecedented role.

Accordingly, democracy is better served if the issue of partisan gerrymandering is addressed outside the federal judiciary than by the least democratic branch of the federal government.

In her dissenting opinion in *Rucho*, Justice Elena Kagan rejected the majority's premise that there were not judicially manageable standards to determine when partisan gerrymanders were so extreme that they became unconstitutional. Federal judges do not need to adopt "contestable notions of political fairness" from which to measure constitutional injury. Instead, the judge should adopt for a baseline the state's own criteria of fairness, as they are articulated in the state's electoral policy (such as compactness, boundaries of local political subdivisions), minus any endorsement of partisan advantage. The judge should then compare all possible electoral maps that satisfy these criteria and compare it to the map adopted by the state legislature. This comparison will give the judge a clear understanding of the degree to which the plan departs from the state's own criteria of fairness for the purpose of gaining a partisan advantage. Only if the adopted plan was an extreme "outlier," only if it served partisan advantage considerably more than the state's articulated goals, only if the adopted plan was far from the median plan that would adequately satisfy all the state's criteria would the judge invalidate the plan as an extreme partisan gerrymander.

Such an approach would be, in Kagan's view, "neutral" and "restrained," thereby preventing any unacceptable judicial intrusion into American political life. Kagan's argument had the potential of having a real impact on partisan gerrymandering because the majority had conceded that state courts did not need to respect the high standards of justiciability required of the federal judiciary. Following *Rucho*, the stage was set for a state court to pursue the path illuminated by Justice Kagan's dissent. The real question was whether a state court would take up this challenge (see Q26).

FURTHER READING

Anand, Easha. "Finding a Path through the Political Thicket: In Defense of Partisan Gerrymandering's Justiciability." *California Law Review* 102 (2014): 917–965.

Chin, Andrew, Herschlag, Gregory, and Mattingly, Jonathan. "The Signature of Gerrymandering in *Rucho v. Common Cause*." *South Carolina Law Review* 70 (2019): 1241–1276.

Cunningham, McKay. "Gerrymandering and Conceit: The Supreme Court's Conflict with Itself." *Hastings Law Journal* 69 (2018): 1510–1544.

Eisler, Jacob. "Partisan Gerrymandering and the Illusion of Unfairness." *Catholic University Law Review* 67 (2018): 229–279.

Foley, Edward B. "Constitutional Preservation and the Judicial Review of Partisan Gerrymanders." *Georgia Law Review* 52 (2018): 1108–1154.

McGann, Anthony J., Smith, Charles Anthony, Latner, Michael, and Keena, Alex. *Gerrymandering in America: The House of Representatives, the Supreme Court, and the Future of Popular Sovereignty*. Cambridge: Cambridge University Press, 2016.

Ross, Bertrall. "Partisan Gerrymandering, the First Amendment, and the Political Outsider." *Columbia Law Review* 118 (2018): 2187–2218.

Seabrook, Nicholas R. *Drawing the Lines: Constraints on Partisan Gerrymandering in U.S. Politics*. Ithaca, NY: Cornell University Press, 2017.

Stephanopoulos, Nicholas O., and McGhee, Eric M. "Partisan Gerrymandering and the Efficiency Gap." *University of Chicago Law Review* 82 (2015) 831–900.

Q26. EVEN IF THE SUPREME COURT WILL NOT CONSIDER THE CONSTITUTIONALITY OF PARTISAN GERRYMANDERING, CAN STATE COURTS STRIKE DOWN GERRYMANDERS FOR VIOLATING STATE CONSTITUTIONS?

Answer: Yes, several state courts have invalidated extreme cases of partisan gerrymandering on the ground that they violate their own state constitutions, not the Constitution of the United States.

The Facts: In recent years, several state courts have taken significant steps to curtail partisan gerrymandering in their respective states. One important example is Florida. In the November election of 2010, Florida voters overwhelmingly passed two amendments to the state constitution: one mandated fair districting for congressional elections (Amendment #6); the other did the same for the two houses of the state legislature (Amendment #5). Known as the "fair districts" amendments, they prohibited any electoral districting in Florida done with the "intent to favor or disfavor a political party or an incumbent." With these amendments in effect, the Republican-controlled legislature redrew Florida's congressional district map following the 2010 decennial census. The map was used in the 2012 election, but the League of Women Voters of Florida filed a lawsuit, claiming that the map violated Amendment #6.

In *League of Women Voters of Florida v. Detzner* (2015), Florida's Supreme Court agreed with the League that Amendment #6 was meant to restore a "core principle of republican government," namely, "that the voters should choose their representatives, not the other way around." If a trial court in the future finds that partisan intent influenced electoral districting, Florida's high court insisted, then the burden of proof "shifted to the Legislature to justify its decisions in drawing the congressional district lines." In *Detzner*, Florida's legislature was not able to meet this burden, in part because the new congressional district map was intentionally based on the 2002 map, which was explicitly gerrymandered to favor the Republican Party because, at the time, gerrymandering was not illegal. As the partisan intent of the 2002 map tainted the 2012 districting plan, the latter could not be used in the upcoming 2016 election. As a result, Florida's legislature was forced to enact a new nonpartisan districting law.

One important dimension of the Florida Supreme Court's decision was its holding regarding the degree of "unlawful intent" requisite for a constitutional violation of Amendment #6. In the past, courts had typically found that a significant degree of partisan intent was permissible, in part because the legislators who approved the maps could not but know the map's political implications for future elections. For this reason, judges generally assumed that an intentional partisan gerrymander had to be "extreme" or "excessive" before it could conceivably be a constitutional violation. In contrast to this earlier approach, the Florida Supreme Court held that under the "fair district" amendments, "'there is no acceptable level of improper intent.' The prohibition on improper partisan intent in redistricting applies, 'by its express terms,' to 'both the apportionment plan as a whole and to each district individually' and does not 'require a showing of malevolent or evil purpose.'" Based on this understanding of "unlawful intent," the state court was clearly acknowledging that the "Florida Constitution now expressly prohibits what the United States Supreme Court has in the past termed a proper, and inevitable, consideration in the apportionment process."

Moreover, according to the Florida Supreme Court, overwhelming evidence of "unlawful intent" was not necessary to trigger a constitutional violation. Certainly, a plaintiff would not have to prove that a majority of the state legislators voted in favor of an electoral map to gain partisan advantage. In this case, the trial court had found that a group of Republican "operatives or consultants did in fact conspire to manipulate and influence the redistricting process," but that it was a "closer question . . . whether the Legislature in general, or the leadership and staff principally involved in drawing the maps, knowingly joined in this plan, or were duped by the operatives in the same way as the general public." However, the trial court was convinced "that the political operatives managed to find other avenues, other ways to infiltrate and influence the Legislature, to obtain the necessary cooperation and collaboration to ensure that their plan was realized, at least in part." Accordingly, these operatives "managed to taint the redistricting process and the resulting map with improper partisan intent," which sufficed to constitute a violation of the state constitution. The Florida Supreme Court accepted the trial court's finding of "unlawful intent," which established the principle that the partisan intent of private individuals sufficed to violate Amendment #6 if their conduct only had a partial, if not minimal, effect on the districting outcome and even if the legislators who actually made the mapping decision did not act with a "malevolent or evil purpose."

Of course, the Florida 2015 litigation involved an amendment to the state constitution that explicitly prohibited partisan gerrymandering. In addition, Florida's Supreme Court did not actually redraw the congressional map, but rather directed the state legislature to do so. Neither of these two aspects of Florida's litigation were present in *League of Women Voters of Pennsylvania v. Commonwealth of Pennsylvania* (2018), a challenge to Pennsylvania's 2011 congressional map. Justices on the Pennsylvania Supreme Court, elected to ten-year terms, have the option of running on a party ticket. As they are elected, they arguably might have some sensitivity to voter dissatisfaction with partisan gerrymandering. Prior to 2015, the Court was solidly Republican. However, in that year three of the seven Supreme Court seats were up for election and on November 3, 2015, all three were filled by Democrats, which produced a 5–2 Democratic majority on the court prior to its consideration of *League of Women Voters* in January 2018.

In this litigation, the League and a group of Democratic voters claimed that the 2011 plan violated the "free and equal elections" principle of the state constitution, a principle dating back to the "Commonwealth's first organic charter of governance in 1776, 11 years before the United States Constitution was adopted." It could be argued that the League's attack on Pennsylvania's 2011 congressional map was significantly compromised by the fact that the principle it was relying on could be traced back to a time frame when the constitutionality of partisan gerrymandering was not seriously questioned. However, in the end, the Pennsylvania Supreme Court agreed with the League, concluding that the plan "clearly, plainly, and palpably violates" the state's constitutional provision mandating that "Elections shall be free and equal; and no power, civil or military, shall at anytime interfere to prevent the free exercise of the right of suffrage." On that "sole basis," the court made it clear, it was invalidating the 2011 congressional map.

It was important that the court rely exclusively on the state constitution because, if it had wholly or partially based its decision on federal law—the U.S. Constitution or a federal statute such as the Voting Rights Act—then the U.S. Supreme Court, as the ultimate interpreter of federal law, would clearly have jurisdiction to review the merits of the ruling. However, as the state court had based its holding exclusively on Pennsylvania's constitution, it had established an "independent and adequate" basis for its decision on state law, thereby precluding substantive review of the decision by the U.S. Supreme Court. The two Republican justices on the Pennsylvania Supreme Court dissented from the majority's decision.

The court invalidated the 2011 map in January 2018, but the primary election for the 2018 general elections was scheduled for May 15. Could the court provide a remedy in such a short span of time? The court's options were to use the unconstitutional map in the primary election; delay the primary; or quickly come up with a new electoral map for the primary, despite the fact that the new map might confuse state officials, candidates, and voters. Despite this latter concern, the court opted to create a new map. It gave the state legislature the opportunity to produce a new map for the governor's consideration by February 9. However, if the legislature chose not to do so or if the governor did not approve the legislature's new map by February 15, then "this Court shall proceed expeditiously to adopt a plan." In light of that possibility, the court invited all parties involved with the case to submit their own electoral maps. The court made it clear no map would be approved unless the congressional electoral districts were "composed of compact and contiguous territory; as nearly equal in population as practicable; and which do not divide any county, city, incorporated town, borough, township, or ward, except where necessary to ensure equality of population."

In an opinion issued on February 7, 2018, the Supreme Court of Pennsylvania elaborated on why it had earlier found the 2011 map in violation of the "free and equal elections" clause of the state's constitution. The Court's premise was the following: "Our autonomous state Constitution . . . stands as a self-contained and self-governing body of constitutional law and acts as a wholly independent protector of the rights of the citizens of our Commonwealth." Armed with this assumption, the Court argued that the "free and equal" Elections Clause "guarantees, to the greatest degree possible, a voter's right to equal participation in the electoral process for the selection of his or her representatives in government." The court, it was true, "has not heretofore held that a redistricting plan violates the Free and Equal Elections Clause," but at the same time the court has "never precluded such a claim in our jurisprudence." The Court felt it had to act because the 2011 map subordinated "traditional redistricting criteria in the service of partisan advantage, and thereby deprives Petitioners of their state constitutional right to free and equal elections." It could not be disputed that the 2011 map had abandoned traditional districting principles of compactness and contiguity. Indeed, critics of the map claimed that the 2011 plan's borders of the 7th District produced a figure bearing a striking resemblance to Goofy kicking Donald Duck (https://commons.wikimedia.org/wiki/File:Pennsylvania_US_Congressional_District_7_(since_2013).tif#/media/File:Pennsylvania_US_Congressional_District_7_(since_2013).tif).

Pennnsylvania's Republican legislature proposed an electoral map to Governor Tom Wolf, a Democrat, but he rejected it. Accordingly, the state's Supreme Court adopted a different map and directed that it be used in the 2018 elections, including the May 15 primary. Republican leaders filed an application for a stay (a suspension) of the decision at the U.S. Supreme Court, but it was denied, and the Pennsylvania Supreme Court's map was used in the 2018 elections. The overall result of the election was to change Pennsylvania's delegation from a 12–6 advantage for the Republicans to a 9–9 tie, which was a significant improvement for the Democrats.

In *North Carolina v. Common Cause* (2019), a three-judge Superior Court, a trial court of first instance, considered whether the 2017 electoral map for the state legislature was an extreme partisan gerrymander that violated an old state constitutional provision. The state court handed down its decision two months after the U.S. Supreme Court had held in *Rucho v. Common Cause* (2019) that partisan gerrymandering of North Carolina's congressional electoral districts was a "political" question outside the jurisdiction of federal courts (see Q25). The state court referred to this federal decision, but noted that the majority opinion in *Rucho* had acknowledged that partisan gerrymanders "are incompatible with democratic principles" and that "state statutes and *state constitutions* can provide standards and guidance for state courts to apply." Accordingly, federal law did not bar the state court from considering the merits of whether North Carolina's 2017 electoral map was consistent with the state constitution. Proceeding on this assumption, the Superior Court found that the map violated state constitutional provisions related to free elections, the equal protection of the law, and free speech. In defending these conclusions, the court relied heavily on the fact that, in its view, partisanship influenced the 2017 map more than the districting principles that the state legislative districting committees had explicitly adopted to guide the preparation of the map, which included contiguity, compactness, and the preservation of boundaries of counties, municipalities, and precincts. In effect, the court's argument was that the 2017 electoral map was an extreme Republican gerrymander because it radically diverged from how the legislative districting committees had said it would draw the map.

In pursuing this line of argument, the state court was following the implicit advice that Justice Elena Kagan had given in her dissent in *Rucho*. The issue was whether a judge could provide a neutral assessment of whether a partisan gerrymander was of an extreme sort. Kagan argued that there was a "neutral baseline," one that "does not use any judge-made conception of electoral fairness—either proportional representation or any other; instead, it takes as its baseline a State's *own* criteria of fairness, apart from partisan gain. And by requiring plaintiffs to make difficult showings relating to both purpose and effects, the standard invalidates the most extreme, but only the most extreme, partisan gerrymanders."

North Carolina Superior Court's reasoning tracked Kagan's to the letter. The Court referred to the charts of the plaintiffs' expert witnesses that showed the degree to which partisanship, rather than the state's districting principles, had shaped the 2017 map. One such chart, prepared by Dr. Jowei Chen, a professor of political science at the University of Michigan, focused on the degree to which the map split municipalities into separate districts, something that the legislative districting committees had explicitly disfavored. Chen's chart compared a thousand possible electoral maps to the 2017 map that the legislature had adopted. It clearly showed that there were one thousand alternative maps that would have split between thirty-eight and fifty-three municipalities, but instead North Carolina's legislature chose a map that split seventy-nine, far above the median of forty-five. The overall impression of the chart was that there were many other maps available to the legislature that would have split fewer municipalities if partisan advantage had not been such an overwhelming consideration in how the map was drawn.

The Court also referred to another of Chen's charts, one that revealed the 2017 adopted plan was also an outlier compared to one thousand other possible maps in terms of the compactness of House districts. In the court's view, these charts constituted undeniable evidence that the 2017 House map greatly subordinated the traditional districting principles that the state had said it would respect in favor of gaining partisan advantage.

North Carolina's 2017 districting plan was largely the work of Dr. Thomas Hofeller, a Republican political strategist, who has been called "the Master of Modern Republican Gerrymandering." Files from Hofeller's computer obtained in a lawsuit showed that he had used election results data from ten previous statewide elections to produce a map that would have the greatest number of districts with a Republican vote share of 53 percent or higher for the 50 seats in the state senate and the 120 seats in the House. According to the court, the "evidence establishes that Dr. Hofeller drew the 2017 Plans very precisely to create as many 'safe' Republican districts as possible, so that Republicans would maintain their supermajorities, or at least majorities even in a strong election year for Democrats." In other words, the electoral map adopted by the North Carolina legislature was designed to ensure that Democrats would not be able to control either house of the state legislature. No Democratic senators voted in favor of either plan and the only Democratic member of the House who voted in favor of both plans became a Republican several months after the vote.

Having found that the 2017 electoral map was an extreme gerrymander, the Superior Court then explained why the map violated the three provisions of the state constitution. Regarding the Free Elections Clause, the court argued that North Carolina's government was one "in which the will of the people—the majority—legally expressed, must govern" and, for that reason, fair and honest elections "are to prevail in this state." Accordingly, "the meaning of the Free Elections Clause is that elections must be conducted freely and honestly to ascertain, fairly and truthfully, the will of the people." The gerrymandered 2017 map clearly violated this Clause because it reflects "a fundamental distrust of voters by serving the self-interest of political parties over the public good" and because it "dilute[s] and devalue[s] votes of some citizens compared to others," with the result that [v]oters are not freely choosing their representatives," but rather "representatives are choosing their voters."

The Superior Court also found that the 2017 map violated the state's Equal Protection Clause and the state's Freedom of Speech/Freedom of Assembly Clauses. It violated the former, in the Court's view, because this partisan gerrymander "treats individuals who support candidates of one political party less favorably than individuals who support candidates of another party." It violated the two latter clauses because voting "provides citizens a direct means of expressing support for a candidate and his views" and because the ability to band "together with likeminded citizens in a political party is a form of protected association" within the right of assembly. In either instance, a government was not permitted to "infringe on protected activity based on the individual's viewpoint" by preferring Republican speakers/voters over Democratic speakers/voters. Indeed, the Superior Court argued, "[v]iewpoint discrimination is *most* insidious where the targeted speech is political."

Relying in part on these equal protection/free speech arguments, the Superior Court opened up new fronts in the ongoing effort to end partisan gerrymandering at the state constitutional level. For example, following the North Carolina decision, the National Redistricting Foundation (NRF), a nonprofit organization affiliated with the National Democratic Redistricting Committee and led by Democratic President Barrack Obama's former Attorney General, Eric H. Holder, Jr., filed a lawsuit (*Harper v. Lewis* [2019]) against North Carolina's current congressional map in the Superior Court of Wake County. Clearly, the NRF was trying to piggyback off the earlier win that had invalidated the state legislative districts (Gardner, 2019). Moreover, a number of states have constitutional provisions comparable to North Carolina's, which state judges could conceivably use to invalidate extreme partisan gerrymanders.

The outlook for such a trend is uncertain. Moderate partisan gerrymanders may very well survive such scrutiny. For example, following the Superior Court's decision, the North Carolina legislature adopted new maps for state legislative districts that experts claimed seemed to give Republicans "a slight political edge" (Wines, 2019). It is not clear how North Carolina's courts will react to such a modest gerrymander. However, it is unlikely that state courts across the country will try to squeeze all partisanship from the process of electoral districting. Redistricting is arguably an inherently political process because it inevitably has partisan consequences. Nevertheless, it is possible that a number of state courts will in the future continue to invalidate extreme partisan gerrymanders on state constitutional grounds.

FURTHER READING

Daley, David. "The Secret Files of the Master of Modern Republican Gerrymandering." *The New Yorker*, September 6, 2019.

Douglas, Joshua A. "State Judges and the Right to Vote." *Ohio State Law Journal* 77 (2016): 1–48.

Elmendorf, Christopher S. "From Education Adequacy to Representational Adequacy: A New Template for Legal Attacks on Partisan Gerrymanders." *William and Mary Law Review* 59 (2018): 1601–1680.

Gardner, Amy. "Holder-affiliated Group Launches New Challenge to Partisan Gerrymandering in North Carolina." *The Washington Post*, September 27, 2019, available at https://www.washingtonpost.com/politics/holder-affiliated-group-launches-new-challenge-to-partisan-gerrymandering-in-north-carolina/2019/09/26/c7574b5a-e0a1-11e9-8dc8-498eabc129a0_story.html.

Kanefield, Joseph. "Partisan Gerrymander Claims: Are State Constitutions the New Frontier." *Arizona Attorney* 55 (2018): 26–31.

Larson, Taylor, and Duden, Joshua. "Breaking the Ballot Box: A Pathway to Greater Success in Addressing Political Gerrymandering Through State Courts." *City University of New York Law Review* 22 (2019): 104–123.

Stewart, Charlie. "State Court Litigation: The New Front in the War Against Partisan Gerrymandering." *Michigan Law Review Online* 116 (2018); 152–164.

Wines, Michael. "In North Carolina, New Political Maps Don't End Old Disputes." *The New York Times*, September 17, 2019, available at https://www.nytimes.com/2019/09/17/us/north-carolina-gerrymandering.html

Q27. IF NO STATE JUDICIAL REMEDY IS AVAILABLE, ARE THERE ANY POLITICAL REMEDIES THAT DISAFFECTED CITIZENS CAN PURSUE TO RECTIFY EXTREME PARTISAN GERRYMANDERING?

Answer: Yes, if their state constitutions permit it, disaffected citizens whose votes have been devalued by partisan gerrymandering can initiate a ballot measure that shifts the power of redrawing electoral districts from the state legislature to a nonpartisan independent redistricting commission. Alternatively, they can band together with citizens from other states to urge Congress to enact appropriate federal legislation.

The Facts: On November 7, 2000, the voters of Arizona approved Proposition 106, an amendment to the state constitution "ending the practice of gerrymandering and improving voter and candidate participation in elections by creating the Arizona Independent Redistricting Commission (AIRC) to oversee the mapping of fair and competitive congressional and legislative districts." The majority and minority leaders of each chamber of the state legislature selected four of the commission's five members from a list of nominees (ten Democrats, ten Republicans, and five independents) provided by the state commission on appellate court appointments. These four members then selected the fifth commissioner from a political party not yet represented on the commission.

Following the 2010 census, the Arizona legislature challenged the congressional map the commission adopted in January 2012. The basis for the challenge was that the "Elections Clause" of the federal Constitution mandated that the "Times, Places, and Manner of holding Elections for Senators and Representatives, shall be prescribed in each State by the Legislature thereof," subject to any revisions that Congress may see fit to enact. This language, the Arizona legislature argued, precluded the use of independent commissions for any policymaking within the purview of the Elections Clause, including the electoral redistricting that followed each national census. In response, the AIRC argued that the reference to "the Legislature" in the Elections Clause encompassed all the legislative authority conferred by the state constitution, not just that conferred to the body of elected representatives. Accordingly, if a state constitution, such as Arizona's, gave citizens the right to amend the state's constitution by way of an initiative, any such amendment that conferred redistricting authority to the AIRC was consistent with the Elections Clause.

The U.S. Supreme Court addressed the constitutionality of Arizona's AIRC in *Arizona State Legislature v. Arizona Independent Redistricting Commission* (2015). Writing for the majority in a 5–4 decision, Justice Ginsburg concluded that the Elections Clause permitted the AIRC to draw congressional district lines because Arizona's constitution "'establishes the electorate as a coordinate source of legislation' on equal footing with the representative legislative body." The federal Elections Clause was no bar to this division of the state's legislative authority. The purpose of the clause was, first, "to empower Congress to override state election rules, not to restrict the way States enact legislation," and, second, to "safeguard against manipulation of electoral rules by politicians and factions in the States to entrench themselves or place their interests over those of the electorate." Accordingly, the "history and purpose of the Clause," in Ginsburg's opinion, weighed heavily against precluding popular control over redistricting, "as does the animating principle of our Constitution that the people themselves are the originating source of all powers of government." For this reason, Ginsburg continued, the Court will "resist reading the Elections Clause to single out federal elections as the one area in which States may not use citizen initiatives as an alternative legislative process," noting that the "people of Arizona turned to the initiative to curb the practice of gerrymandering and, thereby, to ensure that Members of Congress would have 'an habitual recollection of their dependence on the people.'" In doing so, "Arizona voters sought to restore 'the core principle of republican government,' namely, 'that the voters should choose their representatives, not the other way around.'"

Chief Justice Roberts wrote a dissenting opinion joined by the other three dissenting justices. It focused on how the majority had performed "a magic trick" by revising the meaning of the term "the Legislature" in the Elections Clause to mean "the people." In doing so, the majority had dared to do what the framers of the Seventeenth Amendment had not. This amendment had transferred power to choose U.S. senators from "the Legislature" of each state (Article I, Section 3) to "the people thereof." It had been the culmination of "an arduous, decades-long campaign in which reformers across the country worked hard to garner approval from Congress and three-quarters of the States." However, Roberts notes, if the majority's opinion is correct, all this effort embodied in the ratification of the Seventeenth Amendment was unnecessary. Citizens of each state could have elected their senators without the amendment by simply revising "the Legislature" to mean "the people." If such a sleight of hand did not work with the popular election of senators, Roberts argued, it could not work with independent redistricting commissions. No matter that

Arizona's AIRC was "a noble endeavor" to end partisan gerrymandering. "No matter how concerned we may be about partisanship in redistricting, this Court has no power," Roberts insisted, "to gerrymander the Constitution." The citizens of Arizona must either "seek relief from Congress, which can make or alter the regulations prescribed by the legislature" or "follow the lead of the reformers who won passage of the Seventeenth Amendment" by the long and arduous road of ratification.

The slim majority in *Arizona State Legislature* gave frustrated voters in states with ballot measure options (initiatives or referendums) a narrow foothold to expand the use of independent redistricting commissions—and thus restrain partisan gerrymandering by their state legislatures. By the time the Court decided this case, California, Iowa, Ohio, Maine, and Connecticut had already established such commissions, although they varied in terms of their role and significance. California's was a fourteen-person commission composed as follows: a state auditor's panel selected twenty Democrats, twenty Republicans, and twenty others from a pool of applicants; the majority and minority leaders of the state houses have the option of eliminating two nominees from each of the three categories; eight of the commissioners are randomly selected from those remaining in the pool; these eight then select two additional Democrats, two Republicans, and two unaffiliated members. The resulting fourteen-member commission was empowered to draw both congressional and state legislative districts in accordance with the state's constitutional requirement that districts be compact and that local political subdivisions and communities of interests should be kept intact if possible. Approval of new districting maps required nine votes, with three votes required from each of the three categories. The goal of the process was a map that was tolerable and reasonable for all political parties active in the state.

In contrast to California's robust model of a redistricting commission, Iowa's legislature relies on a nonpartisan state agency—the Legislative Services Agency (LSA)—to draw maps for congressional and state legislative districts. The LSA follows a strict set of criteria regarding compactness and contiguity. Interestingly, the Iowa law prohibits any use of political data in drawing district maps, including the addresses of incumbents, the political affiliations of registered voters, previous election results, and other demographic information. In fulfilling its function, the LSA may receive advice from a Temporary Redistricting Advisory Commission (TRAC) that is formed each decade for this purpose. The LSA submits the proposed maps to the state legislature with a report within forty-five days after receiving the census data from the federal government. The proposed map is subject to an up-or-down vote by the legislature. If it is rejected, the LSA proposes a second electoral map. If the legislature rejects the second map, LSA proposes a third, but at this point the legislature may amend the map or propose a map of its own. In response to these options, Iowa's legislature has always adopted one of the plans proposed by LSA without substantive amendment and it has never proposed its own map. Accordingly, although Iowa's legislature yet has final authority to approve new district maps, its model of redistricting has substantially diminished the role that partisanship plays in the redistricting process ("Iowa Model" 2018).

The number of states using redistricting commissions of various types has significantly expanded since the Court's decision in *Arizona State Legislature*. In 2019, fourteen states have commissions in place with primary responsibility for drawing legislative districts (Alaska, Arizona, Arkansas, California, Colorado, Hawaii, Idaho, Michigan, Missouri, Montana, New Jersey, Ohio, Pennsylvania, and Washington); six states have established commissions that only assist and advise the state legislature in its decision (Maine, New York, Rhode Island, Utah, Vermont, and Virginia); and five states have "backup commissions" that will draw and adopt a new redistricting map if the state legislature is unable to agree upon one (Connecticut, Illinois, Mississippi, Oklahoma, and Texas). Only Iowa continues to operate its unique model involving an advisory nonpartisan state agency assisted by a temporary commission.

The selection process for these redistricting commissions varies, considerably, from the designation of certain state officers to those that rely more on random chance. For example, Ohio's commission is composed of the governor, the auditor, the secretary of state, and four people appointed by the majority and minority leaders of the state legislature. In contrast, Michigan's commission, established in 2018 when voters decisively approved a ballot proposal crafted by a statewide grassroots anti-gerrymandering movement, is based on applications that the secretary of state makes available to the public, including ten thousand sent randomly to Michigan residents; the secretary then randomly selects sixty applicants from those in the pool affiliated with each of the two major parties and eighty from those who are unaffiliated. These two hundred names are submitted to four state legislative leaders, each of whom can strike five applicants from any of the three categories, reducing the pool to one hundred and eighty. At that point, the secretary randomly draws the names of two applicants associated with each major political party and one that is unaffiliated, producing a redistricting commission of five members. In short, Ohio's commission requires state officials to serve, while Michigan goes to great lengths to reduce their influence in favor of random selection.

It would be an exaggeration to claim that independent commissions have completely drained the redistricting process of all partisan influence, but those state commissions that have general control over how legislative districts are drawn have sharply increased the partisan competitiveness of state elections. For example, the maps drawn by Arizona's AIRC in 2001 and 2011 "were among the most competitive in the nation" because the average margin of victory was "more than 28 percent lower than that of the United States as a whole." In fact, two of its nine districts "had margins of victory under 5 percent in 2014." California's new commission achieved similar results with its 2011 map, which was "far more competitive than its predecessor drawn by the Democrat-dominated state legislature." The average margin of victory in the post-2011 elections "was 30 percent lower than in races based on the legislature's 2001 maps" and the percentage of districts with a margin of victory under 10 percent jumped from 5 percent to 19 percent (Soffen, 2015). Of course, these results in no way reduce the political salience of the electoral maps adopted by the Arizona and California commissions. The process of redistricting in these states may be less partisan, but the resulting electoral map can yet ignite a partisan firestorm.

Redistricting commissions that play an advisory or backup role cannot be expected to reduce the degree of partisanship in redistricting to the same degree as commissions that are directly empowered to draw and adopt the electoral maps of state legislative and congressional districts. Accordingly, in 2019, only fourteen states have moved in the direction of robust independent redistricting commissions, leaving thirty-six states vulnerable to partisan gerrymandering in varying degrees. Some states have split government, with Republicans and Democrats sharing power, which provides a political buffer to partisan gerrymandering. However, Ballotpedia reports on a webpage titled "State Government Trifectas" that there are, as of 2020, thirty-six states that qualify as "trifectas," which means one party holds the governorship and a majority in both houses of the state legislature, with fifteen states controlled by Democrats and twenty-one by Republicans. Obviously, states that are "trifectas" tend to be more vulnerable to partisan gerrymandering.

Although some of the "trifecta" states have established independent redistricting commissions, many have not. In these states, especially those that have veto-proof majorities in the legislature, the incumbents are the direct beneficiaries of gerrymandered electoral systems and disaffected citizens have little choice but to turn to Congress for any type of political remedy. In that vein, as many as nine bills requiring states to use independent commissions for congressional redistricting were introduced in the 115th Congress and, in early 2019, as many as four bills in the 116th Congress. All of these bills failed to get out of committee except one: the Democrats in the House of Representatives on March 8, 2019, in a party-line vote, passed the For the People Act. This bill included a provision requiring each state to establish an independent redistricting commission, but the Republican-controlled Senate has refused to take any action on the measure. The chances that this bill will become law before the 2020 election are nonexistent and it is worth noting that such a federal law would only apply to congressional, not state, districting. Accordingly, independent commissions have become an important component of the redistricting process in the United States, but partisan gerrymandering has hardly been banished. In addition, there is legitimate concern that the Supreme Court, with the retirement of Justice Kennedy and his replacement by Justice Brett Kavanaugh, might yet overrule *Arizona State Legislature*. Such a ruling would reverse the trend of the last decade and focus more attention on Congress's power to remedy partisan gerrymandering in congressional districting and, possibly, on the need for a federal amendment to remedy unchecked gerrymandering at the state level.

FURTHER READING

Cain, Bruce E. "Redistricting Commissions: A Better Political Buffer?" *Yale Law Journal* 121 (2012): 1808–1844.

Eckman, Sarah J. "Redistricting Commissions for Congressional Districts." *Congressional Research Service Insight*, February 25, 2019, available at https://fas.org/sgp/crs/misc/IN11053.pdf

Gartner, David. "Arizona State Legislature v. Arizona Independent Redistricting Commission and the Future of Redistricting Reform." *Arizona State Law Journal* 51 (2019): 551–591.

Goodman, Josh. "Why Redistricting Commissions Aren't Immune from Politics." *PEW: Stateline*, January 27, 2012, available at https://www.pewtrusts.org/en/research-and-analysis/blogs/stateline/2012/01/27/why-redistricting-commissions-arent-immune-from-politics.

"The 'Iowa Model' for Redistricting: Nonpartisan Staff Draw Map in Iowa—Legislature Votes on Them." *National Conference of State Legislatures*, April 6, 2018, available at http://www.ncsl.org/research/redistricting/the-iowa-model-for-redistricting.aspx.

Lowenthal, Alan S. "The Ills of Gerrymandering and Independent Redistricting Commissions as the Solution." *Harvard Journal on Legislation* 56 (2019): 1–21.

Miller, Peter, and Grofman, Bernard. "Redistricting Commissions in the Western United States." *University of California Irvine Law Review* 3 (2013): 637–668.

"Redistricting Commissions: State Legislative Plans." *National Conference of State Legislatures*, April 18, 2019, available at http://www.ncsl.org/research/redistricting/2009-redistricting-commissions-table.aspx.

Soffen, Kim. "Independently Drawn Districts Have Proved to Be More Competitive." *The New York Times*, July 1, 2015, available at https://www.nytimes.com/2015/07/02/upshot/independently-drawn-districts-have-proved-to-be-more-competitive.html.

Q28. AS STATE COURTS HAVE RECENTLY RULED THAT EXTREME PARTISAN GERRYMANDERING VIOLATES THEIR STATE CONSTITUTIONS (Q26) AND A NUMBER OF STATES HAVE ESTABLISHED INDEPENDENT REDISTRICTING COMMISSIONS (Q27), IS IT LIKELY THAT PARTISAN GERRYMANDERING WILL SOON DISAPPEAR FROM AMERICAN POLITICAL LIFE?

Answer: No, the future of partisan gerrymandering in American elections is uncertain because (1) not all state constitutions have provisions that would justify judicial invalidation of extreme gerrymanders; and (2) Republican Party loyalists continue to resist efforts to eliminate partisan influence on the districting process.

The Facts: The Pennsylvania Supreme Court invalidated gerrymandered state electoral districts on the basis of the state constitution's "free and equal" Elections Clause. Twelve other states (Arizona, Arkansas, Delaware, Illinois, Indiana, Kentucky, Oklahoma, South Dakota, Oregon, Tennessee, Washington, and Wyoming) have identical clauses in their constitutions, but these states historically have not been subject to extreme partisan gerrymanders. In contrast, states often regarded as among those that are gerrymandered—Michigan, Maryland, Ohio, and Wisconsin—have no such clauses in their state constitutions. However, thirteen of the fifty state constitutions do have a requirement that elections must be "free and open," which may provide state judges with a sufficient constitutional basis to follow the example of the Superior Court of North Carolina that ruled against partisan gerrymandering in 2019 (see Q26).

It is impossible to predict how state judges will apply either of these types of constitutional provisions to redistricting maps in the future. One expert who has reviewed state constitutions and relevant state judicial precedents estimates that twenty-two states have a legal background suitable for invalidating partisan gerrymanders on the basis of state law, which would leave twenty-eight yet vulnerable to the problematic effects of partisan redistricting (Elmendorf, 2018). Another issue is enforcement. For decades, state constitutions and laws have on paper required that electoral districts be drawn in accordance with traditional redistricting principles of compactness, contiguity, and respect for local political subdivisions, but partisan gerrymandering has flourished during this period. As state judges have allowed enforcement of traditional redistricting principles to languish for such a period of time, it is not at all clear whether they will have the political will to enforce new interpretations of general electoral guarantees, especially if state judges are elected on party tickets. Will these judges be more loyal to the party that nominated them or the voters who elected them? The future will tell.

State legislators can also respond negatively to state judicial rulings that erode what they think are their prerogatives regarding redistricting. For example, North Carolina's Republican legislature in 2017 required all judicial candidates to identify their party affiliation on the ballot. It was the first time a state reinstituted such partisan judicial elections in nearly a century. Second, as the governor was a Democrat, the legislature reduced the size of the state Court of Appeals, thereby taking away the governor's power to replace three Republican judges who had retired, presumably because the GOP lawmakers feared the replacements would be Democrats. Third, the North Carolina legislature considered amending the state constitution to permit lawmakers to appoint state judges, thereby shifting judicial selection to those who directly benefited from gerrymandered legislative electoral districts. A cynical interpretation would be that the North Carolina legislature was not content to pick the voters who would elect them, but insisted also on picking the judges who would let this practice continue. Although the North Carolina legislature cited South Carolina's and Virginia's systems of legislative judicial appointments as precedents, critics charged that legislative selection would inevitably encourage backroom deals, cronyism, a judiciary overly deferential to the legislature, and legislative retaliation against independent judges (Blythe, 2017). Facing a barrage of criticism, the North Carolina legislature shelved the idea of a constitutional amendment that would have the beneficiaries of partisan gerrymandering pick the judges who would likely be evaluating whether the gerrymander was consistent with the state constitution.

Lastly, North Carolina's legislature redrew the electoral districts for judicial elections of the state's trial court judges. North Carolina's court structure consists of a Supreme Court, an intermediate appellate Court of Appeals (both of which are elected statewide), and trial courts of Superior Court judges and District Court judges, both of whom are elected in local electoral districts. The state legislature shifted the borders of these districts to help Republican judicial candidates, now identified as such on the ballot, get elected. It was, at least in part, a case of gerrymandering the electoral districts of the state's trial courts to decrease the likelihood of future judicial rulings hostile to partisan legislative gerrymandering (Gabriel, 2017). This tactic revealed how far a dominant political party in a state legislature will go to preserve the electoral advantage it has gained through gerrymandering.

The Republican legislature passed the new judicial redistricting system over the veto of the Democratic governor in 2018. In elections held later that year, the new system had a particularly negative impact on African American judges because many of them were placed in majority-white local districts with an incumbent opponent, decreasing the likelihood of their reelection, with a corresponding negative effect on judicial diversity. Two former black judges from Charlotte who lost their seats in the 2018 election sued, claiming that the new districts "are 'deliberately segregated along color and racial lines' in an effort to give white voters more political power." In their case, both judges were placed in a populous but geographically small district in Mecklenburg County that was 82 percent white. The Republican legislature's decision to change judicial elections in North Carolina "coincided with their repeated losses in voting rights cases, including lawsuits over gerrymandering at all levels of government" (Corriher, 2019).

The constitutionality of the new system is doubtful as North Carolina's constitution defines a "court district" as consisting "of one or more entire counties," not as a district within a county. Another constitutional provision mandates that every judge "shall be elected by the qualified voters of the . . . district in which he or she is to serve." As Superior Court and District Court judges served at the county level or higher, they were not being elected by all the qualified voters of the district in which they served, but rather by the qualified voters of a subset of the district in which they served (Corriher, 2019). It is worth noting that these constitutional provisions had little to no effect on the North Carolina legislature's resolve to ward off any judicial threats to its current dominance over the state legislature.

A committee in Pennsylvania's House of Representatives recently began considering an approach to judicial elections different from North

Carolina's. Perhaps because it was the Pennsylvania Supreme Court that invalidated the state's electoral map in 2018, not a trial court as in North Carolina, the committee voted in April 2019 on two proposals to amend the state constitution to shift elections for the state's three appellate courts from statewide contests to a district-based model. Both proposals passed on largely party-line votes. One proposal would divide the state into three regions. The governor would nominate judges for the appellate courts, including the state Supreme Court, from a list composed by a judicial commission, but all nominees would be subject to Senate confirmation and would have to run in a retention election after four years on the bench. The other proposal would elect appellate judges from districts the General Assembly would draw, thereby ensuring geographic diversity on the Supreme Court. The number of districts would depend on the number of judges on the appellate court: seven for the Supreme Court, fifteen for the Superior Court, and nine for the Commonwealth Court.

The Democrats on the committee were not enthusiastic about regional judicial elections. They expressed fears that partisan gerrymandering could easily creep into how the judicial districts were drawn. As the proposals are incompatible with one another, it is at this point not clear which, if any, the full House would support (Scolforo, 2019). However, the committee's actions are a clear signal that the Pennsylvania Supreme Court's 2018 decision invalidating the existing map for congressional elections may not be the last word on the future of gerrymandering in the state. Once again the facts suggest that a political party dominant in a state legislature is not likely to cede power without putting up a fight, whether in a direct or an indirect fashion, such as shifting judicial elections of important state courts from a statewide basis, which cannot be gerrymandered, to a district basis, which are vulnerable to such partisan influence.

On an entirely different front, Republicans have also recently launched legal attacks against newly created independent redistricting commissions that will play an important role in redrawing electoral maps following the 2020 national census. For example, Voters Not Politicians, the Michigan volunteer grassroots organization that initiated the ballot initiative that created the state's new redistricting commission with 61 percent support of Michigan voters, had included in the constitutional amendment a provision that excluded anyone from serving on the commission who had been a partisan candidate, elected official, political appointee, lobbyist, campaign consultant, or a member of a political party's governing body for the last six years. The purpose of these exclusions was to discourage partisanship on the thirteen-member commission, which was to be composed of four Republicans, four Democrats, and five residents unaffiliated with the two major political parties. On July 30, 2019, fifteen citizens of Michigan—in *Daunt v. Benson*—requested a federal judge to enjoin the formation of the commission on the ground that the exclusions were unconstitutional. The Michigan Republican Party formally joined the lawsuit and the Fair Lines American Foundation, a nonprofit with links to the National Republican Redistricting Trust (NRRT), which coordinates Republican redistricting efforts at the national level, provided financial support (Oosting, 2019).

In its complaint and briefs filed at the district court, the plaintiffs in *Daunt* argued that the eligibility rules of the commission violated the rights of those excluded from serving on it, in particular, the right of "free speech and political association" and the right of equal protection of the laws. In their view, such eligibility rules can be squared with First Amendment rights only if they are necessary for "vital interests." Even if the "asserted interests of transparency, impartiality, and fairness" are in some sense "vital," they continued, the exclusions are not necessary because "there is not a sufficient 'fit' between the goals and the exclusions; eligible applicants may be no less partisan than those who fall into the excluded categories." Similarly, the exclusions violate the Equal Protection Clause "because they burden categories of individuals based on perceived 'partisan' biases, but impose no restriction on individuals whose partisan biases may be stronger but who do not fall into one of the excluded categories" (*Daunt v. Benson* [2019]).

In response, the defendant in *Daunt*, Jocelyn Benson, Michigan's secretary of state, noted that the Supreme Court "cited the power of states to enact independent commissions as a remedy to the problem" of partisan gerrymandering. "In fact, the Supreme Court highlighted Michigan's Commission in particular—the very entity under attack by the Plaintiffs in this case." In doing so, the Court thereby recognized that "Michigan's citizens have a constitutional right to structure their sovereign government and choose the qualifications of their officeholders. They do not exceed that right by excluding from the Commission those citizens with a self-interest in thwarting, rather than promoting, a functioning representative democracy" (*Daunt v. Benson* [2019]).

On November 25, 2019, the federal district court denied the plaintiffs an injunction, ruling that the "eligibility provisions at issue do not impose severe burdens on Plaintiffs' First Amendment rights" and that the plaintiffs "do not belong to any suspect classification such as race or religion" under the Equal Protection Clause. Accordingly, Michigan's law excluding certain categories of persons from Michigan's redistricting commission are constitutional because they further "a legitimate state interest in establishing a fair and impartial redistricting process" (*Daunt v. Benson* [2019]). On April 15, 2020, a three-judge panel of the 6th Circuit Court of Appeal affirmed the district court's decision, emphasizing that federal courts generally defer to state efforts to make elections "fair and honest" and that the Supreme Court "has repeatedly held that these types of [eligibility] restrictions [for public office] do not run afoul of the First Amendment or the Equal Protection Clause" (*Daunt v. Benson* [2019]). The plaintiffs responded on May 13, 2020, by petitioning the 6th Circuit for a rehearing *en banc*, that is, a rehearing before all the judges of the 6th Circuit. This new petition highlights the tenacity of the plaintiffs and the high stakes of the litigation.

While this litigation was underway in Michigan, the battle over independent redistricting commissions and gerrymandering continued in the political realm. On June 3, 2019, the National Democratic Redistricting Committee (NDRC), led by Eric Holder, former Attorney General in the Obama Administration, published on its website a Fair Districts Pledge for all candidates and elected officials. The pledge read as follows:

> For too long, partisan gerrymandering has been used as a tool to manipulate electoral districts to benefit political parties instead of voters.
>
> I believe every elected official should be accountable to the people they represent, which means we need to end gerrymandering.
>
> I pledge to support fair redistricting that ends map manipulation and creates truly representative districts.

On the other side of the political spectrum, Scott Walker became the chairman of the NRRT in 2019. Walker, a former governor of Wisconsin, had signed the 2011 redistricting plan that gerrymandered the state's legislature. The gerrymander was so complete that in the 2018 election Republicans won sixty-three of ninety-nine seats in the General Assembly (64 percent of the total) despite the fact that their candidates won only 46 percent of the total statewide vote, which was equivalent to 190,000 fewer votes than their Democratic opponents (Gilbert, 2018).

Walker welcomed the Michigan lawsuit. In a July 30th statement on NRRT's website, Walker wrote ""No American should be barred from holding a government position because they, or someone they are related to, exercised their Constitutional rights. This lawsuit aims to restore the rights of all Michiganders to freely participate in the political process without the threat of government sanction." Regarding Holder's and the NDRC's commitment to "fair redistricting," Walker claimed in a September 27 statement on NRRT's website that this was "the furthest thing from the truth. What they want," he continued, "are maps that elect as many Democrats as possible" and courts "to put a finger on the scale to let them win." Walker summed up his position with the pithy suggestion that, when Democrats cannot win elections, "they sue until it's blue." This rhetorical battle between Holder and Walker over gerrymandering complements the legal argumentation over redistricting commissions found in *Daunt v. Benson*. The intensity of these debates strongly suggests that partisan gerrymandering will not soon be a thing of the past. The stakes for both major political parties are simply too high.

FURTHER READING

Blythe, Anne. "Should NC Lawmakers Create Laws and Select Judges Who Review Them? GOP Senator Asks Why Not." *The News & Observer*, December 9, 2017, available at https://www.newsobserver.com/news/politics-government/state-politics/article188970949.html.

Corriher, Billy. "Lawsuit Targets Racially Gerrymandered N.C. Judicial Elections." *Facing South: A Voice for a Changing South*, August 27, 2019, available at https://www.facingsouth.org/2019/08/lawsuit-targets-racially-gerrymandered-nc-judicial-elections.

Daley, David. *Unrigged: How Americans Are Battling Back to Save Democracy*. New York: Liveright, 2020.

Daunt v. Benson (2019), Case No. 1:19-cv-614, the complaint, the motion to dismiss, and all judicial opinions cited above from this litigation are available at https://www.brennancenter.org/our-work/court-cases/daunt-v-benson.

Elmendorf, Christopher S. "From Educational Adequacy to Representational Adequacy: A New Template for Legal Attacks on Partisan Gerrymanders." *William & Mary Law Review* 59 (2018): 1601–1680.

Gabriel, Trip. "In North Carolina, Republicans Stung by Court Ruling Aim to Change the Judges." *The New York Times*, October 18, 2017, available at https://www.nytimes.com/2017/10/18/us/north-carolina-republicans-gerrymander-judges-.html

Gilbert, Craig. "New Election Data Highlights the Ongoing Impact of 2011 GOP Redistricting in Wisconsin." *Milwaukee Journal Sentinel*, December 6, 2018, available at https://www.jsonline.com/story/news/blogs/wisconsin-voter/2018/12/06/wisconsin-gerrymandering-data-shows-stark-impact-redistricting/2219092002/.

Grofman, Bernard, and Cervas, Jonathan R. "Can State Courts Cure Partisan Gerrymandering: Lessons from *League of Women Voters v.*

Commonwealth of Pennsylvania (2018)." *Election Law Journal* 17 (2018): 264–285.

Keith, Douglas, and Robbins, Laila. "Legislative Appointments for Judges: Lessons from South Carolina, Virginia, and Rhode Island." *Brennan Center for Justice*, September 29, 2017, available at https://www.brennancenter.org/sites/default/files/analysis/North_Carolina.pdf.

Oosting, Jonathan. "Republicans Sue to Block Michigan Redistricting Commission." *The Detroit News*, July 30, 2019, available at https://www.detroitnews.com/story/news/politics/2019/07/30/republicans-sue-block-michigan-redistricting-commission/1860829001/.

Scolforo, Mark. "House Panel Advances Changes in Pennsylvania Judge Elections." *WITF*, April 30, 2019, available at https://www.witf.org/2019/04/30/house_panel_advances_changes_in_pennsylvania_judge_elections/.

5

Ongoing Challenges

The American right to vote is a work in progress. Previous chapters have explored some of the major advancements regarding the right to vote that Americans have achieved, as well as a couple of important challenges: the Supreme Court's decision in *Shelby County v. Holder* (2013) (see Q23), which curbed the federal government's authority to prevent violations of the Voting Rights Act, and the ongoing efforts to remedy extreme partisan gerrymandering following the Supreme Court's ruling in *Rucho v. Common Cause* (2019) (see Q25) that the issue was a "political question" outside the jurisdiction of the federal judiciary.

However, despite these setbacks and controversies, there is no question that the right to vote is more meaningful for more American citizens than it was sixty years ago. There are nevertheless fresh challenges to the American right to vote that have arisen in the last decade or so. Some of these challenges are real and concrete, such as felony disfranchisement and the Russian interference in the 2016 presidential election, while others have more to do with perception, such as the myth that there is rampant voting by illegal aliens or that American elections are "rigged." These latter problems are as worrisome as real ones because how American voters perceive elections is directly linked to voter confidence and the integrity and legitimacy of American democracy. In the end, what American voters think and believe about voting is important whether it is true or not.

The importance of the challenges currently confronting the American voter is magnified by political polarization. The problem of intense partisanship has rarely been so acute. During the 2018 midterm elections, an NBC/Wall Street Journal poll found that 80 percent of Americans felt that the country was "mainly" or "totally" divided. At the same time, as the partisan gulf has widened, nothing has appeared on the horizon that seems capable of reversing this tragic trend. For example, a Quinnipiac poll published on January 17, 2018, indicated that 64 percent of respondents thought that President Trump was doing more to divide the nation than unite it. The Democratic House of Representative's decision in December 2019 to impeach President Trump on a largely party-line vote elevated the problem to new heights. It appeared to partisans on both sides that impeachment was being used by the other party to gain political leverage in the upcoming 2020 presidential election, especially after Trump's acquittal on February 5, 2020, with only Republican Senator Mitt Romney breaking ranks in favor of conviction.

The COVID-19 epidemic that erupted in March 2020 has only exacerbated the situation by raising the possibility that voters may have to choose between exercising their right to vote and avoiding a potentially deadly disease. Wisconsin's primary election on April 7 highlighted this dilemma. Democratic Governor Tony Evans proposed postponing the primary until June 9, but the Republican legislature and state Supreme Court blocked him on April 6. On that same day, in *Republican National Committee v. Democratic National Committee*, the Supreme Court reversed a lower court's extension of when Wisconsin absentee ballots had to be postmarked: switching it from April 13 back to the original date of April 7. The result was that Wisconsin voters who had not requested an absentee ballot had to decide whether to stay safe and not vote or risk their health and vote in person the next day. The election went on as scheduled, and the turnout was unexpectedly heavy. The lines were accordingly long and the delays lengthy, especially because polling places had been consolidated in response to the virus. It will never be known for certain how many Wisconsin voters contracted the coronavirus because they voted in person on April 7, but the *Wisconsin State Journal* reported on May 16, 2020, the Wisconsin Department of Health Services' finding that seventy-one persons who had either voted in person or worked at the polls had later become infected. In effect, the Wisconsin 2020 primary confirmed that the COVID-19 epidemic was not unifying Americans against a common threat, but rather further dividing us into hostile partisan camps. The presidential election of 2020 therefore promises to be a partisan slugfest that will strain and test the American electoral system and highlight many of the ongoing challenges to the American right to vote, especially those bearing upon voter confidence in elections and the integrity of American democracy.

Q29. IS VOTER FRAUD A SERIOUS PROBLEM IN THE MODERN UNITED STATES?

Answer: No. Various types of voter fraud, such as buying votes, intimidating voters, and manipulating absentee ballots, have been serious problems during various eras in the history of the United States, but today such instances occur infrequently and on a very small scale, and they rarely, if ever, change the outcome of a contemporary election, not even at the local level.

The Facts: Voter fraud, such as buying votes, has been a recurrent problem in U.S. electoral history. For example, in 1758 George Washington, who later became the first president of the United States, won his seat in Virginia's House of Burgesses by giving away 160 gallons of liquor to voters who supported him. Using alcohol to buy votes was a common practice well into the nineteenth century. One scholar has described the American polling place between 1851 and 1868 as "a kind of sorcerer's workshop in which the minions of opposing parties turned money into whiskey and whiskey into votes," an "alchemy" that "bought as many, and perhaps far more, votes than the planks in party platforms" (Bensel, 2004). As voting through much of the nineteenth century was not secret and the ballots were printed by the political party in a distinctive style, money incrementally became a more straightforward and effective means of buying votes than alcohol. The vote buyer did not have to expend any funds until the seller had done what he had promised to do. During the nineteenth century, New York City's Tammany Hall, a Democratic Party organization representing recently arrived immigrants, streamlined the process of vote buying by hiring a so-called "striker," someone who could deliver a large number of votes at one negotiated price. Boss Tweed, the leader of the Tammany Hall political machine during the 1860s, once admitted that he didn't "think there was ever a fair or honest election in the City of New York" (Fund, 2004).

The introduction of voting booths and the Australian ballot (one printed and distributed by the government, rather than by political parties) in the 1890s ended the tradition of public voting, which curbed somewhat the practice of brazenly exchanging votes for cash. However, urban political machines in the twentieth century continued to buy votes through a system of patronage. Political bosses such as James Curley of Boston (period of influence: 1914–1950), Ed Crump of Memphis (1915–1954), Frank Hague of Jersey City (1917–1947), Bill Thompson of Chicago (1915–1931), and Tom Pendergast of Kansas City (1925–1939) distributed public patronage to the various ethnic neighborhoods of their cities in accordance with their voting strength. The leader of each ethnic neighborhood would do the same for precinct captains, everyone taking a proportionate share. Because their interests were tied to the political boss, citizens at the bottom of the political machine voted as they were directed by the man at the top. Neither the secrecy of the voting booth nor the partisan neutrality of the Australian ballot eliminated this system of exchanging votes for patronage during the first half of the twentieth century.

Before the secret ballot became commonplace, voter intimidation, such as an employer pressuring an employee whether or how to vote, was also a serious problem. Such intimidation became a systemic practice in Southern states following the end of the Civil War as well. The Ku Klux Klan and other white vigilante groups assassinated black officials in the new Reconstruction governments and used savage violence to keep black voters and their white Republican allies from the polls. Whippings, burnings, mutilations, rapes, race riots, and lynchings were rampant. The situation went from bad to worse after federal troops were removed from the South at the end of Reconstruction in 1876. The Supreme Court was no help, ruling in *United States v. Cruikshank* (1876) that the federal government had no authority to prevent or punish the criminal acts of private white supremacist groups. The decision left African Americans at the mercy of state governments controlled by the white Democratic Party. A respected historian, Eric Foner, has called the era one of "counter-revolutionary terror" (Foner, 1988). The intensity of this system of voter intimidation did not decline appreciably until after the Supreme Court decided *Brown v. Board of Education* (1954) and Congress enacted the Civil Rights Act of 1964 and the Voting Rights Act of 1965. Voter intimidation did not disappear after those historic milestones, but the intervention of the federal government provided considerable relief and the degree of intimidation became less systemic and pervasive.

The election of 1960 suggests that voter fraud could possibly change the outcome of a presidential election, even if it is difficult to prove that this in fact happened. Democrat John F. Kennedy's lead over Republican Richard M. Nixon in the popular vote was just 118,574 out of the almost 69 million votes cast, but he won the Electoral College by a vote of

303–219. However, Kennedy's margin of victory in Illinois was just 8,800 votes and only 46,000 votes in Texas. If Nixon had won these two states instead of Kennedy, he would have won the Electoral College by a vote of 270–252. What made these results somewhat suspicious was that in Illinois, Nixon lost big in Chicago, which was controlled by Mayor Richard Daley, a Democrat and loyal supporter of Kennedy. Robert Dallek has pointed to the fact that Illinois's vote was mysteriously in before Chicago completed its tally. Dallek's inference is that Daley "probably stole Illinois from Nixon" by sending in votes not yet counted. However, Dallek concludes that Kennedy would have won in any case because his 46,000-vote lead in Texas "would have been more than the most skilled manipulator of returns could have hidden" (Zeitz, 2016).

However, Texas's Lyndon Baines Johnson was Kennedy's running mate. Johnson had a reputation for engaging in shady electoral practices, such as stuffing ballot boxes with fraudulent votes and not counting legitimate ones. Robert Caro, a prominent Johnson biographer, examined the evidence and concluded that he only won his Senate seat in 1948 through voter fraud. In addition, Kennedy's margin of victory in Texas in 1960 was especially large in counties under the control of George Parr, Johnson's friend and political ally. Nixon's partisans filed lawsuits challenging the election results in Illinois and Texas and several other states, but in the end they could not prove their case. Though Nixon publicly conceded the election, he claimed privately that "we won, but they stole it from us" (Zeitz, 2016). The truth about whether Nixon was the winner will likely never be known for sure, but the 1960 presidential election does show that voter fraud can plausibly have major consequences.

The presidential election of 2000 between Democrat Al Gore and Republican George W. Bush was highly controversial, but the major issue was the accuracy of vote-counting machines in Florida. A study of the election results by five Florida newspapers and other news organizations found a total of 60,647 undervotes and 111,261 overvotes: the former indicating the number of votes for either candidate that the machines failed to register, the latter the number of votes rejected by the machines because they registered a vote for more than one candidate. By examining these 171,908 ballots manually, the study found that the voter's intent could be determined in 18 percent of these rejected ballots. Poor ballot design (the so-called "butterfly ballot") explained a large percentage of the total number of rejected ballots. In addition, punch cards would not be counted by the machine unless the voter punched the hole cleanly. If the round piece of paper, dubbed a "chad," remained in the hole, then even a manual inspection of the ballot required a choice of a standard to determine the intent of the voter. The study determined that if a strict standard was used to count these punch-card ballots, then Bush would have won by a small margin, from 152 to 407 votes. Under a lenient standard, such that the smallest "dimple" on the chad counted as a vote, Gore would have won by 332 votes. However, Bush won the election before the completion of the above study because Gore never asked for a statewide recount of all the ballots, and the Supreme Court shut down the process, asserting in a 5–4 vote that broke down along partisan lines that what qualified as a legitimate vote in Florida's limited recount varied from one district to another—and thus constituted a violation of the Equal Protection Clause of the Fourteenth Amendment.

Accordingly, the contested presidential election of 2000 in Florida, which decided who won the state's twenty-five electoral votes, was arguably more a matter of voter error (poor ballot design, flawed vote-counting machines, and incompetent election officials) rather than voter fraud. In very close elections, such voting irregularities can change the electoral outcomes, but that does not make them equivalent to voter fraud (Cauchon, 2011). However, prior to the election, Florida also purged the voting rolls of all alleged felons using a haphazard list. Voting rights advocates contended that the purging process disfranchised many eligible voters, especially African Americans (see Q31). Whether this purge was free of all taint has not been conclusively established.

Florida election officials also counted absentee overseas ballots in an arbitrary manner by disqualifying flawed overseas ballots delivered to counties that voted for Gore, but including those from counties favoring Bush. The final tally included overseas ballots that violated state requirements because they lacked postmarks, because they were postmarked after the election, or because they were not signed. Accordingly, voter fraud may well have occurred in Florida's election, but the degree of such fraud was less than the amount of voter error, and it is not clear whether arbitrary miscounting of overseas ballots would have changed the outcome of the election (Barstow and van Natta, 2001).

Since the 2000 presidential election, the perception that voter fraud is a serious problem in the United States has grown steadily. The Heritage Foundation has supported this assertion, maintaining a database that contains 1,217 proven instances of voter fraud across the country. The Foundation does not purport the list to be comprehensive, but rather "just the tip of the iceberg" (Snead, 2019). The Brennan Center for Justice sponsored a 2017 analysis of Heritage's database, however, and found that only 105 of the instances of fraud occurred in the previous five years and 488 within the last ten years; that the number of cases of fraud is a "miniscule portion of the overall number of votes cast" during the time span of the database, which stretches back to at least 1948; and that it includes only forty-one cases involving noncitizens trying to vote or register to vote and only ten cases of voter impersonation fraud (see Q30) (Mehrbani, 2017).

A reasonable conclusion is that voter fraud occurs infrequently and sporadically around the country, mostly in local or state elections, and rarely comes close to changing the outcome of an election. Despite these realities, political rhetoric about voter fraud continues to flare up routinely. A good example is 2008 Republican candidate John McCain's accusation that ACORN, a nationwide community activist group that was associated with Democratic get-out-the-vote efforts, was committing "massive voter fraud" and was "on the verge of maybe perpetrating one of the greatest frauds in voter history in this country," one that "may be destroying the fabric of democracy." The reality was a bit more mundane: a number of ACORN employees had been convicted of submitting false voter registration forms in Colorado, Missouri, and Washington, but their goal was to get paid by ACORN for work they did not do, not in anticipation of committing voter fraud (Newsweek Staff, 2008).

Following his election in 2016, President Trump has repeatedly claimed that there was rampant voter fraud in the 2016 election. His assertion has been widely attributed to unhappiness with the fact that even though he secured the presidency through the Electoral College, he actually lost the popular vote to Democratic opponent Hillary Clinton by almost three million votes. The chair of the Federal Election Commission, Ellen Weintraub, a Democrat, has denied these claims, remarking, "There is no evidence of rampant voter fraud in 2016 or really in any previous election" (Edelman, 2019). The key word in Weintraub's denial is "rampant." Voter fraud continues to occur in the United States, but infrequently and sporadically, and usually with little or no effect upon the outcome of an election.

A recent example of voter fraud that did end with the invalidation of an election was the 2018 election in North Carolina's Ninth congressional district. In this contest, L. McCrae Dowless, Jr., a veteran campaign operative who had earlier worked for both Democratic and Republican candidates, ran an absentee ballot scheme to help elect Mark Harris, the Republican candidate. Dowless paid his friends, acquaintances, and relatives a few dollars for each absentee ballot request form or absentee ballot they could collect from local voters in Bladen County. He then had his minions fill out these forms and ballots and send them in small batches from different post offices to the board of elections before the deadline.

Harris ultimately won the election by a 905-vote margin, but election officials soon discovered that 61 percent of the absentee ballots from Bladen County favored Harris even though only 19 percent came from registered Republicans. Dowless's scheme of voter fraud quickly came to light and the State Board of Elections ordered a new election in February 2019. On July 30, a North Carolina grand jury indicted Dowless and seven others for voter fraud, including "the criminal mishandling of absentee ballots," a type of fraud that undermined "the integrity of the absentee ballot process and the public's confidence in the outcome of the electoral process" (Blinder, 2019).

Voting by absentee ballot may present more of an opportunity for fraud than voter impersonation at the polls, but the Dowless case hardly substantiates any claim that mail-in voting is rampant with fraud. In fact, all states use absentee ballots: two-thirds send a ballot to any voter who requests one; one-third require voters to provide a reason why they cannot vote in-person. However, in either case, voters vote by mail in every state in the country. The practice has become so normalized that five states have shifted to systems of all-mail elections: Colorado, Hawaii, Oregon, Washington, and Utah. However, even though voting by mail is commonplace, the COVID-19 epidemic set the stage for a gross distortion of its character. In March/April 2020, as many states began planning to expand their mail-in voting options as a way to keep their citizens safe during the November general election cycle, a myth began to circulate on social media that mail-in voting is saturated with fraud. How and why this falsehood took root is not entirely clear, but President Donald Trump is undoubtedly partly responsible. On April 7, he characterized mail-in voting as follows: "Mail ballots—they cheat. OK? There's a lot of dishonesty going along with mail-in voting." He added, "Mail ballots are a very dangerous thing for this country, because they're cheaters. They go and collect them. They're fraudulent in many cases" (Timm, 2020). Such statements are patently false. A 2012 *News21* review of voter fraud found only 491 cases of absentee voter fraud among 146 million registered voters over a ten-year period (*News21* Staff, 2012).

At a news conference, Trump revealed, perhaps inadvertently, why he had twisted the facts about the fraudulent nature of mail-in voting when he claimed that Democrats were in control of all mail-in states, implying that Democrats were using COVID-19 as an excuse to promote mail-in voting and "steal" the 2020 election. However, his claim that Democrats control all of the states that exclusively use mail-in voting is false as Colorado is purple and Utah is overwhelmingly red. Although not all Republicans are opposed to mail-in voting, many have joined Trump's crusade, along with conservative news media, and the results are reflected in a recent poll that reports two-thirds of Americans believe that voting by mail would increase voter fraud (Sheffield, 2020). As the epidemic surged, the Supreme Court issued an order on July 2 upholding two of Alabama's requirements for a valid absentee ballot in a July 14 primary runoff election: (1) a voter must show a copy of a photo ID when applying for a mail-in ballot, and (2) to his or her mail-in ballot, the voter must attach a signed affidavit attesting to its validity, one cosigned by either a notary public or two adult witnesses. The four dissenting justices, all of whom were appointed by Democratic presidents, favored abandoning these requirements, presumably on the ground that they unduly burdened vulnerable voters in the context of the COVID-19 epidemic. And so, while the Dowless case confirms that criminal voting fraud involving mail-in voting can occur, it is likely that Trump and other Republicans will continue to promote the myth that such fraud is rampant to discourage any relaxation of current rules governing mail-in voting regardless of the degree to which this myth undermines public confidence in elections. Second, it is doubtful that courts will require states to relax these rules during the upcoming election even though in-person voting will pose significant COVID-19 health risks.

FURTHER READING

Barstow, David, and van Natta, Don, Jr. "Examining the Vote; How Bush Took Florida: Mining the Overseas Absentee Vote." *The New York Times*, July 15, 2001, available at https://www.nytimes.com/2001/07/15/us/examining-the-vote-how-bush-took-florida-mining-the-overseas-absentee-vote.html.

Bensel, Richard Franklin. *The American Ballot Box in Mid-Nineteenth Century.* New York: Cambridge University Press, 2004.

Blinder, Alan. "Election Fraud in North Carolina Leads to New Charges for Republican Operative." *The New York Times*, July 30, 2019, available at https://www.nytimes.com/2019/07/30/us/mccrae-dowless-indictment.html.

Campbell, Tracy. *Deliver the Vote: A History of Election Fraud, an American Political Tradition 1742–2004.* New York: Carroll & Graft, 2005.

Cauchon, Dennis, and Drinkard, Jim. "Revisiting the Florida Vote: Final Tally." *USA Today*, May 11, 2001, available at https://usatoday30.usatoday.com/news/politics/2001-05-10-recountmain.htm#more.

Edelman, Adam. "FEC Chair Slams Trump's 'Baseless' Voter Fraud Claims." *NBC News*, August 19, 2019, available at https://www.nbcnews.com/politics/donald-trump/fec-chair-slams-trump-s-baseless-voter-fraud-claims-n1043951.

Foner, Eric. *Reconstruction, America's Unfinished Revolution, 1863–1877.* New York: Harper Perennial, 1988.

Fund, John. "How to Steal an Election." *City Journal*, Autumn 2004, available at https://www.city-journal.org/html/how-steal-election-12824.html.

Mehrbani, Rudy. "Heritage Fraud Database: An Assessment." *Brennan Center for Justice*, September 8, 2017, available at https://www.brennancenter.org/our-work/research-reports/heritage-fraud-database-assessment.

News21 Staff (data compiled by Corbin Carson). "Election Fraud in America." *News21*, August 12, 2012, available at https://votingrights.news21.com/interactive/election-fraud-database/.

Newsweek Staff. "Factcheck.org: The Truth about McCains' ACORN Accusations," October 17, 2008, available at https://www.newsweek.com/factcheckorg-truth-about-mccains-acorn-accusations-91853.

Sheffield, Carrie. "Two-Thirds of Americans Say Voting by Mail Would Increase Voter Fraud, Poll Finds." *Just the News*, April 30, 2020, available at https://justthenews.com/politics-policy/polling/poll-finds-23-american-voters-say-voting-mail-would-increase-voter-fraud.

Snead, Jason. "More Proof That Voter Fraud Is Real, and Bipartisan." *The Heritage Foundation*, August 28, 2019, available at https://www.heritage.org/election-integrity/commentary/more-proof-voter-fraud-real-and-bipartisan.

Timm, Jane C. "Trump Pushes False Claims about Mail-in Vote Fraud. Here Are the Facts." *NBC News*, April 10, 2020, available at https://www.nbcnews.com/politics/donald-trump/trump-pushes-false-claims-about-mail-vote-fraud-here-are-n1180566.

Tolchin, Martin. "How Johnson Won Election He'd Lost." *The New York Times*, February 11, 1990, available at https://www.nytimes.com/1990/02/11/us/how-johnson-won-election-he-d-lost.html.

Zeitz, Josh. "Worried about a Rigged Election? Here's One Way to Handle It." *Politico*, October 27, 2016, available at https://www.politico.com/magazine/story/2016/10/donald-trump-2016-rigged-nixon-kennedy-1960-214395.

Q30. DO STATE VOTER IDENTIFICATION (ID) LAWS HAVE ANY LEGITIMATE PURPOSE?

Answer: Yes. Voter ID laws can prevent voter impersonation, which is a type of voter fraud, and inspire public confidence in the integrity of U.S.

elections. However, "strict" voter ID laws, such as those that require a government-issued photo ID, negatively affect groups that are less likely to have the requisite ID, such as members of racial minorities, the poor, and the elderly.

The Facts: Voter ID laws have been around for some time, but they have become controversial since the early 2010s because they have become far more strict in character. In 1950, South Carolina was the first state to request that voters show an ID at the polls, but the requested ID only had to include the voter's name. Hawaii added such an ID requirement in 1970, Texas in 1971, Florida in 1977, and Alaska in 1980, but all these states permitted voters to cast regular ballots if they did not have an ID with them. In this early stage, support for such relaxed voter ID laws was bipartisan and there was no significant opposition to them. In response to the contentious 2000 election, Congress enacted the Help America Vote Act of 2002, which mandated that voters registering for the first time or reregistering in a new district must provide a driver's license or the last four digits of their social security number, but did not require an ID for a voter to cast a ballot. Three years later, in 2005, the bipartisan Commission on Federal Election Reform (CFER), cochaired by Democrat Jimmy Carter and Republican James A. Baker, III, recommended that states should require voters to show driver's licenses or personal ID cards established under the REAL ID Act of 2005. These IDs included one's name, date of birth, address, social security number, and proof of U.S. citizenship. The Commission recommended that REAL IDs be made widely available "without expense to any citizen." Any voter who arrived at the polls without such a REAL ID should, the CFER argued, be permitted to cast a provisional ballot, but their vote would not be counted unless they showed a proper form of ID within 48 hours (CFER, 2005).

The initial deadline for state compliance with the REAL ID Act was 2008, but in 2005 the Republican-controlled legislatures in Georgia and Indiana raised the bar higher than the REAL ID Act by requiring voters to present a government-issued photo ID before they could cast a ballot. Eligible voters were able to obtain a free state ID card at specified government offices, and voters without the proper ID had the option of casting a provisional ballot, one that would only be counted if the voter returned with a proper ID in a limited time period. These strict requirements gave voter ID laws a partisan character. Democratic groups condemned them for discriminating against groups whose members were less likely to have a driver's license, passport, or any other form of government-issued photo ID: the poor, racial minorities, and the elderly. It was simply a way, they argued, for Republicans to suppress the right to vote of those least likely to vote for them. Republicans responded that they were not denying any eligible voter the right to vote, but only attempting to prevent voter fraud.

The Democratic Party and several nonprofits representing the elderly, disabled, poor, and minority voters challenged Indiana's law in federal court, and the case made its way to the Supreme Court. In a 6–3 decision, *Crawford v. Marion County Election Board* (2008), the Court upheld Indiana's voter ID law, holding that it was "neutral" and "nondiscriminatory" and that the state's legitimate interests outweighed the burden of requiring that voters have a government-issued photo ID. The first interest that the Court addressed was "the legitimate interest in deterring and detecting voter fraud." Although there was no evidence that anyone has committed "in-person voter impersonation" at any polling place "in Indiana at any time in its history," the Court noted that there were "flagrant examples of such fraud in other parts of the country" and that Indiana had experienced other types of voter fraud. Indiana, the Court argued, also had an interest in protecting public confidence in the "integrity" and the "legitimacy" of representative government. Accordingly, even if little or no voter fraud in fact existed in Indiana, the voter photo ID law was yet justifiable because it might inspire public confidence in the state's elections.

In contrast to these valid and important state interests, the Court reasoned that the burden imposed on voters by requiring a government-issued voter ID would be for most citizens a mere "inconvenience," although it acknowledged that the burden would be "somewhat heavier" for "a limited number of persons." However, the Court had no way "to quantify either the magnitude of the burden on this narrow class of voters or the portion of the burden imposed on them that is fully justified." For this reason, it would be improper for the Court to honor the petitioners' request to invalidate the entire statute. This was so, the Court insisted, even if all the Republicans in Indiana's General Assembly voted in favor of the voter photo ID law and all the Democrats voted against it. The Court conceded that "partisan considerations may have played a significant role in the decision to enact" this law, but that was an insufficient basis to invalidate it. The Court could invalidate it only if the petitioners could establish that partisan considerations were the sole justification for Indiana's voter ID law. But as Indiana apparently also hoped to prevent voter fraud and inspire public confidence in elections, both of which were clearly "valid neutral justifications," the Court had no choice but to uphold the law even if "partisan interests may have provided one motivation for the votes of individual legislators."

Once the Supreme Court decided *Crawford*, Georgia was finally able to implement the voter photo ID law it had enacted in 2005. After the Republican Party swept the 2010 state elections, a number of "red" states, including Kansas, Mississippi, Tennessee, Texas, and one purple state, Wisconsin, adopted strict voter ID laws with minor variations. For example, Kansas permitted the use of a student ID card issued by an accredited postsecondary educational institution located in the state, while Tennessee rejected the use of all student IDs. Mississippi exempted voters who had religious objections to being photographed, while Texas did not, but instead waived the photo ID for those who were disabled.

Civil rights groups challenged a few of these strict voter ID laws in both state and federal court. Litigation on Texas's law was contentious and lengthy. A federal district court found the state legislature had enacted the initial law with discriminatory intent in 2014. The Fifth Circuit Court agreed that the law violated the Voting Rights Act, but eventually upheld a revised form of the law in 2018. The revised law allowed voters to use one of the seven forms of common ID, such as a pay check or utility bill, if they would file, under the penalty of perjury, a "reasonable impediment declaration" stating that they did not have the requisite photo ID for one of seven specified reasons. In addition, the revised law extended the period of time that an expired ID was acceptable and established mobile locations for citizens to obtain state IDs (*Veasey v. Abbott* [2018]).

Civil rights groups attacked other strict voter ID laws as violations of state law. For example, Pennsylvania's Republican-controlled legislature adopted a fairly strict voting photo ID law in 2012, one that permitted the use of certain types of IDs not issued by a government if the name on the ID "substantially" conformed to a name on the official registration list of voters. Relying on an earlier Pennsylvania Supreme Court ruling that any photo ID must "comport with liberal access" to the franchise, the Commonwealth Court of Pennsylvania invalidated the law. In the court's view, the law did not "pass constitutional muster" because there were too few locations where state photo IDs were available and the documentation required for these IDs was excessive. As the right to vote was "fundamental" under the state's Constitution, the only possible conclusion was that the law was unconstitutional because it made the right to vote "so difficult to exercise as to cause *de facto* disenfranchisement" (*Applewhite v. Pennsylvania* [2014]). Tom Corbett, Republican Governor of Pennsylvania, declined to appeal the ruling to the state's Supreme Court.

Despite this decision by Pennsylvania's Commonwealth Court, several states continued to enact and implement voting ID laws that were "strict" in nature, but others opted for nonstrict voter ID laws that did not require a photo or permitted photo IDs of most types, rather than a narrow class of government-issued photo IDs. The result was a spectrum of voter ID laws across the United States. As of January 2020, the National Conference of State Legislatures (NCSL) classifies seven states as having strict photo ID laws; three as strict nonphoto ID; ten as photo ID requested; fourteen as ID requested but photo not required; and sixteen as no physical ID required to vote. Accordingly, there are ten states that have strict voter ID laws and forty that do not. States with strict voter ID laws only permit voters without the required identification to cast a provisional ballot, one that requires the voter to take additional steps for the ballot to be counted. In contrast, nonstrict states permit the voter to cast a ballot that will be counted if election officials can determine voter eligibility without any additional action on the part of the voter (NCSL, 2020).

A key rationale for these voter ID laws continues to be that they prevent voter fraud, an offense that covers a variety of different types of conduct, such as double voting, vote buying, destroying ballots, false registration, and voter impersonation. The voter ID laws are aimed primarily at the last type of fraud. In such an instance, the impersonator pretends to be a registered voter at the polls, whether the person is a nonvoting eligible voter or a voter who is no longer eligible to vote because he or she is a felon, no longer living in the district, or dead. Studies conflict regarding how much election fraud of this type occurs in American elections. A 2007 report by the Brennan Center for Justice claims that voter impersonation at the polls is "an occurrence more rare than getting struck by lightning" (Levitt, 2007). However, in 2013, agents from the Department of Investigations in New York City pretended to be voters who should not have been allowed to vote, but they were able to cast ballots in sixty-one of sixty-three polling stations (Fund, 2014). But what this experiment proved is not clear: even if impersonating eligible voters might be easy, that does not prove that actual impersonation occurs frequently. A 2015 Heritage report, "A Sampling of Election Fraud Cases From Across the Country," argued that prosecuting election fraud was "essential to protecting the integrity of our voting process," but most of the fraud described in the report was fraudulent use of absentee ballots or other types of deception not involving voter impersonation. Only about a dozen cases of voter impersonation were uncovered from 2004 to 2015.

Although election fraud may occur in the United States, it is nonetheless far from clear that voter ID laws do much to address the problem. In fact, in terms of strict voter ID laws, it is very likely that they have suppressed more legitimate votes than the number of instances of voter impersonation, which suggests that they are arguably more problematic than the problem they are meant to solve. Voter ID laws impact turnout by preventing some people from voting and deterring others from even going to the polls. It is, of course, very difficult to find out how many potential voters are in the second category and who they are. One study has tried to address these questions by analyzing the 16,000 voters who were able to vote in Texas's 2016 election by filing a "reasonable impediment declaration" (about 0.18 percent of all votes cast), an option they did not have in the 2014 election. The study found that 11.4 percent of those voting in 2016 were African American voters, but 16.1 percent of the 16,000 voters who voted by filing a "declaration" were African American. A smaller but comparable disparity was found to exist with Latino voters, providing support for the argument that voter ID laws, depending on how strict they are, have a disparate impact on racial minorities (Fraga, 2018). A study of the effect of Michigan's voter ID law on racial minorities in the 2016 election provided additional evidence of a racial disparate impact (Henninger, Meredith, and Morse, 2018).

The overall conclusion is largely one of common sense: the more strict a voter ID law, the more it will have a negative impact on eligible voters of subgroups less likely to possess the requisite ID: racial minorities, the poor, and the elderly. However, despite this disparate impact on these groups, there is strong polling evidence that many Americans believe ineligible voters are yet casting votes (52 percent of Republicans, 33 percent of Independents, and 26 percent of Democrats) and that a photo ID should be required (95 percent of Republicans, 83 percent of Independents, and 63 percent of Democrats) (McCarthy, 2016). These poll numbers suggest that despite the lack of evidence of extensive voter impersonation as well as the disparate impact strict voter ID laws have on vulnerable populations, it is more than likely that many states will continue to enforce voter ID laws of different types for the foreseeable future. States that are Republican-controlled generally favor voter ID laws that are more strict, including those that require government-issued photo IDs, while those controlled by Democrats generally favor more lenient voter ID laws or none at all. Accordingly, one can expect that future changes in state voter ID laws will largely depend on unpredictable political outcomes at the state level.

FURTHER READING

Commission on Federal Election Reform (CFER). *Report: Building Confidence in U.S. Elections*. Washington, DC: Election Assistance

Commission, September 2005, available at https://www.legislationline.org/download/id/1472/file/3b50795b2d0374cbef5c29766256.pdf.

Fraga, Bernard L., and Miller, Michael G. "Who Does Voter ID Keep from Voting?" (A Working Paper), December 14, 2018, available at https://www.dropbox.com/s/lz7zvtyxxfe5if8/FragaMiller_TXID_2018.pdf?dl=0https://www.dropbox.com/s/lz7zvtyxxfe5if8/FragaMiller_TXID_2018.pdf?dl=0.

Fund, John. "Voter Fraud: We've Got Proof It's Easy." *National Review*, January 12, 2014, available at https://www.nationalreview.com/2014/01/voter-fraud-weve-got-proof-its-easy-john-fund/.

Henninger, Phoebe, Meredith, Marc, and Morse, Michael. "Who Votes Without Identification? Using Affidavits from Michigan to Learn about the Potential Impact of Strict Photo Voter Identification Laws." July 13, 2018, available at SSRN: https://papers.ssrn.com/sol3/papers.cfm?abstract_id=3205769.

Heritage Foundation. *A Sampling of Election Fraud Cases from across the Country*. Washington, DC: The Heritage Foundation, 2015, available at https://www.heritage.org/sites/default/files/voterfraud_download/VoterFraudCases_5.pdf.

Hopkins, Dan. "What We Know about Voter ID Laws." *FiveThirtyEight*, August 21, 2018, available at https://fivethirtyeight.com/features/what-we-know-about-voter-id-laws/.

Levitt, Justin. *The Truth about Voter Fraud*. New York: Brennan Center for Justice, 2007, available at https://www.brennancenter.org/sites/default/files/legacy/The%20Truth%20About%20Voter%20Fraud.pdf.

McCarthy, Justin. "Four in Five Americans Support Voter ID Laws, Early Voting." *Gallup News*, August 22, 2016, available at https://news.gallup.com/poll/194741/four-five-americans-support-voter-laws-early-voting.aspx.

National Conference of State Legislatures (NCSL). "Voter Identification Requirements/Voter ID Laws." February 24, 2020, available at http://www.ncsl.org/research/elections-and-campaigns/voter-id.aspx.

Q31. DOES THE FEDERAL CONSTITUTION REQUIRE STATES TO DISFRANCHISE CONVICTED FELONS?

Answer: No. The federal Constitution does not require disfranchisement of convicted felons. Individual states have discretion to decide if convicted felons should be denied the right to vote when they are in prison, on probation or parole, or for the rest of their lives.

The Facts: Today's practice of taking away a convicted felon's right to vote evolved from the medieval tradition of condemning a criminal as an "outlaw," which literally placed the felon outside the law. This penalty was a form of "civil death" that extinguished a felon's legal capacity, rendering him or her "dead in law" without any legal right or privilege, including the right to vote. The American colonists continued this practice of denying felons the right to vote to the point of disfranchising those who were convicted of fornication (Massachusetts) or drunkenness (Maryland). After independence and the ratification of the new Constitution, the right to vote came to be understood as a privilege, one that required evidence of good character, which was typically thought to be a sufficient reason to deny felons the right to vote. As new states came into the union during the nineteenth century, many of them followed this precedent, some limiting the disqualification to "infamous crimes" or crimes that were thought to exhibit an immoral character, such as forgery, bribery, and perjury. Constitutional amendments that barred states from denying the franchise on the basis of race, ethnicity, and sex did not prevent states from continuing the tradition of excluding convicted felons from the franchise, just as they did not bar states from denying the right to vote based on age, lack of residency, and illiteracy. There were few court cases challenging the practice of felon exclusion until the 1960s. It was widely and broadly accepted across the country; its constitutionality and legitimacy largely unquestioned (Ewald, 2002).

After Reconstruction, southern states broadened felon disfranchisement as an indirect way to remove African Americans from the voting rolls. For example, Mississippi revised the scope of its felon disfranchisement provision in its 1890 constitutional convention by shifting it from "infamous crimes," such as murder and robbery, to offenses that were thought to be committed more often by blacks than whites, such as petty larceny, fornication, miscegenation, and wife-beating. One Alabama judge estimated that the last exclusion alone disqualified two-thirds of black male voters, presumably because southern prosecutors had considerable discretion in deciding whether to prosecute cases involving domestic assault. White prosecutors were more likely to file charges against black defendants and drop them against white wife-beaters. Other southern states relied on vague disqualifications, such as crimes "involving moral turpitude," to ensure that the felon disfranchisement provision would be used for the purpose of racial discrimination (Ewald, 2002).

Even as the Supreme Court and Congress began to dismantle the Jim Crow society of southern states in the 1950s, the tradition of felony disfranchisement continued to disproportionately burden the suffrage rights of African Americans. This was true not only in southern states but across the country. As the economic, social, and cultural effects of past racial discrimination often channeled young African Americans, especially males, into innercity poverty, single-parent families, addiction, drug dealing, gangs, and homelessness, they typically committed more crimes than their white counterparts. Accordingly, even when its purpose was not racial discrimination, felon disfranchisement continued to have a detrimental impact on the voting power of the African American community throughout the second half of the twentieth century.

After the Warren Court invalidated a number of voter restrictions in the 1960s, such as the poll tax and the literacy test, the Supreme Court explicitly addressed the constitutionality of felon disfranchisement in *Richardson v. Ramirez* (1974). The question was whether California's voter disqualification of persons convicted of "infamous crimes" who had served their sentences and were no longer on parole was constitutional. The challengers of California's law claimed that such disfranchisement violated Section 1 of the Equal Protection Clause of the Fourteenth Amendment because voting was a fundamental right and the state had no compelling reason to deny it to felons off parole. The Court rejected this argument in its entirety in *Richardson*. It noted that twenty-nine states disqualified felons from voting at the time the Fourteenth Amendment was ratified, that Section 2 of the Amendment allowed denial of voting rights "for participation in rebellion, or *other crime* (emphasis added)," and that courts had indirectly approved voter disfranchisement on a number of occasions. In the Court's view, the "historical and judicial interpretation of the Amendment's applicability to state laws disenfranchising felons" is of "controlling significance in distinguishing such laws from those other state limitations on the franchise which have been held invalid under the Equal Protection Clause." Felon disfranchisement may be "outmoded," as the challengers of California's law claim, but it was consistent with the Equal Protection Clause and it was not for the Court "to choose one set of values over the other."

Felon disfranchisement became more problematic as the number of convicted American citizens increased in the 1980s and 1990s. In 1970, the number was 1,176,234, but by 1980, it was 3,342,586 and by 2000 5,358,282 (Uggen, Larson, and Shannon, 2016). The consequences of a criminal conviction on suffrage rights varied across the country. In 1997, forty-six states disfranchised offenders while they were in prison; thirty-two did so while they were on parole; twenty-nine while they were on probation; and ten states (Alabama, Delaware, Florida, Iowa, Kentucky, Mississippi, Nevada, New Mexico, Virginia, and Wyoming) for as long as felons were alive. It is noteworthy that neither incarceration nor felony conviction was necessary for such disfranchisement to occur. At the time, depending on state law, a person who pleaded guilty to a misdemeanor, such as passing a bad $150 check, might be sentenced only to probation but nonetheless could be barred from voting for life.

A felon could regain the right to vote, but the process was typically a challenging one. In 1997, ten states required either the governor of the state or the state parole board to take action, while in Florida an ex-felon was not eligible for a gubernatorial pardon until ten years after the completion of the sentence. In addition, state prison officials did not generally inform released inmates of the process for regaining their right to vote. Accordingly, few ex-felons knew they could get their voting rights restored and even fewer bothered to try. For example, Virginia during 1996 and 1997 restored the right to vote to only 404 of 200,000 ex-felons (Fellner and Mauer, 1998).

The contested 2000 presidential election in Florida triggered renewed public interest in felon disfranchisement. In this race, Republican George W. Bush defeated Democrat Al Gore by winning all of Florida's electoral votes on the basis of a few hundred ballots, even as more than 500,000 ex-felons living in the state were barred from voting. Many of these ex-felons were African American males who likely would have disproportionately voted for Gore, given the much greater support he enjoyed from African Americans, both in Florida and across the country. To aggravate matters further, before the election state officials had sent county election supervisors a list of over 50,000 persons who were to be purged from the voting rolls, including many who were mistakenly identified as ex-felons. In its report on the election, the U.S. Commission on Civil Rights (USCCR) concluded that 14.1 percent of the names on the purge list were inexact matches; that African Americans had a "significantly greater chance" of being on the list than whites; and, lastly, that the list "resulted in denying countless African Americans the right to vote" (USCCR, 2001). In short, not only were many Floridians barred from voting because they were ex-felons, but many African Americans were barred because they were mistakenly identified as ex-felons. If only a third of these voters had voted in the 2000 election, it is highly likely—if not a near certainty—that Gore would have beaten Bush in Florida and thereby won the presidency.

Governor Jeb Bush attacked the conclusions of the USCCR's report, but Florida's controversial 2000 election sparked a new wave of voting rights activism, including a movement to reform felon disfranchisement laws. After two decades of effort, progress toward easing the harshest restrictions has been slow but steady. For example, since 1997, seven states have repealed their laws disfranchising ex-felons for life or have at least modified them in the direction of expanding voting eligibility; six states have granted voting rights to persons under community supervision; and seventeen states have streamlined the process by which an ex-felon can regain his or her right to vote (McLeod, 2018).

The general results are as follows: on one side of the spectrum, Maine and Vermont allow incarcerated felons to vote; sixteen states immediately restore the voting rights of felons on their release from prison; twenty-one states bar felons from voting while they are incarcerated, on parole, or on probation, but not thereafter; and eleven states refuse to let ex-felons vote indefinitely for certain crimes (e.g., crimes involving moral turpitude or violent crimes) or for some period of time after fully completing their sentence. The states in this last category typically have a process by which an ex-felon can regain the right to vote, such as by receiving a governor's pardon (NCSL, 2019).

Despite the above reforms, the number of American citizens barred from voting because of their status as a felon has not declined. While approximately 4.7 million citizens were barred from voting in 2000, it is estimated that the number rose to 5.4 million in 2004, 5.9 million in 2010, and 6.1 million in 2016, which is about 2.5 percent of the total voting-age population of the United States. Obviously, the percentage of a state's population that are unable to vote is likely to be higher in states that have indefinite disfranchisement of felons. For this reason, Alabama, Florida, Kentucky, Mississippi, Tennessee, and Virginia have more than 7 percent of their adult population disfranchised based on felon status. Among this group, Florida was the extreme outlier, with over 1.5 million citizens disfranchised, which in 2016 was about one-quarter of the national disfranchised felon population.

The impact of disfranchisement on African Americans continues to be disproportionate, with one in thirteen who are of voting age disfranchised in 2016, which is four times greater (7.4 percent) than the average of all other citizens (1.8 percent). The percentages of disfranchised African Americans are particularly worrisome in certain states, such as Florida (21 percent), Kentucky (26 percent), Tennessee (21 percent), and Virginia (22 percent), but it is also noteworthy that twenty-three states in 2016 disfranchised 5 percent or more of their African American voting-age populations (Uggen, Larson, and Shannon, 2016).

The policy of disfranchising felons and ex-felons has partisan, class, and racial overtones, largely because ex-felons are drawn disproportionately from racial minorities and the poor, both of whom generally tend to vote for Democratic candidates. The contested 2000 presidential election in Florida magnified partisan implications of felon disfranchisement (Uggen and Manza, 2002) and these implications have not receded over the last twenty years. For instance, several of the Democratic presidential candidates in the 2020 election supported extending the right to vote to nonviolent offenders or to those who have been released from prison. In an April 23, 2019 virtual town meeting, Senator Bernie Sanders (D-VT) even endorsed the adoption of his home state's policy of permitting imprisoned felons the right to vote at the national level. Most Democrats refuse to go so far, unwilling to give the right to vote to terrorists, serial killers, and murderers incarcerated in prison, but they do support more moderate reforms, such as granting the right to vote to felons released from prison (Rakich, 2019).

Additional steps in the direction of enfranchising ex-felons may well take place, but there will also be resistance. For example, in the 2018 midterm election, Florida voters passed Amendment 4, which granted ex-felons who have completed their sentences (including parole and probation) the right to vote if they had not been convicted of murder or sex offenses. This amendment restored the voting rights to an estimated 1.2–1.5 million citizens, a significant percentage of the total number of 6.1 million ex-felons in Florida who were disfranchised in 2016. However, the Republican state legislature fought back in mid-2019, enacting a law that required ex-felons to pay all fines, fees, and restitution before they could reacquire their right to vote. Civil rights groups immediately challenged the law in state and federal court, but Republican Governor Ron DeSantis argued the new law properly implemented the amendment's provision that ex-felons must complete "all terms" of their sentences, which in his view included financial obligations ordered by courts. In January 2020, the Florida Supreme Court issued an advisory opinion in favor of DeSantis's view that "all terms" of a sentence included payment of financial obligations (Mower, 2020), but a federal district court ruled in May that the new law violated Equal Protection and constituted an unconstitutional poll tax. However, a few months later, on July 1, 2020, the 11th Circuit Court of Appeals suspended the lower court's ruling and granted Florida's request to hear the case, not by a three-judge panel but by all the 11th circuit judges (en banc). Accordingly, four months prior to a presidential election, the right of approximately 774,000 indigent Floridians with felony records to vote is uncertain and unknown (Wines, 2020).

Other states, such as Virginia, Colorado, and Connecticut, have recently lowered their restrictions on ex-felon voting (Rakich, 2019). In addition, in December 2019, the newly elected Democratic governor of Kentucky, Andy Beshear, signed an executive order restoring the right to vote to 140,000 residents who have completed their sentences for nonviolent crimes, leaving Iowa as the only state that strips all former felons of the right to vote. These developments suggest that the trend in favor of expanding the voting rights of ex-felons may well continue, but the process will be slow and uneven, with little prospect that most states will grant violent criminals in prison the right to vote in the foreseeable future.

FURTHER READING

Berman, Ari. "How the 2000 Election in Florida Led to a New Wave of Voter Disenfrachisement." *The Nation*, July 28, 2015, available at https://www.thenation.com/article/how-the-2000-election-in-florida-led-to-a-new-wave-of-voter-disenfranchisement/.

Ewald, Alec C. "'Civil Death': The Ideological Paradox of Criminal Disenfranchisement Law in the United States." *Wisconsin Law Review* 2002 (2002): 1045–1132.

Fellner, Jamie, and Mauer, Marc. *Losing the Vote: The Impact of Felony Disenfrachisement Laws in the United States.* Washington, DC: The Sentencing Project, 1998, available at https://www.sentencingproject.org/wp-content/uploads/2016/01/Losing-the-Vote-The-Impact-of-Felony-Disenfranchisement-Laws-in-the-United-States.pdf.

Manza, Jeff, and Uggen, Christoper. *Locked Out: Felon Disenfranchisement and American Democracy.* Oxford: Oxford University Press, 2006.

McLeod, Morgan. *Expanding the Vote: Two Decades of Felony Disenfranchisement Reforms.* Washington, DC: The Sentencing Project, 2018, available at https://www.sentencingproject.org/publications/expanding-vote-two-decades-felony-disenfranchisement-reforms/.

Mower, Lawrence. "State Supreme Court Agrees with Legislature: Felons Must Pay all Costs to Regain Vote." *Miami Herald*, January 16, 2020, available at https://www.miamiherald.com/news/politics-government/state-politics/article239355253.html.

National Conference of State Legislatures (NCSL). "Felon Voting Rights." October 14, 2019, available at http://www.ncsl.org/research/elections-and-campaigns/felon-voting-rights.aspx.

Rakich, Nathaniel. "How Americans—And Democratic Candidates—Feel about Letting Felons Vote." *FiveThirtyEight*, May 6, 2019, available at https://fivethirtyeight.com/features/how-americans-and-democratic-candidates-feel-about-letting-felons-vote/.

Uggen, Christopher, Larson, Ryan, and Shannon, Sarah. *6 Million Lost Voters: State-Level Estimates of Felony Disfranchisement, 2016.*

Washington, DC: The Sentencing Project, 2016, available at https:// www.sentencingproject.org/wp-content/uploads/2016/10/6-Million -Lost-Voters.pdf.

Uggen, Christopher, and Manza, Jeff. "Democratic Contraction? Political Consequences of Felon Disenfrachisement in the United States." *American Sociological Review* 67 (2002): 777–803.

United States Commission on Civil Rights (USCCR). *Voting Irregularities in Florida During the 2000 Presidential Election.* Washington, DC: Government Printing Office, June 2001, available at https://www.usccr .gov/pubs/vote2000/report/main.htm.

Wines, Michael. "As November Looms, So Does the Most Litigious Election Ever." *The New York Times,* July 7, 2020, available at https://www .nytimes.com/2020/07/07/us/2020-election-laws.html.

Q32. EVEN IF THERE ARE LEGITIMATE REASONS WHY STATES PURGE THEIR VOTER REGISTRATION LISTS, CAN SUCH PURGES BE USED TO SUPPRESS VOTING RIGHTS?

Answer: Yes. States purge their registration lists of voters to delete the names of voters who have died, moved to a different electoral district, or become ineligible to vote for some reason, but such purges have recently devolved into partisan attempts to suppress the rights of eligible voters.

The Facts: With the exception of North Dakota, which has no voter registration requirement, all states require voters to register prior to an election, although a handful permit voters to register on election day itself. Having accurate and up-to-date state registration lists is therefore an important interest because they reduce confusion at the polls and help to detect and deter voter fraud.

The National Voter Registration Act (NVRA), enacted by Congress in 1993, is the key federal law governing voter purges. The law identifies five valid reasons for purging a voter's name from the list: (1) request of the registrant; (2) a disfranchising criminal conviction; (3) mental incapacity; (4) death; and (5) change of residence. However, the NVRA requires that every state voter purge be "uniform, non-discriminatory, and in compliance with the Voting Rights Act of 1965." The federal Help America Vote Act of 2002 (HAVA) added the requirement that states must maintain statewide computerized voter registration databases that are accurate and regularly updated. Accordingly, state purges of registration lists are not in themselves problematic, but are rather required by federal law. The real concern is that states purge their lists responsibly so that eligible voters are not deprived of their right to vote.

Regarding these five grounds for removal of voters from registration lists, federal law does not generally require states to use specified sources of information to make a determination whether a voter can be removed. For example, some states use the Social Security Administration's Death Master File to decide if voters have died since the last election, but this file erroneously often includes the names of people who are still alive. Comparable problems arise with voters who are removed on the basis of felon disfranchisement or mental incapacity. Exclusion based on a change of residence is especially susceptible to error because approximately thirty million voting-age citizens move each year. Federal law permits such a removal if a registrant fails to respond to a notice sent by state election officials and then fails to vote in two federal elections. Sending the notice triggers the two-election rule. Mistakes are of course possible: there may be a typo in the notice's address, the voter's name may not be on the mailbox at the voting address, or the voter may be homeless, temporarily away from his or her residence, or may have separate mailing and residence addresses. Such a mistake can easily lead to the removal of the name of an eligible voter who, for whatever reason, does not vote in the next two federal elections. If that happens, a state may purge the name of the voter from the registration list and bar him or her from voting in the third election post notice.

A troublesome feature of voter purges is that states rarely announce publicly that election officials are implementing a systematic attempt to update the voter registration lists. Voters therefore do not generally know that they should be on the lookout for a possible notice from election officials. Another source of confusion is similar or identical names, especially now that states use computerized databases. The result is that computers are programmed to decide if a name on a list of disfranchised felons, say "John Smith," is the same person as "Johnny Smith" or "Jonathan Smith," assuming that both of these latter names appear on the voter registration list. Date of birth helps to determine which names refer to the same person, but it is not all that unusual for persons with very common surnames (e.g., Baker) to have the same date of birth, especially if the first name has a number of variations, such as Betty, Libby, Liz, Beth, or Elizabeth. Many states do not require exact matches of names before removing someone from the registration rolls. Obviously, the more a state permits inexact matches, the more likely the purge will contain numerous mistakes and errors.

The contested 2000 election in Florida brought the problem of voter purges for partisan purposes to the public's attention. An investigation by the *Palm Beach Post* in 2001 estimated that at least 1,100 eligible voters were wrongly purged on the ground that they were convicted felons, but other estimates were up to twenty times higher. In any case, if the number of voters wrongfully purged could have had their votes counted, it might have changed the outcome of the 2000 presidential election because George W. Bush won Florida's popular vote by a margin of only 537 votes.

Florida repeated its error in 2004, using a list of felons that contained the names of 48,000 Florida residents, but only 61 of the names were Hispanic, while more than 22,000 were African American. These figures were suspicious because black voters in Florida typically vote Democratic, while Hispanics tend to vote Republican. Republican election officials denied any partisan motivation, but curiously used race as one of the required matching criteria: if someone had the same name and date of birth as someone on the list of disfranchised felons, they would not be removed from the registration list if there was a racial discrepancy. However, Florida's registration list included the category of Hispanic, but the list of felons relied only on white, black, Asian, Indian, and unknown. If a felon was classified as white on the felon list, but as Hispanic on the voter registration rolls, he or she would not be removed, while an African American would be removed even if the names did not exactly match. Another problem was that the felon list included the names of thousands of felons who had been granted clemency and were therefore eligible to vote, but were not permitted to do so on election day (Fessenden, 2004).

A 2008 report by a nonpartisan policy institute found that a number of states were purging voter registration lists "through a process that is shrouded in secrecy, prone to error, and vulnerable to manipulation." In fact, the institute found that every recent purge it had reviewed "had been flawed." Along with Florida's 2004 purge, the report identified problems in New Jersey (2005), Kentucky (2006), Mississippi (2008), Georgia (2008), and Louisiana (2008). These states had engaged in poor "matching techniques," inaccurate determinations of voters who had moved to another state, unlawful purges within a week of an election, and felon lists that included the names of people who had never even received a parking ticket (Pérez, 2008).

In 2018, the institute published a follow-up report claiming that purge rates had risen over the last decade, presumably for partisan purposes. Between 2006 and 2008, a total of twelve million voters were removed, with the median jurisdiction purging 6.2 percent of voters and ninety-seven jurisdictions having purge rates above 15 percent. In contrast, between 2014 and 2016, a total of sixteen million voters were removed, with the number of jurisdictions above 15 percent climbing to 205. Of course, the larger number of removals increases the possibility that more eligible voters were removed in error. In this vein, the report found that since 2013 Florida, New York, North Carolina, and Virginia had conducted illegal purges, while Alabama, Arizona, Indiana, and Maine had adopted policies that violated NVRA by not giving notice to voters purged from the rolls and by conducting purges ninety days prior to an election. More than a quarter of registered voters live in these eight states (Brater et al., 2018).

It was in this context that the Supreme Court addressed the lawfulness of voter purges in *Husted v. A. Philip Randolph Institute* (2018), a case involving Ohio's removal of a voter for failing to vote for four years. The voter claimed his removal violated NVRA's failure-to-vote clause, but the Court in a 5–4 decision rejected this reasoning. According to the five conservative justices in the majority, the key fact was that Ohio had sent the voter a notice after a two-year period of voting inactivity and the voter had failed both to return the requisite card and to vote in either of the two successive federal elections. In contrast, "the Failure-to-Vote Clause, both as originally enacted in the NVRA and as amended by HAVA, simply forbids the use of nonvoting as *the sole criterion* for removing a registrant, and Ohio does not use it that way." Instead, "Ohio removes registrants only if they have failed to vote *and* have failed to respond to notice." In doing so, the majority concluded, "Ohio simply follows federal law" and the Court had "no authority to second-guess Congress or to decide whether Ohio . . . [has an] ideal method for keeping its voting rolls up to date." The latter conclusion was important because it suggested that states had considerable discretion to decide what evidence was sufficient to send a notice to a voter. Ohio's practice was to rely on two years of voting inactivity, but other states could rely on sources of evidence that were less reliable in character if they chose to do so.

One source of evidence that became popular among states was the Interstate Voter Registration Crosscheck Program (Crosscheck), which is a multistate database of voters registered in the states that share voter registration lists. Initiated by Kansas in 2005, the program at first had only three other states (Missouri, Iowa, and Nebraska) sharing registration lists to prevent "double voting" by the identification of voters registered in two states. Of course, the assumption that double registrations reflected double voting was dubious. Many Americans who move to a new state do not request the removal of their names from the voter rolls of their departure state. They don't do this because they have any intention of engaging in double voting, but rather because they were busy with the challenges of relocation and assumed that if they didn't vote in their old state of residence there would be no problem with voting in their new state of residence. As Crosscheck does not include reliable registration dates, neither the departure nor the arrival state knows which registration was the most recent. The result is that both states could remove the voter from its rolls, including the state in which the person is a legally eligible voter.

Another problem is that Crosscheck only includes the first name, last name, and date of birth of voters registered in a state. Because a multiple-states database is larger than the database of a single state, participation in Crosscheck significantly increases the likelihood of incorrect matches. For example, in 2017, with twenty-eight states participating in the program, Crosscheck reviewed 98 million voters and found 7.2 million "matches," which supposedly identified 3.6 million voters who were registered and possibly voting in two states. However, in a database of this size the statistical chances that two individuals will have the same name and birthdate "is sufficiently high as to be problematic." In fact, "Stanford professor Sharad Goel found that if applied nationwide, Crosscheck would 'impede 300 legal votes for every double vote prevented'" (Brater, Morris, Pérez, and Deluzio, 2018). Nevertheless, the Court's reasoning in *Husted* suggests that both states could arguably rely on Crosscheck matches to begin the process of purging voters from the rolls by sending out notices, regardless if both voters were eligible voters in their respective states or if one voter had simply moved to another state and had forgotten to request the removal of his or her name from the voting rolls of the departure state.

Indiana took an additional step. It enacted a law that permitted the removal of a voter flagged by Crosscheck without providing notice to the voter or waiting for two federal elections prior to removal. The state's argument was that a Crosscheck flag was equivalent to a registrant's "request" to be removed from Indiana's voting roll or a written confirmation that registrant had moved, either of which would render unnecessary the requisite notice or two-election waiting period. In 2019, the 7th Circuit Court of Appeals dismissed this reasoning and upheld an injunction against Indiana's enforcement of this voting purge law. First, the Court observed that the NVRA's language "at the request *of the registrant*" meant that "the registrant herself makes the request to the state." The Court added, "We cannot twist that language to encompass indirect information from a third-party database." In a similar vein, the Court denied that a Crosscheck flag constituted written confirmation that a voter had moved to another state. In its view, removal violates NVRA "unless *the registrant* confirms in writing that the registrant has changed residence." Crosscheck was obviously "not the resident, nor is it the resident's agent." In closing, the Court emphasized that the NVRA "is designed to ensure that the competing interest in preventing abuse does not wind up disfranchising American voters." The 7th Circuit seemed to imply that Indiana's invalid law had leaned more in the direction of suppressing the voting rights of its citizens than preventing voter fraud.

The nature of recent voter purges has varied considerably. Early in 2019, Texas's chief election officer gave local officials a list of ninety thousand names of "suspected" noncitizens as part of what he described as an effort to clean up the state's voter rolls, but a federal judge held that only eighty persons on the list were in fact questionable. The judge argued that "perfectly legal naturalized Americans were burdened with what the Court finds to be ham-handed and threatening correspondence from the state" (Chokshi, 2019). A few months after this ruling, David Whitley, the state's chief election officer responsible for the purge, resigned. He did so after the state legislature, responding to pressure from voting rights groups, adjourned without confirming his appointment as Texas's secretary of state.

Ohio tried a new approach: during the summer of 2019, it released to voting rights groups, such as the League of Women Voters, the names of 235,000 voters it proposed to remove from its voting list. These volunteers found the list saturated with error: it contained over forty thousand eligible voters, almost one in five names (Casey, 2019). In December 2019, a federal judge in Georgia upheld the plan to remove one hundred thousand names of inactive voters from the state's voter rolls. However, Georgia had given voter notice and, consistent with the NVRA, only voters who had not voted for the past five years were removed (Brown, 2019). Finally, in January 2020, the Wisconsin Court of Appeals halted a purge of more than two hundred thousand voters, approximately 6 percent of the state's voters. As Wisconsin is a battleground state that President Donald Trump won by less than twenty-three thousand votes, the purge had a clear partisan character, especially because it was the Wisconsin Institute for Law and Liberty, a conservative organization, that sued to force Wisconsin's Elections Commission to purge the rolls, something that the three Democrats on the Commission refused to do but that the three Republicans supported. A local newspaper found that most of the persons on the list lived in municipalities that had supported Hillary Clinton in 2016 (Thebault, 2020). Such partisan controversies will likely be a prominent feature of the 2020 presidential race, with the Republican Party prioritizing purging voter lists to keep ineligible voters from voting and the Democratic Party prioritizing not purging voter lists to protect the voting rights of eligible voters.

FURTHER READING

Brater, Jonathan, Morris, Kevin, Pérez, Myrna, and Deluzio, Christopher. *Purges: A Growing Threat to the Right to Vote*. New York: Brennan Center for Justice, 2018, available at https://www.brennancenter.org/sites/default/files/2019-08/Report_Purges_Growing_Threat.pdf.

Brown, Elisha. "Federal Judge Backs Georgia's Purge of Nearly 100,000 Voters." *The New York Times*, December 27, 2019, available at https://www.nytimes.com/2019/12/27/us/elections/georgia-voters-purge.html.

Casey, Nicholas. "Ohio Was Set to Purge 235,000 Voters. It Was Wrong about 20%." *The New York Times*, October 14, 2019, available at https://www.nytimes.com/2019/10/14/us/politics/ohio-voter-purge.html.

Chokshi, Niraj. "Federal Judge Halts 'Ham-Handed' Texas Voter Purge." *The New York Times*, February 28, 2019, available at https://www.nytimes.com/2019/02/28/us/texas-voter-rolls.html.

Fessenden, Ford. "Florida List for Purge of Voters Proves Flawed." *The New York Times*, July 10, 2004., available at https://www.nytimes.com/2004/07/10/us/florida-list-for-purge-of-voters-proves-flawed.html.

Pérez, Myrna. *Voter Purges*. New York: Brennan Center for Justice, 2008, available at https://www.brennancenter.org/sites/default/files/2019-08/Report_Voter-Purges-2008.pdf.

Thebault, Reis. "Court Blocks Planned Purge of More Than 200,000 People from a Swing State's Voter Rolls." *The Washington Post*, January 14, 2020, available at https://www.washingtonpost.com/politics/2020/01/14/court-blocks-planned-purge-more-than-200000-people-swing-states-voter-rolls/.

Q33. IS IT CONSTITUTIONAL FOR A STATE TO REQUIRE THAT AN ELECTOR OF THE ELECTORAL COLLEGE PLEDGE TO VOTE FOR THE PRESIDENTIAL CANDIDATE WHO WON THE STATE'S POPULAR VOTE AND PUNISH THE ELECTOR IF THE PLEDGE IS NOT HONORED?

Answer: Yes. The Supreme Court decided many years ago that it is constitutional for a state to require an elector to pledge to vote for the presidential candidate who won the state's popular vote and has recently upheld the state's power to punish a "faithless elector" who has not honored his or her pledge.

The Facts: Article II of the Constitution requires each state to appoint presidential electors equal to the number of senators and representatives to which it is entitled "in such manner as the Legislature thereof may direct" (see Q1). At first, several state legislatures directly appointed electors, but in the course of the nineteenth century, all the states delegated this function to popular elections, whether they were statewide contests or by districts. The process worked as follows: each political party would select a slate of elector nominees and the popular election of the candidate would determine which slate won. Political parties typically selected their slate of electors at state party conventions or, alternatively, party leaders simply picked the electors. Today, the general rule is that the winner of the statewide popular election determines which party's slate of nominees become the state's electors: a winner-take-all system. The only exceptions are Maine and Nebraska. In these two states, two electoral votes are allocated to the winner of the state's popular vote, but other electoral votes are allocated to the winner of the popular vote in each of the state's congressional districts (of which Maine has two and Nebraska three). In either case, whether electors are chosen in a statewide contest or by districts, the expectation is that each elector, if his or her party's candidate won the popular vote, will cast a vote for that candidate. However, this expectation has not always been fulfilled. It is estimated that there have been 167 so-called "faithless electors" who have cast their electoral votes for someone other than their party's candidate. Although none of these faithless electors have changed the outcome of a presidential election, such a possibility exists. Experts agree that if it occurred, it would not only cause an uproar but trigger a constitutional crisis.

Samuel Miles, a member of the Federalist Party, was the first faithless elector in American history. He voted for Democratic-Republican Thomas Jefferson in 1796 instead of John Adams, the Federalist candidate. As Jefferson lost by three electoral votes, Miles did not change the outcome of the election, but the margin was uncomfortably close. In landslide elections, whimsy can play a part in why an elector does not vote as expected. For example, in 1820, William Plummer, Sr. voted for John Quincy Adams, who was not a presidential candidate, instead of his party's unopposed candidate, James Monroe. Plummer cast his vote for Adams because he was of the view that only George Washington deserved a unanimous vote of the Electoral College. In 1836, twenty-three Democratic electors from Virginia refused to vote for their party's vice presidential candidate because he allegedly lived with an African American woman, making it impossible for the candidate to receive a majority of the electoral votes, which transferred the choice of who would become vice president to the Senate. Preston Parks, a Democrat, refused to vote for Harry Truman in 1948, deciding instead to support Strom Thurmond, the candidate of the States Rights Party who received only 3 percent of the popular vote. Republican Henry D. Irwin in 1960 voted for Harry F. Bird and Barry Goldwater because he "could not stomach" Richard Nixon. Faithless electors also refused to vote for Nixon in 1968 and 1972, giving him the honor of having lost the votes of faithless electors in three separate presidential elections (FairVote, n.d.).

The framers of the Constitution may not have been shocked at the number of faithless electors because they believed presidential electors should exercise their independent judgment in how they voted. For example, Alexander Hamilton wrote in *Federalist No. 68* that the immediate election of the President

> should be made by men most capable of analyzing the qualities adapted to the station, and acting under circumstances favorable to deliberation, and to a judicious combination of all the reasons and inducements which were proper to govern their choice. A small group of persons, selected by their fellow-citizens from the general mass, will be most likely to possess the information and discernment requisite to such complicated investigations.

According to Hamilton, electors were to make a "choice" based on their elevated understanding of the qualifications for presidential office and their insight into the character and attributes of the candidates; they were not simply to mechanically ratify the people's choice. The Supreme Court accepted this understanding of the Founders' intent in *McPherson v. Blacker* (1892), commenting that "electors would exercise reasonable independence and fair judgment in the selection of the chief executive." However, the Court added that the country's experience has "demonstrated that . . . [electors] were so chosen simply to register the will of the appointing power in respect of a particular candidate." For this reason, the Court concluded that in terms of the "independence of the electors, the original expectation may be said to have been frustrated." By the end of the nineteenth century, it was widely believed that electors should vote for the candidate of the party they represented, which meant, by this time, voting for the winner of a popular election.

During the twentieth century, states began to require presidential electors to vote for their party's candidate. This requirement was clearly meant to discourage faithless electors. However, the nature of this requirement varied considerably from state to state; some state laws proclaimed that electors must vote for their party's candidate, while others required electors to sign an oath or a pledge. Other states assumed that a faithless vote rendered the elector's position vacant, one that could then be filled by a faithful elector.

The constitutionality of requiring a pledge came before the Supreme Court in *Ray v. Blair* (1952). This case considered whether the Executive Committee of Alabama's Democratic Party could refuse to certify a potential presidential elector who refused to sign a pledge that he would "aid and support" the party's nominees for president and vice president. The Court's majority opinion argued that nothing explicit in the Constitution "forbids a party to require from candidates in its primary a pledge of political conformity with the aims of the party." Moreover, the "long continued practical interpretation of the constitutional propriety of an implied or oral pledge of his ballot by a candidate for elector as to his vote in the electoral college weights heavily in considering the constitutionality of a pledge, such as the one here required." Even if such a pledge may be "legally unenforceable because violative of an assumed constitutional freedom of the elector under the Constitution," it did not follow that the requirement of a pledge itself was unconstitutional. Requiring a pledge is not equivalent to enforcing one. The Court therefore found "no federal constitutional objection to the requirement of this pledge."

Following the Court's decision in *Ray*, more states began to require pledges from presidential electors, which in time eventually produced today's ratio: thirty-two states (plus the District of Columbia) require them; eighteen states do not. Of the thirty-two states that require them, eleven provide for the faithless elector's vote to be cancelled or the elector replaced, or both, and four impose a penalty (FairVote, n.d.). Of course, *Ray* did not decide one way or the other if a state could enforce an elector's pledge, whether by cancellation of the vote or by fine or some other form of punishment. Accordingly, given the number of states that require no pledge and the number that require a pledge but provide no means of enforcement, one or more faithless electors could yet cause a constitutional crisis. Such an outcome may be unlikely, but it is not farfetched. For example, in 2016, ten electors broke ranks: eight Democratic electors voted for Bernie Sanders, John Kasich, Colin Powell, and Faith Spotted Eagle, a Native American activist and politician, instead of Hillary Clinton, the Democratic candidate, while two Republican electors opted for Kasich and Ron Paul, instead of Donald Trump, the Republican candidate. Although three of these votes were immediately invalidated, seven were counted. It is not inconceivable that seven electoral votes could change the outcome of a closely contested presidential election.

The state of Washington imposed a $1,000 fine on three of the 2016 faithless Democratic electors (Levi Guerra, Esther John, and Peter Chiafalo), all of whom challenged the constitutionality of the penalty, claiming that it violated Article II and the Twelfth and First Amendments. In May 2019, the Supreme Court of Washington rejected their challenge in *In re Guerra* (2019). The electors first argued that because they performed a federal function in casting their electoral votes, the fine was unconstitutional based on *McCulloch v. Maryland* (1819), a landmark decision holding that the Supremacy Clause prohibited a state from taxing the national bank of the United States. Without denying that presidential electors perform a federal function, the state high court noted that the Constitution itself "explicitly confers broad authority on the state to dictate the manner and mode of appointing presidential electors" and that "nothing in article II, section 1 suggests that electors have discretion to cast their votes without limitation or restriction by the state legislature." In similar fashion, the "Twelfth Amendment simply requires the electors to meet at the specified date and time outlined by Congress and to cast two votes for qualified candidates—one for president and one for vice-president." It "does not limit a state's authority in adding requirements to presidential electors," including the authority "to impose a fine on electors for failing to uphold their pledge." For this reason, the court concluded, it was incorrect to claim that the Twelfth Amendment "demands absolute freedom for presidential electors." Lastly, the state court ruled that the First Amendment was not "implicated when an elector casts a vote on behalf of the State in the Electoral College." This was so because the "power of electors to vote [for a presidential candidate] comes from the State, and the elector has no personal right to that role," implying that an electoral vote was a vote of the state, not of the individual voter.

Three months after this state decision, the federal 10th Circuit Court of Appeals came to the opposite conclusion. Colorado's Department of State decided to remove Michael Baca, a 2016 faithless Democratic elector, from his position and discard his vote for John Kasich. The Circuit Court began its analysis of the constitutionality of the penalty imposed on Baca by observing that "*Ray* does not address restrictions placed on electors after appointment or actions taken against faithless electors who have performed their federal function by voting for a different presidential or vice presidential candidate than those they pledged to support." Setting aside this precedent, the Court found that the Supremacy Clause of the Constitution "immunizes all federal functions from limitations or control by the states," including the federal function of a presidential elector. Accordingly, Colorado could remove Baca from his position and discard his vote only if the federal Constitution "expressly permits such acts," which the Constitution did not do. In the Circuit Court's view, Article II granted state legislatures plenary power to appoint electors, but this power does not "include the ability to remove electors in punishment for anomalous votes." In addition, crucial terms used in the Twelfth Amendment, such as "'elector," "vote," and "ballot," have "a common theme: they all imply the right to make a choice or voice an individual opinion." The 10th Circuit Court concluded that "the Constitution ensures that electors are free to perform that federal function with discretion, as reflected in the Twelfth Amendment's use of the terms 'elector,' 'vote,' and 'ballot.'"

Chiafalo and Colorado's Department of State appealed to the Supreme Court, which granted review and, in a unanimous decision, affirmed the Washington Supreme Court's view that "faithless electors" can be punished in *Chiafalo v. Washington* on July 6, 2020. Justice Kagan wrote the majority opinion, one that relied heavily on the "Constitution's text and the Nation's history" to justify the outcome. While the language of Article II describing the role of the Electoral College includes the terms "elector," "vote," and "ballot," these terms, according to Kagan, do not always imply an independent exercise of discretion. In contrast, the Constitution clearly states that each state will appoint electors "in such Manner as the Legislature thereof may direct," which includes a power to condition the appointment, not just by requiring a pledge but also by enforcing the pledge on "pain of penalty." History supports this understanding of the Constitution's text because a "long settled and established practice" may have "great weight in a proper interpretation of constitutional provisions." In this vein, "our whole experience as a Nation," Kagan argues, points in the direction of upholding a state's power to punish faithless electors. In her view, two centuries of experience confirms that "electors are not free agents; they are to vote for the candidate whom the State voters have chosen." Members of the Electoral College therefore "have no ground for reversing the vote of millions of its citizens." That is the only possible conclusion, Kagan concludes, that "accords with the Constitution—as well as the trust of a Nation that here, We the People rule."

The Supreme Court has therefore finally put to rest the question whether a handful of faithless electors could change the outcome of a presidential election. Obviously, such an outcome, had it occurred, would have been a national nightmare. It is somewhat remarkable that this question remained unanswered more than two centuries after the Constitution's ratification, but it has now been finally settled. States are now free to penalize faithless presidential electors, whether by invalidating their votes, replacing them as electors, or imposing a fine or some other penalty. Despite today's partisan polarized environment and concerns about election integrity, an ultimate principle underlying the Court's unanimous decision in *Chiafalo* is clear and straighforward: "here, We the People rule." Even if this principle justifies punishing faithless electors, it is somewhat ironical that the Court invokes it in a decision regarding the Electoral College, an institution marked by well-known undemocratic features (see Q13).

FURTHER READING

Alexander, Robert M. *Presidential Electors and the Electoral College: An Examination of Lobbying, Wavering Electors, and Campaigns for Faithless Votes*. Amherst, NY: Cambria Press, 2012.

FairVote. "Faithless Electors" and "Faithless Elector State Law." n.d., available at https://www.fairvote.org/the_electoral_college#how_the_electoral_college_works_today.

Goldfeder, Jerry H. "Election Law and the Presidency: An Introduction and Overview." *Fordham Law Review* 85 (2016): 965–999.

Gouzoules, Alexander. "The 'Faithless Elector' and 2016: Constitutional Uncertainty after the Election of Donald Trump." *University of Florida Journal of Law and Public Policy* 28 (2017): 215–240.

Liptak, Adam. "Supreme Court to Hear Timely Case on Electoral College Voters." *The New York Times*, January 17, 2020, available at https://www.nytimes.com/2020/01/17/us/supreme-court-electoral-college.html.

Rossiter, Clinton, ed. *The Federalist Papers*. New York: Mentor, 1961.

Sheppard, Stephen M. "A Case for the Electoral College and for Its Faithless Elector." *Wisconsin Law Review* 2015 (2015): 1–11.

Whittington, Keith E. "Originalism, Constitutional Construction, and the Problem of Faithless Electors." *Arizona Law Review* 59 (2017): 903–945.

Williams, Norman R. "Reforming the Electoral College: Federalism, Majoritarianism, and the Perils of Sub-Constitutional Change." *Georgia Law Journal* 100 (2011): 173–248.

Q34. IS THERE ANY WAY TO CIRCUMVENT OR ABOLISH THE ROLE OF THE ELECTORAL COLLEGE IN PRESIDENTIAL ELECTIONS IN FAVOR OF A NATIONAL POPULAR VOTE?

Answer: Yes. Although a constitutional amendment abolishing the Electoral College is very unlikely, the role of the college might be circumvented if state legislatures controlling 270 or more electoral votes committed themselves to casting these votes in favor of the presidential candidate who won the national popular vote.

The Facts: The major concern about the Electoral College is that it permits a candidate to win a presidential election even though he or she has lost the nationwide popular vote. This result has happened five times in American history, including in 2000 and 2016, primarily because forty-eight of the states give *all* their electoral votes to the candidate who receives the most votes statewide, a system known as "winner-take-all." Over the last several decades the level of support for abandoning this state-based "winner-take-all" system in favor of a nationwide popular vote has generally ranged between 55 percent and 66 percent, with members of both major political parties in favor of the switch. For example, prior to the 1968 presidential election, 66 percent of Republicans and 64 percent of Democrats favored abolishing the Electoral College (Newport, 2001). The next year the House passed a proposed amendment to make the shift to a popular presidential election by a vote of 339–70, with both parties solidly behind the measure, but the effort died in the Senate. Small-state senators of both parties filibustered the proposed amendment and it never got to the floor for a vote.

Small states benefit from the Electoral College as they get two electoral votes, one for each senator, regardless of the size of their populations. In the end, this reality is why the 1969 amendment did not come close to passing. The likelihood of an amendment has become even less likely as partisan polarization increased during the 1980s and 1990s and as the Republican Party expanded its control over state legislatures across the country in the twenty-first century. For example, after the 2016 elections, the Republican Party controlled all three branches of twenty-six state governments (referred to as "trifectas"), while Democrats had this degree of dominance in only six. As of January 2020, following losses in 2018 and 2019, Republicans have twenty-one trifectas, while Democrats increased their number to fifteen. However, based on the 2018 elections, Republicans in 2020 yet control thirty-two state legislatures, while Democrats control only thirteen. Lastly, of the twenty least populated states, twelve state legislatures are controlled by Republicans, six by Democrats, and two (Nebraska and Maine) are identified as split or nonpartisan (Mahoney, 2020). Accordingly, any move to a popular presidential election would mean that the Republican Party would lose a significant degree of its influence over presidential elections, which is why the Electoral College has become a partisan issue: Republicans supporting it, Democrats opposing it (Vasilogambros, 2019). In 2000, 73 percent of Democrats favored an amendment in comparison to 46 percent of Republicans, but in 2017, the gap widened, with 81 percent of Democrats in favor of abolishing the Electoral College, but only 19 percent of Republicans. These percentages coincide with the fact that twice in the past five presidential elections the Republican candidate (George W. Bush in 2000 and Donald J. Trump in 2016) won a majority of the votes of the Electoral College even though they lost the popular vote. Accordingly, substantial partisan obstacles stand in the way of any constitutional amendment eliminating the Electoral College.

In the aftermath of the 2000 presidential election, critics of the Electoral College began to explore whether it would be possible to circumvent it without going through the rigorous process of proposing, passing, and ratifying a constitutional amendment. These discussions led to the National Popular Vote Initiative (NPVI), which in 2006 proposed an interstate compact that would commit its members to appoint presidential electors pledged to the candidate who won the nationwide popular vote. If a state joined this compact, then the state's legislature would not appoint electors pledged to the candidate who won the state's popular election, but rather the candidate who won the national popular vote. States could join the compact at any time, but the agreement would not go into effect until states with a majority of electoral votes (270 or more) had joined the initiative.

Proponents of the NPVI argued that it would (1) forever eliminate the possibility of electing a president who was not supported by most American voters; (2) place equal value on every vote across the country; (3) encourage candidates to pay attention to all states, not just those often called "battleground" states; (4) increase voter turnout because voters would be assured that their vote would not be buried in a "winner-take-all" state-based system; and, finally, (5) restore trust in American elections and the legitimacy of U.S. democratic institutions. Opponents of the proposal responded that the NPVI would (1) be an "end run" around the Constitution, violating both its letter and spirit; (2) elect a plurality winner of the nationwide popular vote, while the Electoral College required a majority vote of the electors; (3) diminish the status of states in the constitutional structure; (4) undermine a president's authority if his or her margin of victory in the popular vote was paper thin; and, lastly, (5) lead to more contested elections in every voting precinct in the country if the margin of victory in the nationwide vote was small.

Only Maryland joined the NPVI in 2007; followed by New Jersey, Illinois, and Hawaii in 2008; Washington in 2009; Massachusetts and the

District of Columbia in 2010; Vermont and California in 2011; Rhode Island in 2013; New York in 2014; Connecticut in 2018; and Colorado, Delaware, New Mexico, and Oregon in 2019. Together, these jurisdictions account for 196 electoral votes, 74 less than the 270 required for the agreement to go into effect. It is worth noting that, as of January 2018, no "red" state controlled by the Republican Party has agreed to join this initiative, although three "purple" states (New York, Colorado, and Connecticut) have joined the pact (Mahoney, 2020). However, one legislative chamber in nine additional states in control of eighty-eight electoral votes (Arkansas, Arizona, Maine, Michigan, Minnesota, North Carolina, Nevada, Oklahoma, and Virginia) has passed the NPVI and legislative committees have approved it unanimously in two other states in control of twenty-seven electoral votes (Georgia and Missouri) (see https://www.nationalpopularvote.com/state-status). Accordingly, it is arguable that there are currently 115 electoral votes in play and the NPVI only needs 74 of them to go into effect. It, therefore, may seem that the prospects for the NPVI are bright, but it may also be true that this initiative will encounter more resistance the closer it gets to the 270 threshold.

The NPVI will have a difficult time convincing Republican "red" states to join the initiative unless the Democrats are able to flip both houses of several state legislatures. In this regard, it is noteworthy that Virginia's Democratic Party in 2019 was able to flip the state legislature, one the Democrats had not controlled since 1994. It is therefore possible that the Democrats will "flip" additional state legislatures in the 2020 election, thereby increasing the possibility that the NPVI might be successful, but it would be too much to say that such a result is likely, much less a sure thing. At the same time, "purple" states with a substantial number of electoral votes, such as Michigan, Ohio, Florida, Wisconsin, or Pennsylvania, may also be reluctant to join the NPVI because, as "battleground" states, they receive a substantial amount of attention from both Republicans and Democrats under the existing "winner-take-all" system. Moreover, opposition has begun to build against the NPVI. Legislators in Connecticut, Hawaii, Maryland, Massachusetts, New Jersey, and Washington have introduced legislation to repeal membership in the NPVI. In addition, an advocacy group in Colorado, "Protect Colorado's Vote," has initiated a referendum repealing membership on the 2020 ballot. Although no state has yet withdrawn from the NPVI, it is likely that opponents will commence similar countermeasures if and when the NPVI comes closer to its goal of controlling 270 electoral votes. And even if the NPVI goes into effect, a state legislature, if it does not support the winner of the nationwide popular vote, might attempt to withdraw from the agreement based on its constitutional authority to change "the manner" of appointing presidential electors. It is doubtful whether any interstate compact can set aside this authority, even during a presidential election, if the change in "the manner" of appointment occurs before presidential electors cast their votes, which typically takes place on January 6 after the November election.

Contemporary public opinion polls on the NPVI are split: a March 27, 2019 *Politico/Morning Consult* poll reported a 43 percent to 33 percent preference for the NPVI over the current Electoral College, with 23 percent having no opinion. In contrast, a May 2019 Gallup poll found that 55 percent to 43 percent favored a constitutional amendment abolishing the Electoral College, but that only 45 percent favored the NPVI in contrast to 53 percent who opposed it (Neale and Nolan, 2019). Of course, these conflicting polling results may reflect shifts in public opinion or subtle differences in the specific questions asked of the respondents in the two polls. In either case, the overall conclusion is that the future of the NPVI is uncertain and unpredictable.

However, even if Democratic victories in the 2020 elections encourage additional states to join the NPVI and thereby trigger its implementation, it is likely that Republicans will go to court to stop the initiative. The foremost legal objection to the NPVI is based on the fact that Article I of the Constitution provides that "no State shall, without the Consent of Congress . . . enter into any Agreement or Compact with another State." In *Cuyler v. Adams* (1981), the Supreme Court noted that the purpose of this clause was "to ensure that Congress would maintain ultimate supervisory power over cooperative state action that might otherwise interfere with the full and free exercise of federal authority." Such interstate compacts are not uncommon, numbering approximately two hundred in 2019, and they are quite diverse, addressing such issues as boundary disputes, disaster assistance, and pollution control. As Congress has not yet endorsed the NPVI, it is currently unsettled whether it is the sort of interstate compact that requires congressional approval. In *Virginia v. Tennessee* (1893), the Supreme Court narrowed the scope of the constitutional prohibition to interstate compacts "tending to the increase of political power in the States, which may encroach upon or interfere with the just supremacy of the United States." Accordingly, if Republicans ever attempt to seek an injunction against the implementation of the NPVI, the key issue will be whether the compact expands the political power of states in such a way that it shrinks the lawful role of the federal government. If a federal court finds that it does, it will likely issue an injunction against the implementation of the NPVI unless and until it has been approved by Congress, an unlikely scenario if senators from states with relatively small populations uniformly oppose the measure, just as they have opposed the abolition of the Electoral College.

Another possible constitutional objection to the NPVI is that the framers of the Constitution clearly envisioned the Electoral College as an institutional mechanism that would protect states with small populations in the presidential selection process from being dominated by those with large populations. It seems somewhat counterintuitive that this constitutional guarantee could be circumvented by a compact of populous states. On the other hand, Article II states quite clearly that each state shall have the authority to choose its presidential electors "in such manner as the Legislature thereof may direct," suggesting that a state with a relatively small population has no right to complain if more populous states come to an agreement to appoint electors who support the presidential candidate who has won the national popular vote. If this issue arises in future litigation concerning the constitutionality of the NPVI, a court will have to decide if the significance of this textual language outweighs the purpose of the Electoral College: to protect small states.

One last concern is whether the NPVI would violate Section 2 of the Voting Rights Act by diluting the voting strength of racial and ethnic minorities. The votes of minorities in states with strong electoral constituencies will arguably be diminished in value if they are simply added to the national totals, rather than determining which candidate will receive all of the state's electoral votes in a statewide "winner-take-all" election. However, one of the explicit goals of the NPVI is to make sure that every person's vote in a presidential election is equal throughout the United States. Accordingly, while courts have prevented states from diluting the value of the votes of racial and ethnic minorities in statewide elections, these precedents, according to the supporters of the NPVI, have little or no weight if states join a compact for the very purpose of equalizing the value of everyone's vote (Neale and Nolan, 2019). It is anyone's guess how courts will decide these controversial issues regarding the constitutionality of the NPVI, but it is almost a certainty that courts will have to resolve them if the NPVI ever attracts enough state support to trigger its implementation.

FURTHER READING

Amar, Akhil Reed, and Amar, Vikram David. "How to Achieve Direct National Election of the President without Amending the Constitution." *Findllaw's Writ*, December 28, 2001, available at https://supreme.findlaw.com/legal-commentary/how-to-achieve-direct-national-election-of-the-president-without-amending-the-constitution.html.

Gringer, David. "Why the National Popular Vote Plan Is the Wrong Way to Abolish the Electoral College." *Columbia Law Review* 108 (2008): 182–230.

Jones, Jeffrey M. "Americans Split on Proposals for Popular Vote." *Gallup News Service*, May 14, 2019, available at https://news.gallup.com/poll/257594/americans-split-proposals-popular-vote.aspx.

Koza, John R., et al. *Every Vote Equal*. 4th ed. Los Altos, CA: National Popular Vote Press, 2013, available at http://www.every-vote-equal.com/sites/default/files/everyvoteequal-4th-ed-2013-02-21.pdf.

Mahoney, John. "State Partisan Composition." *National Conference of State Legislatures*, January 20, 2020, available at http://www.ncsl.org/research/about-state-legislatures/partisan-composition.aspx.

Neale, Thomas H., and Nolan, Andrew. "The National Popular Vote (NPV) Initiative: Direct Election of the President by Interstate Compact." *Congressional Research Service*, October 28, 2019 (R43823), available at https://fas.org/sgp/crs/misc/R43823.pdf.

Newport, Frank. "Americans Support Proposal to Eliminate Electoral College System." *Gallup News Service*, January 5, 2001, available at https://news.gallup.com/poll/2140/americans-support-proposal-eliminate-electoral-college-system.aspx.

Samples, John. "A Critique of the National Popular Vote Plan for Electing the President." *Cato Institute*, October 13, 2008, available at https://object.cato.org/sites/cato.org/files/pubs/pdf/pa-622.pdf.

Skelley, Geoffrey. "Abolishing the Electoral College Used to Be a Bipartisan Position. Not Anymore." *FiveThirtyEight*, April 2, 2019, available at https://fivethirtyeight.com/features/abolishing-the-electoral-college-used-to-be-bipartisan-position-not-anymore/.

Vasilogambros, Matt. "Trump Alters Electoral College Debate in States." *Pew: Stateline*, April 19, 2019, available at https://www.pewtrusts.org/en/research-and-analysis/blogs/stateline/2019/04/19/trump-alters-electoral-college-debate-in-states.

Q35. DID RUSSIA INTERFERE IN THE 2016 PRESIDENTIAL ELECTION TO UNDERMINE AMERICAN CONFIDENCE IN U.S. ELECTIONS AND THE VALUE OF THE RIGHT TO VOTE?

Answer: Yes. Even if Russian interference did not alter any actual votes in the 2016 U.S. election, its purpose was to undermine American voter confidence in U.S. elections, the integrity of U.S. elections, and the value of American democracy itself.

The Facts: A number of studies have documented the scope and degree of Russian interference in the 2016 presidential election. The first of these was the American Intelligence Community's (IC) declassified interagency assessment published on January 6, 2017, just two months after the election and two weeks before President Donald Trump's inauguration as the forty-fifth president of the United States. The IC is a collection of seventeen governmental agencies engaged in intelligence gathering activities on behalf of the foreign policy and national security of the United States, including the Federal Bureau of Investigation, the Central Intelligence Agency, and the National Security Agency.

The IC assessment concluded that "Russian President Vladimir Putin ordered an influence campaign in 2016 . . . to undermine public faith in the US democratic process, denigrate Secretary [Hillary] Clinton, and harm her electability and potential presidency." The campaign was a multifaceted one that "featured disclosures of data obtained through Russian cyber operations; intrusions into US state and local electoral boards; and overt propaganda." Targets of unlawful Russian cyberattacks included primary campaign organizations, think tanks, lobbying groups, and the networks of the Democratic National Committee (DNC) and the Democratic Congressional Campaign Committee (DCCC). In addition, Russian intelligence agencies disclosed documents harmful to Clinton's election efforts through various media outlets, including Guccifer 2.0, DCLeaks, and WikiLeaks.

Although the IC found there were Russian intrusions into U.S. state and local electoral boards in multiple states beginning as early as 2014, its assessment was that Russia did not manipulate vote tallies in 2016. The propaganda dimension of the Russian influence campaign included its own domestic media channels, international outlets, such as Russia Today (RT), as well as a "network of quasi-government trolls" that amplified negative views of Clinton through internet blogs and social media. The IC concluded that the 2016 Russian influence campaign was the "boldest" effort of cyber intrusion it had yet seen and that it constituted the "new normal" of foreign electoral interference (Office of Director of National Intelligence).

Despite the IC's report, President Trump expressed doubts about Russian interference in the 2016 election, claiming that the allegation was merely a partisan ploy to undermine the legitimacy of his presidency. However, in June 2017, *The Intercept* disclosed the existence of a classified National Security Agency (NSA) report dated May 5, 2017. This report claimed that Russian military intelligence hacked at least one U.S. voting software supplier in August 2016. The "Russian plan was simple," the report claimed. First, they "sent spoofed emails purporting to be from Google to employees of . . . VR Systems, a Florida-based vendor of electronic voting services and equipment whose products are used in eight states." At least one employee's e-mail account at VR Systems was compromised, which enabled the hackers to set up a Gmail account in the employee's name in October 2016. The Russians then used this account to send e-mails to local state officials responsible for voter registration rolls that included an attached "trojanized" Microsoft Word document that, if opened, would give the Russian hackers a "backdoor" to enter the state's computer, steal data, and deliver additional malware. The NSA report concluded that the Russians were seeking capability to remove eligible voters from registration lists. They may not have achieved this goal, but it was likely one of their objectives (Cole et al., 2017).

In September 2017, the Department of Homeland Security (DHS) admitted that the scope of the Russian intrusion into state voting systems had been broader than what initial reports had claimed. Russian intelligence agencies, DHS alleged, had targeted the electoral systems of twenty-one states. In most cases, the targeting focused on voter registration systems, not tallying software. There "were some attempts to compromise networks but most were unsuccessful." Illinois admitted "that hackers had succeeded in breaching its voter systems," thereby gaining access to the records of tens of thousands of voters in the state's centralized registration database. In turn, Arizona conceded that Russian hackers had acquired the password and other credentials of a county elections worker. Once again, investigators found no evidence that Russian hackers had manipulated the vote count of any election, but they did acquire information and expertise that could be used in a future attempt (Mulvihill and Pearson, 2017).

In July 2018, Special Counsel Robert Mueller indicted twelve Russian nationals for computer hacking of political campaigns and institutions, the public dissemination of hacked e-mails, and attempts to penetrate state electoral systems. The indictment indicated that the Russian conspirators targeted over three hundred individuals affiliated with Hillary Clinton's campaign organization, successfully stole thousands of the organization's e-mails, and installed malware on the computer networks of the DCCC and the DNC. The malware enabled the Russians to monitor screenshots and keystrokes of individual computers, acquire passwords, and steal documents involving fundraising, voter outreach projects, and opposition research. To disseminate the stolen documents, the conspirators created fake websites named "DCLeaks" and "Guccifer 2.0." The latter was responsible for sending 2.5 gigabytes of data to a Republican lobbyist, including "donor records and personal identifying information for more than 2,000 Democratic donors," an e-mail to a U.S. reporter with an offer to provide access to emails stolen from "Hillary Clinton's staff," and an e-mail to Roger Stone, who was in regular contact with senior members of the Trump campaign. Starting in June 2016, WikiLeaks, a website operated by Julian Assange, contacted Guccifer 2.0, offering to help disseminate the material the Russians had stolen from the DNC. In response, Guccifer 2.0 gave WikiLeaks access to a gigabyte of stolen DNC documents, twenty thousand of which WikiLeaks published on July 22, 2016, just three days before the Democratic National Convention, and another fifty thousand during the weeks and days before the election itself (*United States v. Internet Research Agency, et al.* [2018]).

In March 2019, Special Counsel Mueller issued his long-awaited report on Russian interference in the 2016 election. Volume I described in detail the various dimensions of this interference effort, which included a social media campaign, a hacking operation, and a series of contacts with members of the Trump campaign organization. Mueller's investigation found that in 2014, the Internet Research Agency (IRA), a Russian organization funded by a close associate of Russian President Vladimir Putin, launched a campaign of "information warfare" through social media sites, such as Facebook and Twitter, that reached millions of American citizens. The purpose of this campaign was twofold: to undermine the U.S. electoral system and elect Donald Trump president of the United States. The contacts with Trump's campaign consisted of "business connections, offers of assistance to the Campaign, invitations for candidate Trump and Putin to meet in person, invitations for Campaign officials and representatives of the Russian government to meet, and policy positions seeking improved U.S.-Russian relations." Although Mueller's final report indicated that its investigation had "identified numerous links between individuals with ties to the Russian government and individuals associated with the Trump Campaign, the evidence was not sufficient to support criminal charges." However, the Mueller investigation did charge a number of individuals affiliated with the Trump campaign organization with lying to Congress and federal officials about "their interactions with Russian-affiliated individuals and related matters." These lies and deceptions implied that Mueller's report was not able to yield "a complete picture of the activities undertaken by the subjects of the investigation" (Mueller, 2019).

In mid-2019, the Senate Select Committee on Intelligence (SSCI) declassified two volumes of its report on "Russian Active Measures Campaigns and Interference in the 2016 U.S. Election." Volume I focused on election infrastructure and confirmed much of what has been discussed above. There was no evidence that the Russians had actually altered voting tallies on election day, but the SSCI admitted that its "insight into this [issue] is limited." In any case, new intelligence bolstered the conclusion "that all 50 states were targeted" in 2016 and that the Russians had successfully extracted voter data from two states, including personal information from fifteen million voters in Illinois. The SSCI report concluded that the Russians likely interfered with the 2016 election "to further their overarching goal: undermining the integrity of elections and American confidence in democracy" and recommended that the federal government provide the states with funds to replace outdated and vulnerable voting systems with "[p]aper ballots and optical scanners." Any voting "machine purchased going forward," the SSCI admonished, "should have a voter-verified paper trail and remove (or render inert) any wireless networking capability."

Volume II of the SSCI report examined in depth the IRA's use of social media to influence American public opinion by deceiving "tens of millions of social media users in the United States" for the purpose of polarizing "Americans on the basis of societal, ideological, and racial differences," provoking "real world events," and providing "covert support" for Donald Trump, "Russia's favored candidate in the U.S. presidential election." The most frequently targeted individuals, the SSCI found, were African Americans. "Evidence of the IRA's overwhelming operational emphasis on race is evident in the IRA's Facebook advertisement content (over 66 percent contained a term related to race) and its targeting (locational targeting was principally aimed at African-Americans in key metropolitan areas . . .)." One of the IRA's top-performing Facebook pages, "Blacktivist," generated 11.2 million engagements. In the same vein, five of the top ten Instagram accounts of the IRA highlighted African American issues; its Twitter content focused on hot-button issues with racial undertones, such as the NFL kneeling protests; and 96 percent of its YouTube content targeted racial issues and related policy issues (SSCI, 2019).

In March 2018, Congress appropriated $380 million in funds to help improve the security of state voting systems, but Mitch McConnell (R-KY), majority leader of the Senate, resisted any further increase in funding. He refused to allow Senate votes on additional appropriations for this purpose despite warnings from the IC that Russia and other countries, such as China and Iran, were gearing up for expansive election meddling in the 2020 presidential election. Frustrated critics began calling McConnell "Moscow Mitch," implying that he did not oppose foreign election interference if he thought it would benefit Trump and the Republican Party. Stung by this criticism and nickname, McConnell relented in September 2019 by supporting a new appropriation of $250 million, but he continued to oppose federal requirements on how states should spend the money. In December, Congress approved an additional $425 million for election security reforms, but once again the legislation did not include federal mandates, such as paper ballots or postelection audits. Democrats complained that appropriating additional money without federal safeguards allows state and local governments to continue to purchase voter machinery plagued with cyber vulnerabilities. According to the Brennan Center for Justice, a progressive nonpartisan policy institute, the $900 million Congress has appropriated for election security since 2018 amounts to "less than half of the $2.2 billion needed to fully upgrade the nation's aging and vulnerable election infrastructure" (Marks, 2019).

In early 2020, U.S. intelligence and law enforcement officials warned that Russian interference in the upcoming presidential election "could be more brazen than in the 2016 presidential race or the 2018 midterm election." William Evanina, director of the National Counterintelligence and Security Center, claimed that the Russians will use "social media and many other tools to inflame social divisions, promote conspiracy theories and sow distrust in our democracy and elections." He guaranteed that "they'll keep up their influence campaigns and utilize new vectors of disinformation." The Office of the Director of National Intelligence added that "Moscow may employ additional influence toolkits—such as spreading disinformation, conducting hack-and-leak operations, or *manipulating data* [Emphasis added]—in a more targeted fashion to influence US policy, actions, and elections" (Strohm, 2020).

One recent example of a Russian attempt at disinformation would be the headline that appeared on the website of the Russian television channel RT during the spring 2020 Democratic primary season: "Coronavirus is coming, hide the ballots! Calls to cancel campaigns & voting erode already-thin trust in US primaries." By exaggerating the potential vulnerabilities to mail-in voting, such disinformation will likely raise doubts about the integrity of the 2020 election, especially when such distortions are amplified through social media. As one Justice Department official put it, Russia does not need to "hack the vote to hack people's perception of the vulnerability of the vote." All it needs do is "seed enough doubt about the legitimacy of a vote." Once the seed is planted, Russian hackers and conspiracy theorists can spread and weaponize the disinformation through social media, even up to the point of claiming that Democrats are hyping forecasts of a second wave of COVID-19 simply to "rig" the election by replacing in-person voting with a mail-in election (Tucker and Seitz, 2020).

Given the vulnerability of the U.S. electoral system and the reality that other countries, including China and Iran, have joined Russia in trying to influence the 2020 presidential election, it is hardly surprising that the American public has expressed considerable anxiety about the 2020 election. A January 2020 NPR/PBS/Marist poll indicated that 41 percent of adults believe that the United States is not very prepared or not prepared at all to keep the November elections secure, that almost 40 percent think that it is likely a foreign country will tamper with the votes to change the result, that 82 percent believe that foreign nations will spread false information about candidates, and that 35 percent believe that this type of disinformation is the biggest threat to the upcoming election, followed by voter fraud at 24 percent and voter suppression at 16 percent. Finally, the poll also found that 38 percent of Americans currently think elections are unfair (Neely, 2020). Regardless of this poll's margin of error, these results suggest that there is an ongoing crisis in voter confidence in U.S. elections. The degree of partisan polarization afflicting America further heightens the problem. In mid-February 2020, when intelligence officials warned the House Intelligence Committee that Russia was already interfering in the 2020 election, President Trump complained that the Democrats would "weaponize" the information to defeat his reelection (Goldman et al., 2020). Clearly, restoring voter confidence to the level a healthy democracy should have will be a major challenge for the next president, regardless of who wins the 2020 election.

FURTHER READING

Cole, Matthew, Esposito, Richard, Biddle, Sam, and Grim, Ryan. "Top-Secret NSA Report Details Russian Hacking Effort Days before 2016 Election." *The Intercept*, June 5, 2017, available at https://theintercept.com/2017/06/05/top-secret-nsa-report-details-russian-hacking-effort-days-before-2016-election/.

Goldman, Adam, Barnes, Julian E., Haberman, Maggie, and Fandos, Nicholas. "Lawmakers Are Warned That Russia Is Meddling to Re-elect Trump." *The New York Times*, Februrary 20, 2020, available at https://www.nytimes.com/2020/02/20/us/politics/russian-interference-trump-democrats.html.

House Permanent Select Committee on Intelligence (HPSCI). "Report on Russian Active Measures." House of Representatives, March 22, 2018, available at https://docs.house.gov/meetings/IG/IG00/20180322/108023/HRPT-115-1_1-p1-U3.pdf.

Marks, Joseph. "The Cybersecurity 202: Pressure Still on McConnell after $425 Million Election Security Deal." *The Washington Post*, December 17, 2019, available at https://www.washingtonpost.com/news/powerpost/paloma/the-cybersecurity-202/2019/12/17/the-cybersecurity-202-pressure-still-on-mcconnell-after-425-million-election-security-deal/5df7b70288e0fa32a5140757/.

Mueller, Robert S., III. *Report on the Investigation Into Russian Interference in the 2016 Presidential Election*. 2 Vols. Washington, DC: Department of Justice, 2019, available at https://www.justice.gov/storage/report.pdf.

Mulvihill, Geoff, and Pearson, Jake. "Federal Government Notifies 21 States of Election Hacking." *Associated Press*, September 22, 2017, available at https://apnews.com/cb8a753a9b0948589cc372a3c037a567/Federal-government-notifies-21-states-of-election-hacking.

Neely, Brett. "NPR Poll: Majority of Americans Believe Trump Encourages Election Interference." *NPR*, January 21, 2020, available at https://www.npr.org/2020/01/21/797101409/npr-poll-majority-of-americans-believe-trump-encourages-election-interference.

Office of the Director of National Intelligence. "Assessing Russian Activities and Intentions in Recent US Elections: Intelligence Community Assessment." January 6, 2017, available at https://www.dni.gov/files/documents/ICA_2017_01.pdf.

Senate Select Committee on Intelligence (SSCI). "Report on Russian Active Measures Campaigns and Interference in the 2016 U.S. Election: Volume I: Russian Efforts Against Election Infrastructure with Additional Views." United States Senate, July 2019, available at https://www.intelligence.senate.gov/sites/default/files/documents/Report_Volume1.pdf.

Senate Select Committee on Intelligence (SSCI). "Volume II: Russia's Use of Social Media with Additional Views." United States Senate, July 2019, available at https://www.intelligence.senate.gov/sites/default/files/documents/Report_Volume2.pdf.

Strohm, Chris. "U.S. Probes If Russia Is Targeting Biden in 2020 Election Meddling." *Bloomberg*, January 10, 2020, available at https://www.bloomberg.com/news/articles/2020-01-10/u-s-probes-if-russia-targeting-biden-in-2020-election-meddling.

Tucker, Eric, and Seitz, Amanda. "Vote-by-Mail Debatet Raises Fears of Election Disinformation." *Associated Press*, May 5, 2020, available at https://apnews.com/ee8dd4051a53b5e7471c8a6a2ca1b8f3?utm_campaign=wp_the_cybersecurity_202&utm_medium=email&utm_source=newsletter&wpisrc=nl_cybersecurity202.

United States v. Internet Research Agency, et al., No. 18-cr-32 (D.D.C.). 2018, available at https://www.justice.gov/file/1035477/download.

Q36. APART FROM FOREIGN INTERFERENCE IN THE 2016 PRESIDENTIAL ELECTION, ARE THERE ADDITIONAL REASONS WHY VOTERS HAVE LOST CONFIDENCE IN THE VALUE OF THE RIGHT TO VOTE AND THE INTEGRITY OF AMERICAN DEMOCRACY ITSELF?

Answer: Yes. For a number of interrelated reasons, such as a sense of political inefficacy, the prominent role of money in American elections, and the erosion of the concept of "truth" itself, American voters have lost a significant degree of confidence in the value of the right to vote and of the integrity of American democracy itself.

The Facts: Voter confidence in U.S. elections and democracy cannot be disentangled from voter trust in government and politics. Voting may be a personally rewarding experience for an individual, but voters also cast votes for the purpose of remedying society's problems through political institutions and processes. Accordingly, if voters over time lose their trust in government and political decision-making because nothing or very little is done to address society's ills, then that failure slowly but surely erodes the public's confidence in the value of the right to vote.

At this point in time, turnout rates for national elections strongly suggest that many American voters simply do not think voting is worth the time it takes. Since 1950, participation rates in presidential elections have fluctuated between approximately 50 percent of potential voters to 63 percent, while turnout in midterm elections ranges between 37 percent and 50 percent. This degree of political apathy is not typical of western democracies. For example, although voter turnout has fallen in established European democracies, it has declined from a far higher degree of participation, approximately 84 percent in 1945, to a figure in 2015 that is lower yet still much higher than in America—70 percent of potential voters. These statistics strongly suggest that American voters suffer from voter apathy to a considerably greater degree than their European counterparts (Solijonov, 2016).

Of course, many Americans do not vote because they are ineligible to register due to felon disfranchisement or other factors. But there are a sizable number of American potential voters who can register to vote but deliberately choose not to. For example, only about 20 percent of young adults generally vote because a majority of them "don't think voting is an effective way to change society." Lower-income individuals with a high school education or less have a similar point of view. As a forty-two-year-old fast-food worker who has not voted in years explained, "What good does it do . . . when they'll promise you anything and then it's a lie?" It is estimated that a majority of the nonvoters in the 2016 election had only a high school education or less and made less than $30,000 (Khalid, Gonyea, and Fadel, 2018). Lastly, voter participation varies with different ethnic groups: 52 percent of Hispanics do not vote; 51 percent of Asians; 43 percent of African Americans, and 33 percent of whites. The director of the California Civic Engagement Project explains, "But if you don't see how or why . . . politicians and the political landscape matters for you . . . you don't think you have agency" (Khalid, Gonyea, and Fadel, 2018). The depressing reality is that millions of Americans do not think voting matters and they do not vote for that reason.

However, doubts about the efficacy of voting are not confined to young adults, lower-income/less educated Americans, or ethnic minorities. The public's trust in the federal government has been decreasing for a generation. A 2019 poll by the Pew Research Center found that two-thirds of adults believe that Americans have little or no confidence in the federal government. A majority also agreed that public confidence is shrinking. The poll found that the following comment was typical across the political spectrum: "Many people no longer think the federal government can actually be a force for good or change in their lives. This kind of apathy and disengagement will lead to an even worse and less representative government." The public's lack of confidence in elected officials is especially striking: while over 80 percent of the respondents expressed trust in the members of the military and scientists, 63 percent reported that they had little confidence in elected officials and 56 percent said they had the same opinion of business leaders. One major reason for the lack of trust of elected officials was that two-thirds of Americans find it hard to tell when an elected official is telling the truth and the same percentage believe that the federal government holds back important information from the public. In the end, 41 percent of the poll's respondents described the public's level of trust in the federal government to be a "very big problem," placing it on par with racism and illegal immigration and above terrorism and sexism (Rainie, Keeter, and Perrin, 2019).

Polls have also found high levels of doubt and frustration about the priorities of American corporations and business in general. The American lack of confidence in business leaders is arguably a reflection of the relatively low rate of wage increases over the last forty years, especially in comparison to the radical increase in wealth inequalities that has occurred since 1980. During this time period, the rich have enriched themselves, while the poor have become more impoverished and the working middle class has fought to maintain its standard of living. Minimum-wage jobs and minimal cost-of-living wage increases have often forced working men and women to take on second and third jobs to make ends meet. The resulting picture of wealth inequality presents a bleak picture of America's future: three Americans (Bill Gates, Jeff Bezos, and Warren Buffett) own as much as the bottom half of Americans; the richest Americans in 2018 are worth thirty-one times as much as their predecessors in 1982; the richest 5 percent of Americans own two-thirds of the wealth of the country; the richest 1 percent own more than 50 percent of all stocks and mutual funds (Inequality.org).

Income inequality mirrors wealth inequality: each year the richest 0.1 percent of Americans take in 188 times as much as the bottom 90 percent, a level of income that is twice that of the wealthy in 1980, even though the number of Americans living in poverty has not declined. The after-tax income of the top 1 percent has grown faster than that of the bottom 20 percent of Americans, a rate of growth that further increased with President Trump's 2017 tax cut, which disproportionately benefited the wealthy. Also, the rich receive more of their income from investments, which is taxed at a lower rate (capital gains rate) than other income. The annual paychecks of the top 0.1 percent have gone from $600,000 in 1980 to over $2.5 million in 2017—over a 200 percent increase—while the bottom 90 percent have seen just a 22 percent increase over that same period of time. Lastly, CEOs of corporations are paid nearly nine times more than what they were paid in 1980, while Congress has not raised the minimum wage in more than a decade (Inequality.org).

Persistent inegalitarian trends of this character help explain why so many Americans have no trust in corporate business leaders. The overall impression is that the economic system is "rigged" against ordinary men and women and they have considerable doubt whether anything can be done about it through voting. One reason why this is so is because of the role that money plays in American politics (lobbying) and electoral political campaigning. The vast majority of Americans support limits on campaign spending, in part because there is broad and bipartisan consensus among the public that large donations to candidates buy political influence over policy. In 2018, 77 percent of respondents in a Pew Research Poll endorsed limits on campaign expenditures, while only 20 percent claimed that candidates and their supporters should be able to spend as much as they want (Jones, 2018).

The Supreme Court has been at least partly responsible for the current public perception that money in U.S. elections is out of control by significantly weakening laws regulating campaign financing. This process began with *Buckley v. Valeo* (1976). Although the Court conceded in this decision that reasonable regulations of campaign contributions were constitutional, it ruled that limits on campaign expenditures, whether by an individual candidate or his or her campaign organization, violated freedom of speech. For the same reason, the Court held that expenditures of a political party/committee were free of any limits unless they were coordinated with a candidate's organization, in which case the expenditure became a contribution subject to reasonable limits. At first, a corporation was prohibited from making any independent political expenditures for the express benefit of a political candidate, but this rule was completely abandoned in *Citizens United v. FEC* (2010). In this decision, the Court permitted politically oriented nonprofit corporations to spend unlimited amounts of money either attacking candidates or advocating for them so long as the expenditures were made independently of the candidate's campaign organization. In *McCutcheon v. FEC* (2014), the Court turned to contribution limits, holding that the current federal limits on aggregate contributions that an individual donor could make to all federal candidates was unreasonably low. The decision allowed more money to flow to candidates in addition to all the money spent on their behalf by wealthy supporters, including corporations.

The amount of money spent in federal elections, including both the candidate's expenditures and independent expenditures by corporations and political committees, has mushroomed as a result of these Supreme Court decisions. The total cost of U.S. elections has gone from $1.6 billion in 2000, to $5.2 in 2008, and reached $6.5 in 2016. Presidential races for these elections cost $1.4, $2.7, and $2.3 billion, while congressional races cost $1.6, $2.4, and $4.1 billion. The average winner of a seat in the House of Representatives spent $800,000 in 2000, $1.3 million in 2008, and $2.0 million in 2018. Senate seats were usually more expensive than House seats, the average cost climbing to almost $16 million in 2018. And the amount of money spent in these elections generally made a difference: 88 percent of the candidates who spent the most won in the House, while 83 percent won in the Senate (see https://www.opensecrets.org/overview/index.php).

These facts and statistics have buttressed the cynical view that money has as much, if not more, influence over public policy than voting. This kind of cynicism may be unwarranted in terms of specific individual candidates and legislators, but it is the overall impression that has eroded American confidence in government and elections. Merging the results of four questions about voter perceptions of government and politicians into one number, the American National Election Survey reports that voter trust on a scale of 100 has fallen from 61 in 1966 to 17 in 2016.

As American voter cynicism becomes more extreme, it explains, in part, why many Americans support outsider politicians who promise to "shake up" the system and who have little or no respect for traditional political conventions (Koerth, 2019). An obvious example of such a politician is President Trump, who has gone out of his way to defy presidential conventions. His lack of respect for the system is reflected in his rhetorical attacks on American intelligence and law enforcement agencies as the "deep state" and the news media as the "enemy of the people." Throughout his 2016 presidential campaign, Trump claimed that the election was "rigged" and he refused to confirm that he would accept the election's results if he lost. As soon as he took office in January 2017, he claimed he lost the popular vote in 2016 only because three to five million illegal votes had been cast. In the 2018 midterm election, he insisted that Republicans were having elections stolen from them (Graham, 2019). Obviously, such attacks on the legitimacy of U.S. elections by a president of the United States is itself a force that undermines voter confidence and trust in the integrity of American democracy.

Political rhetoric of this nature is arguably more damaging in today's polarized environment where the ever-expanding internet permits bad actors to spread half-truths and falsehoods to the far corners of American society. The Russian interference campaign in the 2016 presidential election was a harbinger of how misinformation and deception might well become the new normal. Not only is it likely that other foreign countries will join Russia in trying to influence the 2020 presidential election, it is clear by now that domestic groups on both sides of the political spectrum are spreading innuendo, distortions, and outright lies. The rise in the number of "fact checkers" in today's media world may, of course, rectify some of this misinformation but it also confirms the degree to which falsehoods have flooded the marketplace of ideas.

A 2018 report by the Rand Corporation refers to these developments as "truth decay," which is defined as "a set of four related trends: increasing disagreement about facts and analytical interpretations of facts and data; a blurring of the line between opinion and fact; an increase in the relative volume, and resulting influence, of opinion and personal experience over fact; and declining trust in formerly respected sources of factual information." According to the report, the consequences of "truth decay" are an "erosion of civil discourse, a political paralysis, alienation and disengagement of individuals from political and civic institutions, and uncertainty over national policy" (Kavanaugh and Rich, 2018). All of these consequences of "truth decay" have a direct bearing on voter confidence, not only in government, politicians, and election results but also in the assumption that "truth" can function as the common ground on which American voters can build this country's future through democratic policymaking.

FURTHER READING

Atkeson, Lonna Rae, and Saunders, Kyle L. "The Effect of Election Administration on Voter Confidence: A Local Matter?" *Political Science and Politics* 40 (2007): 655–660.

Graham, David A. "Democracy, Interrupted." *The Atlantic*, January 13, 2019, available at https://www.theatlantic.com/politics/archive/2019/01/trump-continues-to-attack-rigged-elections/580030/.

Jones, Bradley. "Most Americans Want to Limit Campaign Spending, Say Big Donors Have Greater Political Influence." *Pew Research Center*, May 8, 2018, available at https://www.pewresearch.org/fact-tank/2018/05/08/most-americans-want-to-limit-campaign-spending-say-big-donors-have-greater-political-influence/.

Kavanaugh, Jennifer, and Rich, Michael D. *Truth Decay: An Initial Exploration of the Diminishing Role of Facts and Analysis in American Public Life*. Santa Monica, CA: Rand Corporation, 2018, available at https://www.rand.org/pubs/research_reports/RR2314.html.

Khalid, Asma, Gonyea, Don, and Fadel, Leila. "On the Sidelines of Democracy: Exploring Why So Many Americans Don't Vote." *National Public Radio*, September 10, 2018, available at https://www.npr.org/2018/09/10/645223716/on-the-sidelines-of-democracy-exploring-why-so-many-americans-dont-vote.

Koerth, Maggie. "In American Politics, Everyone's A Cynic." *FiveThirtyEight*, December 17, 2019, available at https://fivethirtyeight.com/features/in-american-politics-everyones-a-cynic/.

Leighley, Jan E., and Nagler, Jonathan. *Who Votes Now?: Demographics, Issues, Inequality, and Turnout in the United States*. Princeton, NJ: Princeton University Press, 2014.

Rainie, Lee, Keeter, Scott, and Perrin, Andrew. "Trust and Distrust in America." *Pew Research Center*, July 22, 2019, available at https://www.people-press.org/2019/07/22/trust-and-distrust-in-america/.

Solijonov, Abdurashid. *Voter Turnout Trends around the World*. Stockholm: International Institute for Democracy and Electoral Assistance, 2016, available at https://www.idea.int/sites/default/files/publications/voter-turnout-trends-around-the-world.pdf.

Index

Abbott v. Perez (2018), 104
Absentee ballots, 162–169, 174
ACORN, 167
Adams, John, 4, 190
Adams, John Quincy, 190
Affirmative action, 106–107
African Americans, 21, 29, 82–87, 106, 155, 164, 205
    free, right to vote, 8–19, 21, 28, 40, 54–55, 82–89, 95–97, 100–101, 107–109, 115, 119, 166, 175, 177–180, 185, 210
    military service and right to vote, 12, 31
    slave, denied right to vote, 10–13
Alabama Legislative Black Caucus v. Alabama (2015), 103
Alaskan Natives, 112–113, 115
Albright, Madeleine, 29
Allen v. State Board of Elections (1969), 100
American National Election Survey, 213
American Woman Suffrage Association (AWSA), 26
Anthony, Susan B., 26
Applewhite v. Pennsylvania (2014), 173
Apportionment
    relative to population, 44–52, 57–62, 65–75, 126, 128, 133–137
    relative to race/ethnicity, 45, 53–56, 58–62, 107, 109, 126, 136–137
Apportionment Act, 47–48
Arizona State Legislature v. Arizona Independent Redistricting Commission (2015), 148–152
Ashcroft v. Georgia (2003), 109–110
Asian Americans, 20–24, 112–114, 185, 210
Assange, Julian, 204
Australian ballot, 163–164
Avery v. Midland County (1968), 73
AWSA. *See* American Woman Suffrage Association

Baca, Michael, 193–194
Bailout provision. *See* Voting Rights Act of 1965
Baker, James A., III, 171
Baker v. Carr (1962), 57–62
Ballot, 2, 194
   absentee, 162–169, 174
   Australian, 163–164
   butterfly, 165
   mail-in, 121, 167–169, 206
   overseas, 166
   provisional, 97, 171, 174
   punch-card, 165–166
   secret, 163–164
Bartlett v. Strickland (2009), 102
Beer v. United States (1976), 105
Beshear, Andy, 181
Bezos, Jeff, 211
Bilingual elections, 97, 111–115
Bird, Harry F., 191
Birthright citizenship, 22–23
Black, Hugo, 33, 52
Blackwell, Henry, 26
Bloody Sunday, 85
Board of elections, 97, 167–168, 202
Breedlove v. Suttles (1937), 40, 76
Brennan, William, 58–60
Brennan Center for Justice, 166–167, 174, 206
Brown v. Board of Education (1954), 82, 164
Buckley v. Valeo (1976), 212
Buffett, Warren, 211
Bull Moose Party, 38
Burr, Aaron, 4–5
Bush, George W., 6, 165–166, 179, 185, 197
Bush, Jeb, 179
Bush v. Vera (1996), 108
Butterfly ballot, 165
Buying votes, 36, 163–164, 174

Campaign financing, 130, 211–212
Caraway, Hattie Wyatt, 29
Caro, Robert, 165
Carter, Jimmy, 171
Catholics, 8–9, 20
Census, 45, 48, 57, 63, 73, 109, 115, 128–129, 139, 147–149, 156
Census Bureau. *See* U.S. Census Bureau
Central Intelligence Agency (CIA), 202
CFER. *See* Commission on Federal Election Reform
Chad. *See* Punch-card ballot
Chae Chan Ping v. United States (1889), 22
Chen, Jowei, 144
Chiafalo, Peter, 193–194
Chiafalo v. Washington (2020), 194–195
China, interference in 2020 election, 205–207
Chinese Exclusion Act of 1882, 22–23
CIA. *See* Central Intelligence Agency
Citizens United v. FEC (2010), 212
Citizenship, requirements for, 20–24, 26–27, 31
City of Mobile v. Bolden (1980), 56, 100
City of Richmond v. J. A. Croson Co. (1989), 106–107
Civil Rights Act of 1866, 15
Civil Rights Act of 1875, 15–16
Civil Rights Act of 1957, 82
Civil Rights Act of 1960, 82
Civil Rights Act of 1964, 83–84, 164
Civil Rights Cases (1883), 16, 83
Civil Rights Division (DOJ), 82, 98
Civil rights movement, 29, 81–88
Civil Service Commission, 95
Civil War, 1–2, 9–13, 20, 25, 30–31, 164
Clark, Jim, 84
Clark, Tom C., 68–69

Clinton, Hillary, 29, 167, 188, 192, 202
Colegrove v. Green (1946), 51–54, 58–59
College students, right to vote, 33–34, 74
Commission on Federal Election Reform (CFER), 171
Compromise of 1877, 16
Conscription, 31–32
Constitution of the United States of America, 1–40
  Article I, 6–8, 33, 37, 39, 45, 47, 61, 63–64, 75, 83, 148, 199
  Article II, 3, 7, 21, 64, 190, 193–194, 200
  Article IV, 49–52
  Article V, 64
  Elections Clause, 142, 145, 147–148, 153
  Equal Protection Clause, 17, 40, 54, 57–80, 100, 103, 105–110, 134, 136, 145, 157–158, 166, 178
  Fifteenth Amendment, 9, 13–24, 31, 54–56, 58–59, 76, 84, 89–96, 99–106, 118–120
  First Amendment, 15, 157–158, 193
  Fourteenth Amendment, 13, 16, 18, 22–26, 40, 57–62, 67, 73, 78, 103, 105–110, 134, 166, 178
  Necessary and Proper Clause, 78
  Nineteenth Amendment, 25–29
  Republican Guarantee Clause, 49–52, 57, 59
  Seventeenth Amendment, 35–37, 43, 148–149
  Supremacy Clause, 193
  Thirteenth Amendment, 13–14
  Twelfth Amendment, 5, 193–194
  Twenty-Fourth Amendment, 36, 40, 76
  Twenty-Second Amendment, 35, 37
  Twenty-Sixth Amendment, 30–34
  Twenty-Third Amendment, 35, 39
Constitutional Convention of 1787, 2, 9, 45, 61, 65
Cooper v. Harris (2017), 103
Corbett, Tom, 173
Coronavirus, 162, 206
Corruption, 4, 36
COVID-19, 162, 168–169, 206
Cracking electoral districts, 102, 127
Crawford v. Marion County Election Board (2008), 172–173
Crosscheck. *See* Interstate Voter Registration Crosscheck Program
Crump, Ed, 164
Curley, James, 164
Cuyler v. Adams (1981), 199
Cyber intrusion, 202
Cyberattacks, 202

Daley, Richard, 165
Dallek, Robert, 165
Daunt v. Benson (2019), 157–159
Davis v. Bandemer (1986), 134
Dawes Act of 1887, 24
DCCC. *See* Democratic Congressional Campaign Committee
DCLeaks, 202–203
Declaration of Sentiments, 25
Democratic Congressional Campaign Committee (DCCC), 202–203
Democratic National Committee (DNC), 202–204
Democratic National Convention, 204
Democratic Party, 34, 83, 109, 130, 134, 163–164, 172, 188, 192, 198
Democratic-Republican Party, 4, 125

Department of Homeland Security (DHS), 203
DeSantis, Ron, 181
Dewey, Thomas, 38
DHS. *See* Department of Homeland Security
Disfranchisement, xiv
  African Americans, 10, 14–19, 83, 115, 166, 180
  Asian Americans, 20–23, 114
  felons, 161, 166, 176–182, 184–185, 209
  Hispanic Americans, 102, 114–115
  illiterate, 20–21, 177
  illiterate in English language, 112–115, 177
  immigrants, 20–22, 27
  indigent (poor), 20–21
  Mexican Americans, 20–21, 56
  Native Americans, 20, 23–24, 31, 112, 114
  slaves, 10–13
  women, 25–29
District of Columbia Voting Rights Amendment, 39
DNC. *See* Democratic National Committee
Dorr rebellion, 50
Dowless, L. McCrae, Jr., 167–169
Draft. *See* Conscription
Dred Scott v. Sandford (1857), 11–13
Dunn v. Blumstein (1972), 80

Eastland, James, 87
Edmund Pettus Bridge, 85–88
Eisenhower, Dwight D., 31, 39
Election integrity, 209–214
Election interference, foreign, 201–207
Elections Clause, 142, 145, 147–148, 153
Electoral College, 4–6, 13, 39, 63–66, 164–167, 189–200
  faithless electors, 189–195
  winner-take-all, 5–6, 190, 196–200
Electoral districting
  based on political partisanship, 125–159
  based on population, 43–80
  based on race/ethnicity, 53–56, 100–110
  cracking of districts, 102, 127
  multimember districts, 43, 46–47, 55–56, 72, 101–102
  packing of districts, 102, 127–128
  single-member districts, 43–48, 101–103, 127
Electoral maps, 130–144, 150–151, 156
Elk v. Wilkins (1884), 23
Emancipation Proclamation, 12
Enforcement Act of 1870, 15
Equal Protection Clause, 17, 40, 54, 57–80, 100, 103, 105–110, 134, 136, 145, 157–158, 166, 178
Equal Rights Amendment, 29
Evanina, William, 206

Facebook, 204–205
Failure-to-Vote Clause (NVRA), 186
Fair Districts Pledge, 158
Fair Lines American Foundation, 157
Faithless electors, 189–195
FBI. *See* Federal Bureau of Investigation
Federal Bureau of Investigation (FBI), 202
Federal Election Commission, 167
Federal examiners and observers. *See* Voting Rights Act of 1965
Federal Fugitive Slave Act, 11
Federalist Papers, 3, 36–37, 45, 50, 191
Federalist Party, 4–5, 125, 190
Felon disfranchisement, 161, 166, 176–182, 184–185, 209

Fifteenth Amendment, 9, 13–24, 31, 54–56, 58–59, 76, 84, 89–96, 99–106, 118–120
First Amendment, 15, 157–158, 193
Foner, Eric, 164
For the People Act, 152
Foreign election interference, 201–207
Fortson v. Dorsey (1965), 55
Fourteenth Amendment, 13, 16, 18, 22–26, 40, 57–62, 67, 73, 78, 103, 105–110, 134, 166, 178
Frankfurter, Felix, 51–52, 59–60
Free Elections Clause, 145

Gaffney v. Cummings (1973), 75, 133
Gates, Bill, 211
Gerry, Elridge, 125
Gerrymandering. *See* Partisan gerrymandering
Gill v. Whitford (2018), 136
Gingles test, 101–104
Ginsburg, Ruth Bader, 120, 136, 148
Goldwater, Barry, 191
Gomillion v. Lightfoot (1960), 54–55, 58–59
Gore, Al, 165–166, 179
Government-issued photo ID, 171–175
Grandfather clause, 17–18, 54
Grant, Ulysses S., 13, 15–16, 26, 38
Grassley, Charles E., 121
Gray v. Sanders (1963), 60–61
Great Depression, 38, 40
Grovey v. Townsend (1935), 18–19
Growe v. Emison (1993), 102
Guccifer 2.0, 202–204
Guerra, Levi, 193
Guinn v. United States (1915), 18

Hadley v. Junior College District (1970), 73
Hague, Frank, 164

Hamilton, Alexander, 3–4, 37, 45, 191
Hand, Learned: "Spirit of Liberty" speech, xiii–xv
Hare, James, 84
Harman v. Forssenius (1965), 76
Harper v. Lewis (2019), 145
Harper v. Virginia Board of Elections (1966), 40, 77
Harris, Mark, 167–168
Harrison, William Henry, 47
HAVA. *See* Help America Vote Act of 2002
Hayes, Rutherford B., 13, 16
Heart of Atlanta Motel, Inc. v. United States (1964), 83
Help America Vote Act of 2002 (HAVA), 97, 171, 183, 186
The Heritage Foundation, 166, 174
Hispanic American, 102, 114–115, 175, 185
Hofeller, Thomas, 130, 144
Holder, Eric H., 145, 158–159
Home Rule Act, 39
Hoover Commission, 38
House Intelligence Committee, 207
Hunt, Ward, 26
Hunt v. Cromartie (2001), 108
Hunter v. Pittsburgh (1907), 53–54
Husted v. A. Philip Randolph Institute (2018), 186–187

IC. *See* Intelligence community
Immigrants, right to vote, 20–22, 27, 114, 163
Immigration Act (1952), 23
Impeachment, xv, 7, 162
In re Guerra (2019), 193
Income inequality, 211
Independent redistricting commissions. *See* Redistricting commissions
Indian Citizenship Act of 1924, 24
Instagram, 205

Intelligence community (IC), 202–207, 213
The Intercept, 202
Interstate Voter Registration Crosscheck Program (Crosscheck), 186–188
Intimidation, voter, 16, 21, 112, 117, 163–164
Iran, interference in 2020 election, 205, 207
Irwin, Henry D., 191

Jackson, Jimmie Lee, 85
Jefferson, Thomas, 4–5, 190
Jewish American, 8–9, 20, 105–106
Jim Crow Era, 16, 177
John, Esther, 193
Johnson, Frank, 86
Johnson, Lyndon Baines, xiv, 83–88, 89, 165
Johnson v. De Grandy (1994), 102

Kagan, Elena, 137–138, 143, 194
Kasich, John, 192–193
Katzenbach v. Morgan (1966), 78
Kavanaugh, Brett, 136, 152
Kennedy, Anthony, 135–136, 152
Kennedy, Edward, 32
Kennedy, John F., 39, 83, 164–165
Kilgarlin v. Hill (1967), 72
King, Martin Luther, Jr., 84–88
Kirkpatrick v. Preisler (1969), 73–75
Klobuchar, Amy, 29
Korean War, 31
Kramer v. Union Free School District No. 15 (1969), 79
Ku Klux Klan, 16, 164
Ku Klux Klan Act, 15

Lane v. Wilson (1939), 54
Language minorities, xvi, 21–22, 78, 93, 95, 97–98, 102, 111–115, 117, 121–122, 125

Lassiter v. Northampton County Board of Elections (1959), 19, 77–78, 91
Latino American, 102, 114–115, 175, 185
League of United Latin American Citizens v. Perry (2006), 103, 136
League of Women Voters, 28–29, 139–141, 188
League of Women Voters of Florida v. Detzner (2015), 139
League of Women Voters of Pennsylvania v. Commonwealth of Pennsylvania (2018), 140–141
LEP. *See* Limited English proficiency
Lewis, John, 84–85
Limited English proficiency (LEP), 114
Lincoln, Abraham, 12, 30–31, 60
Literacy tests, 14, 17–21, 27, 40, 54, 77–79, 84, 90–92, 111, 178
Lucas v. Forty-Fourth General Assembly of Colorado (1963), 67–70
Luther v. Borden (1849), 50

Madison, James, 3, 36, 45–46, 50
Mahan v. Howell (1973), 74
Mail-in voting, 121, 167–169, 206
Malapportionment. *See* Apportionment
Mansfield, Mike, 87
Marshall, John, 90
McCain, John, 167
McConnell, Mitch, 205–206
McCulloch v. Maryland (1819), 90, 193
McCutcheon v. FEC (2014), 212
McPherson v. Blacker (1892), 191
Mexican American, 20–21, 56, 112
Mexican War, 20
Miles, Samuel, 190

Index

Military service and the right to vote, 12, 30–32, 74
Miller v. Johnson (1995), 108
Minor, Virginia, 26
Minor v. Happersett (1875), 26–27
Mississippi v. Williams (1898), 17
Mobile v. Bolden (1980), 56, 100–101
Monroe, James, 190
Mott, Lucretia, 25
Mueller, Robert, 203–204
Multimember districts, 43, 46–47, 55–56, 72, 101–102

National American Woman Suffrage Association (NAWSA), 27–28
National Conference of State Legislatures (NCSL), 174
National Counterintelligence and Security Center, 206
National Democratic Redistricting Committee (NDRC), 145, 158
National Popular Vote Initiative (NPVI), 197–200
National Redistricting Foundation (NRF), 145
National Republican Redistricting Trust (NRRT), 157–159
National Security Agency (NSA), 202–203
National Voter Registration Act (NVRA), 97, 183–188
  Failure-to-Vote Clause, 186
National Woman Suffrage Association (NWSA), 26
Native American, 9, 20, 22–24, 31, 112–115, 192
Naturalization Act of 1790, 11
Naturalization Act of 1870, 21
Naturalized citizenship, xiii, 11–13, 20–24, 26, 188
NAWSA. *See* National American Woman Suffrage Association
NCSL. *See* National Conference of State Legislatures

NDRC. *See* National Democratic Redistricting Committee
Necessary and Proper Clause, 78
News21, 168
Nineteenth Amendment, 25–29
Nixon, Richard M., 32, 39, 128, 164–165, 191
Nixon v. Condon (1932), 18
Nixon v. Herndon (1927), 18, 54
North Carolina v. Common Cause (2019), 143
Northwest Austin Municipal Utility District No. One v. Holder (2009), 117–118
NPVI. *See* National Popular Vote Initiative
NRF. *See* National Redistricting Foundation
NRRT. *See* National Republican Redistricting Trust
NSA. *See* National Security Agency
NVRA. *See* National Voter Registration Act
NWSA. *See* National Woman Suffrage Association

Obama, Barack, 34, 87–88, 121, 130
O'Connor, Sandra Day, 29
One person, one vote, 44, 60, 63–70, 71–75, 133–134
Oregon v. Mitchell (1970), 32–33, 79–80
Overseas ballots, 166
Ozawa v. United States (1922), 22–23

Pacific States Telephone and Telegraph Company v. Oregon (1912), 51
Packing electoral districts, 102, 127–128
Palm Beach Post, 185
Parks, Preston, 191
Parr, George, 165
Partisan gerrymandering, 125–159, 161

Partisan polarization, xv, 110, 131, 162, 194, 196, 207, 213
Paul, Ron, 192
Pelosi, Nancy, 29
Pendergast, Tom, 164
Pew Research Center, 34, 210–211
Plessy v. Ferguson (1896), 16
Plummer, William, Sr., 190
Political bosses, 164
Poll tax, 17–18, 20–21, 36, 40, 76–77, 84, 178, 181
Pope v. Williams (1904), 16–17
Popular election, 2–7, 16, 36–37, 43, 65–66, 73, 148, 164, 167, 185, 189–200, 213
Populist Party, 37
Powell, Colin, 192
Powell, Lewis, 106
Preclearance requirement. *See* Voting Rights Act of 1965
Property qualifications, 1, 4, 8, 10–11, 20, 40, 79
Puerto Ricans, 55, 78–79, 111–112, 115
Punch-card ballot, 165–166
Putin, Vladimir, 202, 204

Racial districting, 53–56, 100–110
Radical Republicans, 13–14
Randolph, Jennings, 31
Rankin, Jeannette Pickering, 29
Ray v. Blair (1952), 192–193
REAL ID Act of 2005, 171
REAL IDs, 171–172
Reconstruction Acts of 1867 and 1868, 15
Reconstruction Amendments, 15–16
Reconstruction Era, 13–16, 20, 164
Redeemer Democratic Party, 16
Redeemers, 16
Redistricting. *See* Electoral districting
Redistricting commissions, 132, 147–153, 156–159

Redistricting Majority Project (REDMAP), 130
REDMAP. *See* Redistricting Majority Project
Reeb, James J., 85
Regents of the University of California v. Bakke (1978), 106
Reno, Janet, 29
Republican Guarantee Clause, 49–52, 57, 59
Republican National Committee v. Democratic National Committee (2020), 162
Republican Party, 13, 15–16, 18, 34, 38, 128–130, 133, 139, 153, 157, 173, 188, 196, 198, 205
Republican Redistricting Committee, 29
Republican State Leadership Committee (RSLC), 130
Residency requirement, 1, 4, 8, 10–11, 16, 18, 20, 24, 33, 80, 177
Reynolds v. Sims (1964), 61–66, 68, 70, 71, 77, 133–134
Richardson v. Ramirez (1974), 178
Roberts, John, 118–119, 136–137, 148–149
Rogers v. Lodge (1982), 100
Romney, Mitt, 162
Roosevelt, Franklin Delano, 31, 38
Roosevelt, Theodore, 38
RSLC. *See* Republican State Leadership Committee
Rucho v. Common Cause (2019), 136–138, 143, 161
Russell, Richard, 83
Russia
    interference in 2016 election, xv, 161, 201–205, 213
    interference in 2020 election, 205–207, 213
Russia Today, 202

Russian Internet Research Agency (IRA), 204–205
Ryder, John, 129

Sanders, Bernie, 34, 181, 192
School district elections, 76, 78–79
Secret ballot, 163–164
Selma, Alabama, 84–88
Senate Select Committee on Intelligence (SSCI), 204–205
Separation of power, 3, 58
Seventeenth Amendment, 35–37, 43, 148–149
Shaw v. Hunt (1996), 108
Shaw v. Reno (1993), 107
Shelby County v. Holder (2013), 82, 98, 104, 110, 116–122, 161
Sherman, William Tecumseh, 31
Single-member districts, 43–48, 101–103, 127
Slaves, 7, 10–13, 25–26, 45
Smith v. Allwright (1944), 19
Social media, 168, 202–207
South Carolina v. Katzenbach (1966), 78, 89–93, 117, 119–120
Southern Christian Leadership Conference, 84
Special provisions. See Voting Rights Act of 1965
Spotted Eagle, Faith, 192
SSCI. See Senate Select Committee on Intelligence
Stanton, Elizabeth Cady, 25–26
States Rights Party, 191
Stewart, Potter, 68–69
Stockton, John P., 37
Stone, Lucy, 26
Stone, Roger, 204
Strict scrutiny, 79, 103, 106–107
Student Nonviolent Coordinating Committee, 84
Supremacy Clause, 193
Swann v. Adams (1967), 72

Symm v. United States (1979), 34
Tammany Hall, 163
Taney, Roger B., 11–13
Tax-paying requirements, 1, 7–8, 10–11, 17–18, 20–22, 36, 40, 76–77, 79, 81, 84, 178, 181
Taylor and Marshall v. Beckham (1900), 51
Term limits, 6–7, 35, 37–39
Thirteenth Amendment, 13–14
Thompson, Bill, 164
Thornburg v. Gingles (1986), 101–104
Thurmond, Strom, 83, 191
Tilden, Samuel J., 16
Treaty of Guadalupe Hidalgo, 20
Trifectas, 130, 151, 196
Truman, Harry, 38, 191
Trumbull, Jonathan, Jr., 38
Trump, Donald, xv, 6, 122, 162, 167–169, 188, 192, 197, 202, 205, 207, 211, 213
   campaign organization, 204–205
Trust, lack of
   in corporate business leaders, 211
   in government, 135, 145, 197, 206, 209–210, 213
Truth decay, 209–210, 213–214
Tweed, Boss, 163
Twelfth Amendment, 5, 193–194
Twenty-Fourth Amendment, 36, 40, 76
Twenty-Second Amendment, 35, 37
Twenty-Sixth Amendment, 30–34
Twenty-Third Amendment, 35, 39
Twitter, 204–205
Tyler, John, 48

United Jewish Organization of Williamsburg, Inc. v. Carey (1977), 105–106
United States Department of Commerce v. Montana (1992), 63
United States v. Bhagat Singh Thind (1923), 23

United States v. Cruikshank (1876), 15, 164
United States v. Internet Research Agency, et. al. (2018), 204
United States v. Reese (1875), 15
United States v. Wong Kim Ark (1898), 22
USCCR. *See* U.S. Commission on Civil Rights
U.S. Census Bureau, 96, 113–115, 129
U.S. Commission on Civil Rights (USCCR), 82, 115, 179

Vandenberg, Arthur, 31
Veasey v. Abbott (2018), 173
Vieth v. Jubelirer (2004), 135–136
Vietnam War, 30–32
Virginia v. Tennessee (1893), 199
Voinovich v. Quilter (1993), 102
Vote, popular. *See* Popular election
Vote-counting machines, 165–166
Voter apathy, 209–210
Voter confidence, 161–163, 201–214
Voter Education Project, 96
Voter fraud, 80, 163–169, 170–175, 183, 188, 207
Voter identification (ID) laws, 121, 170–175
Voter impersonation, 167–168, 170–175
Voter intimidation, 16, 21, 112, 117, 163–164
Voter participation rate, 8, 209–210
Voter registration, 17, 26, 34, 80, 83–88, 90, 92–98, 108–109, 112–119, 167–174, 209
Voter registration lists, 33, 203
  purges, 183–188
Voter turnout, xv, 29, 34, 119, 175, 197, 209–210
Voting age, 30–34
Voting Rights Act of 1965, 81–122, 141, 161, 164, 173, 183, 200
  Amendments of 1970, 32–33, 93, 117
  Amendments of 1975, 93, 95, 97, 111–113, 117
  Amendments of 1982, 93, 99–101, 113–114, 117
  Amendments of 2006, 93, 115, 117–120
  bailout provision, 117–118
  federal examiners and observers, 92–98, 113
  preclearance requirement, 91, 99–100, 105–110, 117–122
  special provisions, 90–98, 104, 110–117
Voting Rights Advancement Act, 122
Voting Rights Language Assistance Act of 1992, 114
Voting systems, 46–47, 56, 75, 100, 203–205
  booths and machines, 163–166, 205–206
VR Systems, 203
VRA. *See* Voting Rights Act of 1965

Walker, Scott, 158–159
Wallace, George, 84
Warren, Earl, 43–44, 68
Warren, Elizabeth, 29
Warren Court, 43–80
Washington, D.C., citizens right to vote, 36, 39–40
Washington, George, 2, 4, 37–38, 163, 190
The Washington Post, 85
Wealth inequality, 210–211
Weintraub, Ellen, 167
Wells v. Rockefeller (1969), 74
Wesberry v. Sanders (1964), 60–63
West Virginia State Board of Education v. Barnette (1943), 68
Whig Party, 47
White supremacists, 15–16, 164

White v. Regester (1973), 56, 75
White v. Weiser (1973), 75
White vigilantes, 15–16, 85–86, 164
Whitley, David, 188
WikiLeaks, 202, 204
Wilson, Woodrow, 28
Winner-take-all. *See* Electoral College
Wisconsin Institute for Law and Liberty, 188
Wisconsin State Journal, 162
Wolf, Tom, 142
Women's suffrage movement, 25–29
Wood v. Broom (1932), 48
World War I, 28, 31
World War II, 23, 31, 38
Wright v. Rockefeller (1964), 55

YouTube, 205

About the Author

H. L. Pohlman is the A. Lee Fritschler Professor of Public Policy and professor of political science at Dickinson College. He received his PhD from Columbia University in 1982. Professor Pohlman's teaching interests include American constitutional law, other law-related courses, and political and legal philosophy. His published works include *Terrorism and the Constitution: The Post-9/11 Cases* (2008), *U.S. National Security Law: An International Perspective* (2018), *Free Speech and Censorship: Examining the Facts* (2019), and titles on such subjects as civil rights and liberties, the justice system, and governmental authority and accountability.

Printed in the USA
CPSIA information can be obtained
at www.ICGtesting.com
LVHW012357280624
784238LV00001B/79